CHILDREN OF THE STRUGGLE AND THE ANCESTORS WHO STAYED

CHILDREN OF THE STRUGGLE AND THE ANCESTORS WHO STAYED

The Tuskegee Institute High School Class of 1964

Edited by
Sonjia Parker Redmond
and Beatrice J. Adams

Foreword by
Fred D. Gray

The University of Alabama Press
Tuscaloosa

The University of Alabama Press
Tuscaloosa, Alabama 35487-0380
uapress.ua.edu

Typeface: Janson Text LT Std

Cover image: *Singing Windows*, stained glass designed by J&R Lamb, located in the chapel at Tuskegee University, Tuskegee, Alabama; George F. Landegger Collection of Alabama Photographs in Carol M. Highsmith's America, Library of Congress, Prints and Photographs Division
Cover design: Sandy Turner Jr.

For more information, please visit childrenofthestruggle.com.

Cataloging-in-Publication data is available from the Library of Congress.
ISBN: 978-0-8173-6232-4 (paper)
E-ISBN: 978-0-8173-9581-0

Contents

Foreword

The writers of this volume illuminate the lives of their ancestors "who stayed" in the South before, after, and especially during the Great Migration, when millions of Black Americans were leaving the South for northern and western cities. They describe how many of their parents participated in the Civil Rights Movement and the fight for freedom and justice in Alabama and how their actions promoted Black upward mobility in a southern town. It was my honor to have been the attorney for several of the writers and/or their families. Anthony T. Lee, Willie B. Wyatt Jr., and the sisters of Palmer Sullins Jr. and Gerald W. Billes were four of the twelve students who successfully desegregated schools in the *Lee v. Macon County Board of Education* case. In that case, we defeated Governor George Wallace and effectively desegregated all public schools in Alabama. I also had the privilege of representing several of their parents, including Detroit Lee and Della P. Sullins, in the *Gomillion v. Lightfoot* case, which was argued before the US Supreme Court. The court ruled that gerrymandering based on race violated the Fourteenth and Fifteenth Amendments to the US Constitution.[1]

It is an inspiration for me to read the stories presented herein from the "children of the struggle" about their lives and the lives of their parents and grandparents "who stayed" and helped to advance human rights and create an upwardly mobile class in the South. It is also heartening to read how they, who were mere teenagers during the heat of the struggle, have taken advantage of opportunities created by it.

On a personal note, I am also one of "those who stayed" and became a part of the struggle for equal justice. As I wrote in my autobiography, *Bus Ride to Justice*, I was born in Montgomery, Alabama, on December 14, 1930; grew up in Alabama; attended high school at Nashville Christian

Institute in Nashville, Tennessee; became a preacher; returned to Montgomery in 1948 and enrolled in what was Alabama State College for Negroes (now Alabama State University) to become a teacher.[2] I observed that Black people were having problems of racial discrimination on the public buses. I decided to become a lawyer in Alabama and "destroy everything segregated I could find."[3]

I moved to Tuskegee, Alabama, in 1964 after being admitted to practice law in Alabama in 1954. For seventy years, I have been counsel of record in cases that eliminated racial discrimination in almost every aspect of American life, including the right to use public transportation, to vote, to protect the membership of organizations, to public education without discrimination, to equal access to farm subsidies, to health care, and to serve on civil juries. Four of the precedent-setting cases were filed by residents of Macon County, including some of the members of the Tuskegee Institute High School class of 1964.

Understanding the past can give us encouragement and a vision for what we need to do in the future. Toward that end, in 1997, I cofounded the Tuskegee Human and Civil Rights Multicultural Center, also known as the Tuskegee History Center or the center in downtown Tuskegee, as a permanent memorial to the victims of the US Public Health Service Syphilis Study at Tuskegee and Macon County. The center also educates the public on the contributions made by Native Americans, European Americans, and African Americans in developing this country and offers a brief history of the struggles of African Americans from enslavement to the present. This center contains information you can see and hear, including some of the authors herein, their parents, and grandparents. I invite you to visit and support the center at www.tuskegeecenter.org.

Racism and inequality still lead to poor educational outcomes for children, overpopulated jails, and inadequate housing and health care. Vast fortunes are being spent to maintain the status quo by stacking the courts with judges who favor restricting voting rights and limiting health care access. Such forces work against the common good. But, as the stories in this book suggest, we cannot sleep. We must remain vigilant to protect the rights of every citizen.

The class of 1964 and their ancestors are typical of what many other African Americans who "stayed" have done to complete the job so that

all American citizens can truly enjoy all the rights and privileges of the US Constitution. For those of us who stayed in the South, the journey was not always easy, but it was necessary and rewarding. I hope that the writers' recollections of their and their ancestors' journeys will inspire readers to fight on for equality and the destruction of racism.

In the spring of 2025, scholars and community leaders came from twenty-three states and fifteen universities to launch the Fred Gray Institute for Human and Civil Rights. Utilizing the foundational principles of my legal work, the institute will convene an annual symposium to create actionable strategies for change in areas including medical racism, voting rights, human and civil rights laws, and equal access to quality education.

At ninety-four years of age, I am grateful to have played a role in enhancing the social, political, and economic freedoms and opportunities for current and subsequent generations.

Fred D. Gray, Esquire
Presidential Medal of Freedom Recipient

Acknowledgments

In the African tradition, we must begin by honoring all the ancestors who gave us their stories, our lives, and our opportunities . . . with special thanks to my maternal grandparents, Jodie and Johnnie Mae Parker, and my mother, Robenia Parker Bass, who all taught me to love learning—and justice.

Next, the highest respect is offered to a supreme elder who stayed, Attorney Fred D. Gray, whom Martin Luther King Jr. called the "chief counsel for the Civil Rights Movement." Thank you for lending your enormous prestige to this work in which some of the narrators and their families were plaintiffs in civil rights cases you tried during the 1950s and '60s.

My deepest gratitude goes to my brave and adventurous octogenarian classmates—Ray, Barbara, Gerald, Earline, Mattie, Nancy, Rosa, Margaret, Anthony, Douglas, Annie Jean, Alex, Alma Jean, Palmer, Harold, Marian, Lorenzo, Carolyn, Willie B., and Milton, who shared your family histories to make this book possible. You accepted the enormous challenge of critiques and rewrites with grace, laughter, and the joy of reconnecting. Thanks to each of you for adding your authentic voice to history.

To my coeditor, Dr. Beatrice J. Adams, assistant professor of history at Princeton University, we could not have done it without you. Your extraordinarily thorough knowledge of African American history and historiography, with a specialty in southern migration, has been invaluable. Thank you for joining us on this wondrous journey.

To my California State University East Bay faculty colleagues, Dr. Benjaman Bowser and Dr. Gale Young, as well as other longtime friends and colleagues Dr. Elaine Parker Adams and Dr. Frances Smith Foster,

"Thank you!" is not enough. I am truly grateful for your time. Your readings, critiques, and encouragement kept us moving toward the prize.

Much appreciation goes to my grandchildren, Jeremy, Sasha, Miya, Khensu, and Abi, for being inspirations during this project. Gratitude to all my classmates' children, grandchildren, and great-grandchildren whose technological assistance helped usher the manuscript to fruition. May this book motivate all of you to contribute to the ongoing journey toward justice and equality in the world.

Thanks to my Alabama family for caring about the book. Your constant query, "Is the book done yet?" always reminded me to get back to it.

To my son, Shaka Jamal Redmond, an ingenious documentarian, thank you for sharing your talents, beginning with producing the first narrator recruitment video, filming narrator interviews at the class reunion, and producing content for our digital archive at childrenofthestruggle.com. And thank you to my son, Gregory Jr., whose intellect and courage always inspire me.

To Gregory Charles Redmond, my husband of fifty-five years, thank you for your interminable support throughout my academic career and especially during my work on this book. You knew how much it meant to all of us.

And finally, thanks to the University of Alabama Press and the finest editor-in-chief ever, Dan Waterman, for believing in this project and supporting the revelation of untold stories of "those who stayed."

Dr. Sonjia Parker Redmond

FIRST, I MUST THANK MY ancestors and family, especially my paternal grandparents, Robert and Juanita Brown, and their siblings. Their stories about coming of age in Jim Crow–era Arkansas helped cultivate my interest in history and continue to shape how I approach the past.

I also owe my coeditor, Dr. Sonjia Parker Redmond, my deepest thanks. This project is a dream come true, and I will forever be humbled by your willingness to let me serve as its coeditor. You and this project have brought joy and new ways of engaging with the past into my life, along with the late nights and Zoom meetings. Additionally, thank you so much to the contributors for trusting me with your treasures and welcoming me into your community.

I would also like to thank my friends and colleagues from the College of Wooster, the James Weldon Johnson Center at Emory University, and Rutgers–New Brunswick for their advice, encouragement, and support throughout the research and writing processes. In a broader sense, I would like to thank my formal and informal academic advisors and mentors from Fisk University to Rutgers–New Brunswick, who have poured so much into me.

Finally, a very special thanks to my parents, Patricia and Billy Adams, for their support and encouragement, especially your grace in catching the dozens and dozens of balls I dropped while working on "the book." And to my partner, James Watkins, whose unwavering confidence in me has provided me with a solid foundation on this journey.

Dr. Beatrice J. Adams

CHILDREN OF THE STRUGGLE
AND THE ANCESTORS WHO STAYED

Introduction

Origins of the 1964 Reunion Class Narratives Project

Nineteen sixty-four was an eventful year. With the passage of the Civil Rights Act of 1964 and Freedom Summer, the year marked fundamental changes to the politics, economics, and culture of the American South. It was also the year that an exceptional group of students graduated from Tuskegee Institute High School. The children of college professors, health care professionals, rural schoolteachers, small landowners, and sharecroppers, members of this class had already made history themselves by helping to desegregate the all-White high school—Tuskegee High School. They also helped to desegregate Alabama public schools because of Attorney Fred Gray's *Lee v. Macon County Board of Education* case. Furthermore, they had also witnessed their parents claim the right to vote in Macon County when Mr. Gray took *Gomillion v. Lightfoot* to the US Supreme Court and won in 1960. Over the next few years, they would continue to serve as eyewitnesses to some of the most influential events of the Civil Rights Movement—the murder of Sammy Younge Jr., the march from Selma to Montgomery, and Bloody Sunday.

These students forged powerful bonds in this fiery time in American history. Despite all the social and emotional turbulence of the 1960s, or maybe because of it, the Tuskegee Institute High School graduating class of 1964 developed a closeness that remains over sixty years later. These connections informed their decision to record their life narratives illuminating an understudied aspect of Black history—the decision to remain in the South before, during, and after the Great Migration.

The Tuskegee Institute High School 1964 Reunion Club is part of a larger group, the Tuskegee Institute High School Stone Age Reunion Group, which is open to anyone who attended Tuskegee Institute High School between 1955 and 1965. The 1964 Reunion Club helps to sponsor the more expansive Stone Age Reunions every two years. The 1964 Reunion Club plans social activities for its members and awards scholarships to graduates of the current high school in Tuskegee, Booker T. Washington High, as well as Notasulga High, the Macon County school that was integrated by our classmates.

The idea to record their stories originated at a 1964 Reunion Club business meeting Zoomed during the COVID pandemic in the fall of 2021. At the meeting, classmates began reminiscing about the group's special bonds forged across decades as they met formally and informally at reunions, business meetings, funerals, weddings, and barbecues for six decades. It was also mentioned that the group was exceptional because their ancestors stayed in the South, lived through, and made significant contributions to southern society during some difficult times in American history—Jim Crow and the emergence of the Civil Rights Movement.[1] The group expressed gratitude for the sacrifices our ancestors had made, especially in getting us to the advantaged positions we now enjoy in our lives. Then, Dr. Sonjia Parker Redmond suggested writing "stories" about coming of age in Tuskegee and the ancestors who stayed. The group consented enthusiastically to engage in the project.

Narrative Collection Methods

With the encouragement of her classmates, Redmond as a professor emeritus, having taught and conducted social research, volunteered to serve as editor on the project. As the project grew, she invited Dr. Beatrice J. Adams, a historian of race and migration in the American South, to join the project as coeditor. They devised a qualitative research method approach with first-person written or oral narratives as the proposed data source. With the help of Redmond's son, Shaka Jamal Redmond, a documentary filmmaker, a recruitment video describing the project's purpose was sent to classmates, inviting them to participate in the project. Each classmate received a copy of the video, along with the themes, questions, and proposed timeline for the project. The video was also shown at one of the Reunion Club's business meetings. Questions and suggestions were addressed during the introductory discussion, and feedback from classmates during the club's monthly business meetings became an essential element in the project's development.

Eventually, twenty-one of seventy classmates volunteered to participate in the project. While some of the narrators learned about the project during our monthly meetings, others learned about the project through emails sent to the Reunion Club email list. Classmates were advised that they could either write their narratives with the use of the themed questionnaire or participate in recorded interviews. There was so much excitement around the project, as classmates saw it as an opportunity to tell their ancestors' and their own life stories for future generations.

Since the narrative collection phase of the project occurred during the COVID-19 pandemic, there were travel and face-to-face meeting restrictions. As a result, the editors relied heavily on technology, which was sometimes challenging for some of the septuagenarians. Most of them had grown up with typewriters and landline phones and, depending on their profession, had only learned the basics about cell phones, computers, and software applications. Their children and grandchildren were often the heroes and sheroes who came to the rescue. They helped participants install Zoom; sign onto Zoom sessions; create, open, and save Microsoft Word documents; attach files; use Google Docs; and convert PDF photo files to JPG files.

As Redmond collected the narratives, she smiled knowingly when she heard, "I need to wait until my granddaughter gets home from school so she can set the computer up for my Zoom interview," or "this computer is so old, I really need to take it to the shop," or "that's not my email, I was just using my granddaughter's email, and she has gone back to college now," or "I am typing my story on my phone because I can't do anything with that computer!" Seventy-five years of living life and the welcomed opportunity to work together on something special brought patience, perseverance, and lots of laughter to the process for both the coeditors and the participants. The moments spent together during interviews and discussing the project at meetings inspired all of us to continue our work on the project.

The questions addressed a variety of themes related to ancestors' reasons for coming to, staying, or leaving Tuskegee; ancestors' experiences living in the Jim Crow South; and ancestors' participation in the Civil Rights Movement. Questions also covered narrators' experiences growing up in Tuskegee and the surrounding rural areas during the Jim Crow era; their participation in the Civil Rights Movement; their adult lives, and careers, and whether and why they had stayed, left, or returned to Tuskegee or the South. Narrators were also asked what advice they wanted to pass on to their children and future generations regarding "the struggle." Narrators' responses resulted in the four thematic chapters in the book.

Several months into the project, only ten of the twenty-five classmates who had initially expressed interest were in various stages of writing. It became apparent to the editors that they needed to use the qualitative research method of recursivity and reach out to the group to determine if they wanted to be interviewed. Recursivity refers to the process by which the researcher examines the data to ascertain whether a change in process or collection method is needed to improve the outcome. As described in *SAGE Encyclopedia of Qualitative Research Methods*, while quantitative research methods depend on strict adherence to the initial methodology used, qualitative researchers can use a more dynamic approach to their search for answers.[2] In the case of this project, it became clear that many of the participants were not writing because they felt uncomfortable with their writing methods, styles, or abilities. The amelioration was to remind the remaining participants that they had the option of participating in oral interviews.

Michelle Butina, in "A Narrative Approach to Qualitative Inquiry," explains how the main purpose of narrative inquiry is to allow participants to tell their stories to obtain data related to the who, what, when, how, and why of a particular subject for a particular purpose.[3] In facilitating the written and oral narratives, the data collection methods at times merged. Both methods necessitated follow-up interviews for clarification of the written story or for missing data in either the written or oral narratives. Approximately half of the twenty-one participants chose to be interviewed by their classmate coeditor. The process required the use of Zoom. Interview lengths varied from one-and-a-half to three hours, depending upon the loquaciousness of the interviewee. The interviews were recorded on Zoom and Microsoft Dictate and transcribed in-house.

Transcription was time consuming as it required playing the Zoom recording and editing the Microsoft Dictate document simultaneously, a process that could take up to forty hours, depending upon the length of the interview and the clarity of the narrator. Accuracy was enhanced by using both applications, especially when either one was unintelligible. After the transcription process, the narratives were then edited for readability.

Edited narratives, whether written or oral, were always sent to the narrators to review for accuracy, deletions, or additional information. It was clear during this process that both Microsoft Dictate and Grammarly fell short in honoring their Black southern accents and phrases. Therefore, we took care to use Grammarly mostly for clarifying spelling and punctuation rather than for rephrasing. The oral and written narratives were also examined for any discernible differences in content based on the data collection method utilized. The editors did not find any, possibly because all participants were interviewed either entirely or partially.

Much has been written about the role of the interviewer in qualitative methods, essentially how power dynamics between the interviewer and interviewee can shape oral narratives.[4] Surmising that there was very little, if any, difference between the oral and written narratives, thoughts turned toward the effect of the two methods on the interviewer. As both editor and classmate, Redmond enjoyed the interviewing process, whether it was for the total interview or to complete a written narrative. The idea of reconnecting with a classmate, sometimes after sixty years, was fascinating. Often it felt like connecting the dots of life or finishing a long overdue conversation with a cup of coffee laced with knowing compassion. For others, it was like starting a conversation that as teenagers we were probably too shy to even initiate.

The Reunion Club's monthly Zoom business meetings helped to keep the project on track. The coeditors' monthly progress reports in the Old Business section of the agenda kept interest high. The reports included applause for those who had finished their stories and next steps. Requests from classmates to share completed stories with the group went unheeded to prevent cross contamination of the stories. However, a fun game of "Guess That Classmate" was developed from tidbits selected from classmates' narratives. A sample question, "Whose grandmother became a bootlegger to help feed her family?" elicited laughter from the group and pride from the classmate that his beloved grandma possessed such gumption. "Guess That Classmate" became a much-anticipated part of the monthly project update.

Three ancillary projects were designed to help maintain participant interest. The first project involved the development of a PowerPoint presentation of photographs of ancestors and narrators accompanied by music by distinguished composer William L. Dawson and the famed Tuskegee Institute Choir Director.[5] The second project involved a formal presentation by narrators of their work at the Tuskegee Institute High School Stone Age Reunion held in Montgomery, Alabama, in the summer of 2023. The third project is a digital history project featured on the book's website, childrenofthestruggle.com and hyperlinked to the University of Alabama, Tuskegee University, and other university archives. This will contain artifacts, photographs, and narrator interviews.

These seventy-nine-year-old classmates tell stories of their great-grandparents, grandparents, and parents who were either born in the area, stayed, returned to, or migrated to Tuskegee to be part of an extraordinary moment and place in American history. Although they faced daily racism, discrimination, and the threat of violence, they remained in the South because of the educational, employment, social, and cultural activities that Tuskegee Institute made possible. The ability to be close to family was extremely important to some who stayed. While other studies have discussed the importance of landownership as a reason for staying in the South, this project also shows the importance of home and business ownership as essential factors for staying as well.[6] Some ancestors saved money to buy land, while others inherited land from their ancestors. Some ancestors were even assisted by their enslavers to buy land.

In the 1940s and 1950s, many parents of the narrators were able to acquire new brick homes built by Black Tuskegee-trained construction craftsmen. Some later ancestors traveled to Detroit every few years to buy new cars or bought cars from the local Black car dealership in Tuskegee. The ancestors engaged their children in sports, cultural, travel, and intellectual activities that fostered upward mobility. They taught them the value of taking care of their money, hard work, and community involvement. Practically all the ancestors were able to provide better lives for their families, building upon the foundations their ancestors had created for them, as they emerged from enslavement.

The narrators in this study basked in the upward mobility that Tuskegee Institute and their ancestors had provided them. Growing up under Jim Crow, witnessing their ancestors' commitment to social justice, and their own involvement in the Civil Rights Movement have left a mark on them. They continue to pass on the teachings and values of their ancestors to their progeny. Members of the class of 1964 exemplify how the adoption of Booker T. Washington's philosophy of Black upliftment through education, hard work, and self-sufficiency can lead to social and economic progress.[7]

Historical Context for Ancestors and Narrators

The Founding and Early History of Tuskegee Institute

Tuskegee, Alabama, has played a singular role in American history. Well-known as the home of the Tuskegee Institute and Booker T. Washington, it has been pivotal in Black history since Reconstruction.[8] However, the historical importance of Tuskegee expands beyond its most famous resident and even Tuskegee Institute. A haven for Black people seeking safety and economic opportunities during the years of formal racial segregation in the American South, the Black community of Tuskegee flourished and grew through the twentieth century.

Tuskegee Institute was established as Tuskegee Normal School in 1881, and Booker T. Washington, an alumnus of Hampton Institute, became its first principal. It was founded in the wake of Reconstruction—only sixteen years after emancipation—as newly freed people worked to make their freedom real.[9] The founding of the school was revolutionary since most Black people in the area could not read or write, and most, like narrator Marian Quinn Williams's great-grandparents, were sharecroppers. Although Washington was the school's first principal, Lewis Adams, a leader in the Black community in Tuskegee and the great-great-grandfather of narrator Raymond Adams, was responsible for the school's founding. Asked by two local White politicians to guarantee the Black vote in 1880 in their favor, Adams agreed to deliver the Black vote if the

White politicians, in turn, provided support for the establishment of a school for Black people in Macon County. [10] Keeping their promise, on July 4th 1881, the newly reelected Alabama state legislators introduced legislation for teacher training through the creation of the Tuskegee Normal School, which would later become Tuskegee Institute and later Tuskegee University.[11]

During its first academic year, the school was located in Butler Chapel Church. The following year, Washington purchased a one-hundred-acre former plantation with a loan from Hampton Institute, his alma mater.[12] Students at the school with the help of some community ancestors constructed new buildings and grew food on the school's farm. Early immigrants from other parts of the South, including narrator Carolyn Earline Foster Bivins's great-grandparents, settled near Tuskegee Normal, learned building trades, and assisted in the building of the school. The course of study at Tuskegee included teacher preparation courses and practical trade-related skills. Several of the narrators' ancestors, including the mothers of Barbara White Atkinson-Liggins, Margaret Meadows Jones, Carolyn Bivins, and Nancy Hooten Garrison, became primary school teachers and taught mainly in rural communities surrounding Tuskegee. As part of Washington's educational outreach programs to Black communities throughout the South, Garrison's ancestors became teachers and founded small institutes in the South, including Snow Hill Institute.[13] Several of her ancestors also created construction businesses that built housing developments for the newly upwardly mobile Black classes in Tuskegee.

As Washington worked to build a parallel set of educational, economic, social, and cultural institutions for Black people in Macon County, the agricultural and industrial skills developed by graduates of Tuskegee Institute helped the growing community.[14] Washington's connection to Hampton deeply informed the educational system he devised at Tuskegee. This model of education would become known as the Hampton-Tuskegee model. While this model of industrial and agricultural education has often been critiqued, Washington focused on both the development of trade skills and the education of teachers.[15] Furthermore, his concentration on Black economic development as opposed to political empowerment is often criticized; however, he believed economic development was necessary for Black people to have and skillfully wield political power. Consequently, despite the frequent critiques, he supported liberal education for Black people, employing an all-Black faculty before many other historically Black colleges and universities (HBCUs) had even one Black professor, but he did so within a broader curriculum that could attract funding for Black education. In fact, he used his influence with philanthropists to secure funding for the establishment and support of other Black liberal arts colleges in the country. [16]

As the school grew, so did the public persona of Washington. By 1895, the year of his famed "Atlanta Compromise" speech, he emerged as one of the foremost leaders of the Black community. His embrace of self-help and technical skills garnered donations from numerous philanthropists, including Andrew Carnegie, John D. Rockefeller, and Julius Rosenwald. Thus, as the twentieth century dawned, Tuskegee Institute was one of the nation's most prominent and best-funded historically Black colleges.

Building a Parallel World

As the twentieth century progressed, Washington's moniker as a "builder of a civilization" became a reality as Tuskegee Institute became the economic and social foundation of the city's dynamic Black community—a world within a world.[17] This world starkly contrasted with the broader political changes occurring in Alabama and beyond. By this time, Jim Crow racial segregation codes intertwined with Alabama law, and the social dictates of White supremacy shaped every aspect of southern society. Nonetheless, Washington and Tuskegee Institute continued to attract some of the most accomplished Black people of the era. In fact, he actively recruited top Black graduates from colleges and universities across the nation, and he maintained an all-Black faculty during his tenure as president.[18] For example, Robert Robinson Taylor, the first Black graduate of the Massachusetts Institute of Technology and the first professionally educated Black architect in the United States, spent most of his professional career at Tuskegee after being invited by Washington. Taylor oversaw the industrial training programs and designed several buildings on the campus, including the famous chapel.[19]

Famous artists and educators such as Langston Hughes; Zora Neale Hurston, who had been born in rural Notasulga just ten miles from

Tuskegee; and even W. E. B. DuBois found their way to Tuskegee to teach, study, or meet with Washington. Of course, the most famous scholar invited to Tuskegee by Washington was George Washington Carver. Carver earned his master's degree from Iowa State Agricultural College and became Iowa's first Black faculty member. Washington invited him to head the Agriculture Department at Tuskegee Institute in 1896. During his tenure, Carver grew the department into a leading research center and traveled to farms across the region to share practical insights from his research, including insights about crop rotation and soil erosion. During this time at Tuskegee, he became one of the most influential scientists in the United States—coordinating with and working with some of the most prominent people of the times, including Henry Ford.[20]

In addition to the agricultural extension work, rural areas benefited from Tuskegee Institute's educational outreach. Starting in 1912, Washington encouraged his friend Julius Rosenwald, a co-owner of Sears and Roebuck, to form the Rosenwald School Program to make elementary education available to Black Americans in rural communities. The program built six of the earliest schools in Macon County, Alabama, beginning in 1913. The Shiloh Rosenwald School, a school attended by coeditor Redmond, was built in 1922 in Notasulga. Some famous attendees of Rosenwald schools include John Lewis, Medger Evers, and Maya Angelou. Local Black communities helped to construct these schools with their labor or monetary donations. Initially, Tuskegee Institute's extension department assisted in locating teachers from the campus to staff them. By the 1940s, there were over five thousand Rosenwald schools in the South, with nearly four hundred in Alabama.[21]

Continuing its commitment to improving lives of people in Macon County and beyond, Tuskegee Institute opened the first hospital for Black people in Alabama and a home for Black American veterans.[22] In addition to providing access to medical services, these institutions provided employment opportunities for Black people from a variety of economic classes and served as economic engines of Tuskegee's Black community. The Tuskegee Institute Hospital and Nurse Training School opened in 1892 as a teaching hospital that trained nursing students and provided medical care to members of the Tuskegee community. It also ran clinics in the surrounding rural communities. In 1902, John A. Kenney Sr. became the hospital director, and under his guidance, it grew and expanded.[23] As part of this expansion, it was renamed John A. Andrew Memorial Hospital.[24] One of only a handful of places in the South where Black people could receive postgraduate medical training and Black patients could receive first-rate care, the hospital exemplified the fundamental social good that Tuskegee Institute meant to create.[25] The hospital employed several narrators' relatives, including the fathers of narrators Raymond Adams and Harold White. Later in 1949, Tuskegee Institute became the first university in the state of Alabama to establish a bachelors in nursing program, graduating fourteen students in 1953.[26] Three students who had finished all coursework for the bachelor's degree prior to the formal announcement of the program, graduated early in 1949. Narrator Palmer Sullins's mother, Della Sullins, was the first of the three to receive the degree, becoming the first nurse in Alabama to get a bachelor's of nursing degree.

Furthermore, a hospital for sick and injured Black World War I veterans, which later became the Tuskegee Veterans Administration Medical Center, was established in 1923. Like John Andrew Hospital, the VA Medical Center provided medical services unavailable to Black veterans across many regions of the nation and provided stable employment opportunities to Tuskegee's Black community. As Black soldiers returned from World War I, the NAACP and other organizations had been calling for a veteran's home to serve the needs of Black veterans in the South. Once Congress authorized the construction of such a facility, the second president of Tuskegee, Dr. Robert Russa Moton (1915–35), believed that Tuskegee would be an ideal location for the new hospital.[27] With a connection to the president of the United States, Warren Harding, and the leading Black Americans of the era, Dr. Moton succeeded in getting Tuskegee named as the location for the new hospital. In the process, he agreed to provide three hundred acres of land for the building of the hospital. Then, encouraged by the NAACP and National Medical Association, he also convinced President Harding (1921–23) to agree that any jobs created by the new facility would be open to Black doctors and nurses, a situation that some powerful White groups vehemently opposed.[28] Nonetheless, even after Harding died in 1923, President Calvin Coolidge

(1923–29) ensured that Black people staffed the hospital.[29] Among the Black professionals and staff members who the medical center would employ were parents and grandparents of several of the narrators, including the fathers of Stokes, Atkinson-Liggins, Jones, Lee, Billes, Woodard, and Sullins's mother, who worked as a nurse for the VA for over thirty years. Narrator Milton Donald's family moved from Mississippi to Tuskegee to get treatment for his grandfather at the new veterans hospital.

Unfortunately, an infamous incident in the history of Tuskegee Institute grew out of its commitment to improving the public health of Black Americans in Macon County. The US Public Health Service (USPHS) Study of Untreated Syphilis at Tuskegee and Macon County documented the long-term effects of syphilis on a group of Black men located in Macon County.[30] The project sought to understand the long-term effects of syphilis on Black men. After meeting with several doctors from the USPHS, Dr. Eugene Dibble, the director of John A. Andrew Memorial Hospital, was convinced of the scientific importance of the study as it was presented at the time and saw it as an opportunity to improve public health and provide valuable training for Black nurses and interns. Unfortunately, even after penicillin became widely available as a treatment after 1943, the researchers at the USPHS refused to treat the participants of the study.[31] The study continued because a group of White federal government researchers purposefully kept information about the study, its purpose, and the participants' medical diagnoses and treatment options from them. Even after the situation was exposed, the White researchers fought to justify its continuance. The study only ended after its ethical and legal violations were reported in the press three decades after discovering a reliable treatment for the disease.[32] Tuskegee's support of the USPHS study at Tuskegee and Macon County began as other positive Tuskegee community improvement projects had in the past. Unfortunately, the university has suffered adverse publicity effects because its name is most noticeably associated with the study and because of its inability or its failure to intervene. At least one narrator had a relative who was part of the study.

During World War II, Tuskegee would again serve as an economic engine by playing host to progressive projects related to the Black community and the military. Specifically, it hosted the first segregated flight training program, which produced the famed Tuskegee Airmen. The program at Tuskegee for flight training started as a civilian program by Tuskegee professor of mechanical engineering G. L. Washington.[33] Then with the passage of the Selective Service Act of 1940, there was a legal basis for the War Department to provide facilities to train Black draftees for every branch of the military. With the legal basis established, the NAACP initiated a lawsuit, and the following year, the War Department announced that it would establish a new military airfield near Tuskegee.[34] Like the hospital, the airport brought new jobs for Black people and attracted new residents to the city.[35] One of the narrators, Sullins, began his flight training at age nine at Moton Field with Tuskegee Airman Chief Alfred Anderson who famously took Eleanor Roosevelt for a flight. Furthermore, the Tuskegee Airmen provided compelling examples of Black achievement that undercut the prevailing logic among many White people at the time of Black inferiority and White supremacy.

Tuskegee during the Civil Rights Movement and Beyond

As Tuskegee Institute grew, so did the surrounding community. By the 1940s, the community included over a thousand Black professionals who provided a solid economic, social, and cultural foundation for Black people in Tuskegee and the surrounding rural areas.[36] Members of this community also served as teachers in all Black schools that dotted the more rural areas of Macon County. Like historically Black colleges and universities (HBCUs) across the South, including those in Nashville, Durham, Prairie View, and Atlanta, Tuskegee Institute became the anchor of a dynamic Black community that challenged the logic of White supremacy in the Jim Crow South. In fact, HBCUs served as the economic, social, and cultural engines of their regions' most successful and influential Black communities, including communities labeled as the "Capital of the Black Middle Class" and the "Black Mecca."[37] Consequently, they served as foundational institutions in the parallel Black world Black people developed as both a response and resistance to Jim Crow segregation.

These educational institutions also provided leadership for social and civic organizations, such as the Tuskegee Civic Association (TCA). The TCA, established in 1941, was founded by Dr. Charles G. Gomillion, who was then the dean of students at Tuskegee.[38] Gomillion, a professor of sociology and social research, also taught many of our narrators. They learned social activism firsthand from him in classes and research methodology while interviewing participants in civil rights marches in Atlanta and Montgomery. He gave narrator Redmond her first official job as a student researcher interviewing Black mothers in rural areas in Macon County. After Gomillion spent several years attempting to register to vote before being successful, he and the TCA worked to increase the number of Black voters in Tuskegee. Black men's right to vote had been eroded through a combination of laws with barriers, such as literacy tests and poll taxes, as well as through outright intimidation and fraud. They had successfully voted in 1880 to help Lewis Adams bring a school for Black people to Tuskegee. Thus, Gomillion's efforts and commitment to "civic democracy" served as the opening act of the Modern Black Freedom Movement in Tuskegee.[39]

Gomillion and the TCA were at the center of one of the most important legal cases during the Civil Rights Movement, *Gomillion v. Lightfoot*, which helped to lay the foundation for the Voting Rights Act of 1965.[40] As Black people in the area became more educated and demanded their rights to vote in 1957, local White officials attempted to maintain their power in Tuskegee through a plan to gerrymander the city's boundaries to exclude Tuskegee Institute and its surrounding areas. White people were demographically in the minority and fearful of the political transformation occurring because of the Modern Black Freedom Movement. As leaders of the movement encouraged Black citizens to register to vote and become more civically engaged, local White leaders' and officials' anxieties led to the passage of Local Act. No. 140 in the Alabama Legislature, which upheld the city's gerrymandering plan.

As many of the narratives in this study recount, the gerrymandering case also led to the Tuskegee Boycott that lasted more than three years. The TCA led the boycott, and the families of many of the narrators were active with the TCA and participated in the boycott. During the boycott, the TCA encouraged Black people in Macon County to refuse to shop at White-operated businesses in Tuskegee.[41] The boycott required that Black people from different classes work together; however, it affected them differently. Many Black laborers, especially sharecroppers and tenant farmers from the rural communities surrounding Tuskegee, depended on credit offered by local White merchants to buy groceries.

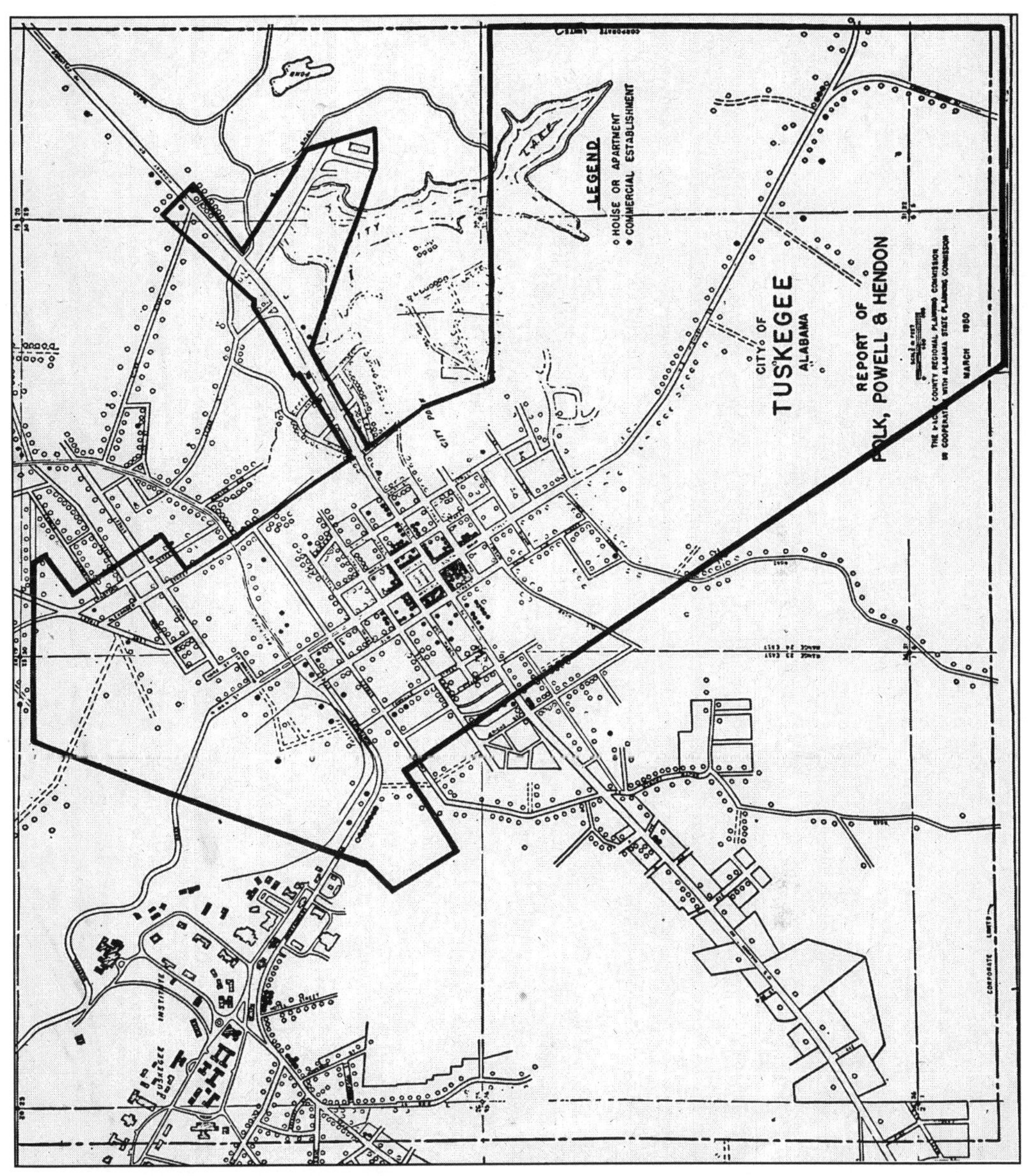

City of Tuskegee 1957 gerrymandering map. This map shows the 1957 twenty-eight-sided gerrymandered figure of Tuskegee City limits designed to disenfranchise Black voters. Areas shown outside the gerrymandered lines were included within Tuskegee City limits before the gerrymander attempt. Courtesy Tuskegee University Archives, Tuskegee University.

Narrator Roosevelt Lorenzo Williams tells the story of how his grandparents depended on credit from White store owners during the boycott. His grandparents eventually ceased this practice upon discovering how one White business owner was cheating them. Lower income citizens also could not afford to drive to Montgomery, Alabama, or Columbus, Georgia, to buy groceries. Some still did not even own cars and were using horse-drawn wagons for transportation at that time. Nonetheless, despite some tensions between rural working-class and middle-class Black people who lived in the city, the TCA worked to provide carpools and shopping co-ops to ensure most could unite to protect Black voting rights.[42]

Residents in Tuskegee and surrounding areas using their buying power to challenge the gerrymander, eventually led to White-operated businesses in Tuskegee closing and going bankrupt. Gomillion also became the lead plaintiff in the legal battle against redistricting. This battle ended with *Gomillion v. Lightfoot* being argued before the Supreme Court.[43] The attorneys for the case included veteran civil rights attorney Fred Gray; Robert L. Carter, lead counsel for the NAACP; and Arthur D. Shores, a prominent Black lawyer from Alabama. The US Supreme Court accepted their argument that redistricting discriminated against Black people. Thus, the court declared that the gerrymandering violated the Fifteenth Amendment by denying Black people the right to vote.[44] Many of the life narratives featured in the collection discuss the boycott and how it influenced their development and thinking as members of the civil rights generation. Several narrators' relatives were plaintiffs in the case, including the parents of Sullins and Lee and Marian Quinn Williams's aunt.

Another important legal battle in the local Civil Rights Movement in Tuskegee and Alabama was *Lee v. Macon County Board of Education*. The case sought to integrate the all-White Tuskegee High School, eventually leading to the desegregation of every school in Alabama. Civil rights attorney Fred Gray filed and argued the lawsuit.[45] Among the group of students seeking admission to Tuskegee High School were brothers Anthony, one of the narrators, and Henry Lee. Their father, Detroit Lee, a staunch community activist, served as the lead plaintiff in the case. Lee, an active member of the TCA and founding member of the local NAACP chapter, was committed to social justice. In his narrative in this volume, Anthony describes his father's activism and his own experience integrating rural Notasulga High School after Governor George Wallace closed the all-White Tuskegee High School.

In addition to Lee, several other narrators discuss their connection to the case as part of their life narratives. Willie B. Wyatt, also a plaintiff in *Lee v. Macon County*, describes his experiences integrating rural Notasulga High School and his and Anthony's attempts as teenagers to integrate local White churches. Lee and Wyatt also write about being among the first Black students to integrate Auburn University—a bastion of racial hostility at the time. Furthermore, Sullins and Billes, who had siblings as plaintiffs in the case, relate the effects on their families who were committed to the movement.

While the case initially sought to integrate schools in Macon County alone, it eventually led to the integration of schools across the state because of the legal maneuvering of Gray and missteps by then-Governor of Alabama George Wallace. Seeking to live up to his infamous declaration of "segregation now, segregation tomorrow, segregation forever," Wallace closed the all-White Tuskegee High School in September 1963 to keep it from integrating.[46] His actions proved that the governor, as opposed to local school boards, controlled educational policy in districts across the state. Therefore, Gray and other civil rights attorneys did not need to file and pursue separate cases against each local school board. Instead, a panel of three judges declared that the state must desegregate schools across the state—an order the court expanded to trade and vocational schools, junior colleges, and all other schools under the control of the state Board of Education.[47]

In addition to the narrators being at the center of two of the most important legal cases of the Civil Rights Movement, they were also witnesses to one of the most infamous events of the movement—the killing of Sammy Younge Jr. It happened in Tuskegee during the college years of the narrators, most of whom knew Younge personally. On the evening of January 3, 1966, when Younge tried to use the bathroom at the Standard Oil service station, he was shot by Marvin Segrest, a service station attendant. Younge was the first Black student murdered for their support of the Civil Rights Movement.[48]

Younge grew up in Tuskegee, Alabama, as the son of prominent members of its Black middle-class community. His mother, Renee Younge, was a schoolteacher, and his father, Sammy Younge Sr., was an occupational therapist at the Veterans Hospital. Although he attended boarding school in Massachusetts for several years, he graduated from Tuskegee Institute High School in 1962. He then served in the navy for two years before returning to Tuskegee Institute to study political science.[49] Upon returning to Tuskegee, he became involved with the Modern Black Freedom Movement. He was a member of the Student Nonviolent Coordinating Committee (SNCC). He participated in several important campaigns led by SNCC, including the march from Selma to Montgomery and helping the Mississippi Democratic Party register people to vote in Mississippi. Furthermore, he was also a leader on the campus of Tuskegee and served as an outspoken voice for desegregation in the city.[50]

Much like the death of Emmett Till in August 1955, the killing of Younge was the catalyst for a generation of activists. Many of the life narratives featured in this volume discuss the killing of Younge and the effects it had on them and their commitment to the movement. Some remember him walking the campus in his SNCC uniform of blue denim overalls and brogan boots and talking about the movement to anyone who would listen. Milton Donald says they were friends, and Carolyn Woodard remembers walking home after high school with him. Additionally, many narrators participated in the silent march the night of and the day after Younge was murdered.[51] Marian Quinn Williams captures many of their feelings when she wrote, "We all put our hurt, grief, and anger into the march. Many of us knew Sammy personally."[52]

The lasting impacts of the Modern Black Freedom Movement on Tuskegee were varied. Although the campaign to desegregate Tuskegee High School led to the desegregation of schools across the state of Alabama, a decade later, the county was home to only one truly integrated school—Notasulga High School.[53] Furthermore, the segregated academies in Auburn and Montgomery formed in the 1960s by White parents fleeing desegregation remain almost all-White today.[54]

As a result of the movement, Tuskegee could boast of Black officials holding most of the top offices in the city and county including mayor and county commissioners, but the promises of Black electoral power were primarily left unfulfilled. Black electoral power had promised economic development and opportunities for all of Tuskegee's Black community. Instead, as federal and state support for the local economy dried up during the 1980s and '90s, the economy stagnated.[55] The rise of Black political power also accelerated the rate of White flight from Tuskegee, along with their wealth and businesses. Unwilling to live under Black politicians, the flight of White residents further shrank the city's limited tax base.[56] In addition, the Modern Black Freedom Movement opened vast professional opportunities for the children of the struggle nationally and internationally. Their professional accomplishments far and wide made their parents and grandparents proud, but it also contributed to the brain and tax base drain on the city of Tuskegee as the children fulfilled the hopes and dreams their parents had for them, as well as the dreams they had for themselves. However, the uneven impact of the struggle was not unique to Tuskegee. Across the Black Belt and beyond, the leaders of the movement had turned to Black electoral power politics as the obvious next step in the movement and had been disappointed by the outcomes.[57]

Narrative Findings

Why Ancestors Stayed or Returned to Tuskegee

The narratives provide significant insights into the question that fueled the origin of the project: Why did some Black families stay in the South broadly, and Tuskegee specifically, before, during, and after the Great Migration? In conversation with a range of sociological and historical projects that address why Black people stayed in the South during the Great Migration, including William Falk's *Rooted in Place*, Luther Adams's *Way up North in Louisville*, and Bernadette Pruitt, *The Other Great Migration: The Movement of Rural African Americans to Houston*, this project adds to still-emerging discussions that highlight the key role education and educational institutions played in shaping African Americans' decisions to remain in the South.[58]

Furthermore, the narratives herein also highlight how education and educational institutions became the catalysts for other significant reasons for staying—employment, land, home and business ownership, and family. The group of narrators, at its center, was brought together by the educational resources available in Tuskegee. Many of the ancestors featured in the narratives, whether formally educated or not, valued education and shared this value with their children. While White's father and Woodard's and Donald's grandparents were not college educated, the narrators describe how they read newspapers daily. Lee recounts how his parents, neither with college degrees, required their children to read the newspaper every day and discuss the articles they read at breakfast. Many Tuskegee families proudly displayed in their homes the gold standard of conspicuous educational aspirations at that time, the *World Book Encyclopedia*. Billes's father bought a set of encyclopedias and required him to read the entire set, although he had not reached "Z" by the time he went off to college.

Therefore, the experiences of the Black residents who stayed in Tuskegee and Macon County more broadly provide distinctive answers to why Black people remained in the Jim Crow South during the Great Migration. Interestingly, access to education was often high on the list of reasons why Black people fled the South. Many rural schools operated on shortened calendars, inadequate facilities, and substandard educational supplies. Additionally, most southern communities did not have high school facilities for Black people. Black people in rural areas in the South often had to travel long distances to attend high school, or they had to leave home and move to the nearest city or town to attend an all-Black high school.[59] For most students, leaving home meant boarding with relatives or strangers in their new setting, a practice some more conservative Black parents found untenable; thus, truncating the hopes and dreams of many southern Black Americans at that time. However, because of Tuskegee Institute and its emphasis on educating not only the citizens of Tuskegee but people in surrounding rural areas, the educational injustices of Jim Crow segregation were not as acutely felt in the area. In fact, other educational institutions, including local elementary and high schools, were also important sites of employment and community development. Washington's partnership with Rosenwald to form the Rosenwald school program led to several elementary schools for Black children in Macon County.[60] Home to one of the best Black high schools in the South, two private primary through eighth grade schools, and with public primary and secondary schools staffed by graduates of Tuskegee Institute, access to education did not drive Black people to leave Tuskegee but instead drove them to stay in the city.[61]

Some grandparents and great-grandparents of this cohort had been enslaved and born in Macon County, Alabama, in the early 1800s. Others moved there around the time of the founding of the Tuskegee Institute to take advantage of the opportunities promised by Washington. Some of the ancestors became skilled tradesmen and even helped to construct buildings on the one hundred acres of land Washington purchased to establish the new school when he moved from the leaky lean-to at Butler Chapel Church.

While migration to Tuskegee in the early 1900s continued to be centered upon gaining access to education, Washington also heavily recruited faculty and other staff to meet the school's growing instructional needs. The latter stages of migration to Tuskegee involved not only those seeking education and employment at Tuskegee Institute but those who were seeking employment at the institutions and organizations it had helped to spawn, such as the Veterans Administration Hospital, the campus and community John Andrew Hospital, and Moton Airfield, which served the Tuskegee Airmen. Those ancestors recruited to Tuskegee by Washington or others, including parents of narrators, were most often already well educated or well skilled. Many, like Douglas Mayberry's father, went on to obtain advanced degrees at prestigious institutions in the North and returned to teach and work at Tuskegee Institute.[62]

These highly educated professors, health care professionals, engineers, and their spouses formed the foundation for the Civil Rights Movement in the Tuskegee area. Tuskegee Institute and its affiliates also created well-paying skilled and unskilled employment that supported a certain level of activism. Narrator Wyatt credits his father's well-paying job as a professor, where his father had also received his degree, as one of the reasons for the family's staying in the South. His father's place of employment also shielded the family from retribution when they became deeply involved in the Civil Rights Movement.

Along with the need for highly educated and skilled employees, the parallel world also had opportunities for less skilled employment. Narrator Rosa McWilliams Henderson was thankful for the maintenance job her father eventually secured at Tuskegee Institute High School. It helped him turn their two-room home into one with several bedrooms and a separate kitchen. Marian Quinn Williams stated that the job her father acquired in food services at Tuskegee Institute helped the family enormously and made it possible for her to attend the university at a reduced cost. Thus, since economic opportunities often topped the list of reasons why Black people migrated out of the South, the Tuskegee Institute's dynamic economic landscape for the surrounding area helped to anchor residents to the community.[63]

Another major reason for ancestors staying in the area was the ability to gain ownership of land, homes, and businesses. Landownership was highly valued by the ancestors in this project and seemed to be an exclamation point on their freedom. Marian Quinn Williams wrote about how her parents always asked relatives who had migrated North if they owned their homes or any businesses. In most cases, they did not. They were renting. These southern ancestors also often worried if those who had migrated had paid taxes on the land they sometimes left behind. Williams and Redmond wrote of the pride their parents and grandparents had in landownership. Stokes wrote about how proud her grandfather was to be able to entertain generations of family on his property for special occasions. Roosevelt Lorenzo Williams wrote with pride about how his great-grandfather donated land to Tuskegee for the building of a local elementary school. He also wrote of how his family was able to sell some of the land in difficult economic times, especially when his grandfather was elderly and became ill. Annie Jean Baker Reed wrote sadly about the family lore of her great-grandfather "losing hundreds of acres of land to White people," his migration to Tuskegee, his acquisition of more land, and becoming one of Washington's "humble friends." The pride of the narrators' ancestors in landownership highlighted the momentousness of an emancipated person owning property, rather than being owned like property. The ancestors "who stayed" also saw landownership as a way of having something to pass on to future generations, creating intergenerational wealth.

Landownership often led to home and business ownership. Sullins writes that his aunt owned one of the most successful dry-cleaning businesses in Tuskegee. Roosevelt Lorenzo Williams talks about the pride the community had in the first Black man to own a service station near campus. Mayberry writes about his ownership of a pizza parlor, although short-lived.

Many ancestors and some of their progeny stayed or returned to the South because of the desire to live close to family or to care for aging family members. Atkinson-Liggins states that her parents would not have migrated because of the closeness of their family. Narrator White stayed because of his love for his family and being able to help care for his aging parents. He also became very involved in the life of the community through politics and as a leader in its spiritual community. He admits that even after traveling the world, he had not found another place that nourished him as much as Tuskegee and being close to his family have done. Narrator Marian Quinn Williams writes that she was proud and honored to stay in the South to take care of her aging parents to repay them for all the sacrifices they had made for her.

Although counterintuitive, some people might have stayed in the South because of the relative security they felt in their community. While most Black communities offered some protection for its dwellers during the Jim Crow era, Tuskegee Institute and the parallel world that Washington and his supporters created was in many respects an oasis. It shielded the Black populace from some of the harshest everyday effects of Jim Crow that those in other southern spaces experienced, even those in small rural towns only a few miles away from Tuskegee. Narrators Stokes, Donald, Bivins, and several other narrators acknowledge the protected environment within which they lived in Tuskegee. The protectiveness offered by this parallel world, although not all-encompassing, might also have made some residents more comfortable staying in the South.

Lastly, some parents and grandparents in this study stayed in the South for highly personal reasons. It was home, it was what they knew, and they did not have a desire for what city life would have required of them. Redmond writes of her grandfather's love of his ability to move freely in wide open spaces without the screeching noise of cars, buses, trains, and upstairs neighbors. Reed returned home due to difficulties in finding jobs and managing city life. Roosevelt Lorenzo Williams returned home because he had some personal and professional interests related to his hometown that he wanted to fulfill. Mattie Davis Blizzard came home to retire and help with aging parents. Personal factors join employment and educational opportunities, landownership, and family as major variables why ancestors in this study stayed in the South, particularly in the Tuskegee area.

Organizing Narratives into Thematic Sections

Organizing the narratives by themes presented some issues. The selected categories are neither exhaustive nor exclusive. They reflect the editors' attempt to organize the narratives in a way that makes essential points more accessible to the reader. Since all narrators were presented with the same questions, the narratives sometimes reflect the similarity of experiences, as they all cover a specific time in history within a relatively small geographical area. However, each narrative is unique in that it contains the rich and unique lived experiences of the narrator and their family. While many of the narratives address similar incidents, the context is always different, considering their individual and family experiences in the Tuskegee area. Some of the narratives cover over one hundred years of family history, including some ancestors who lived through enslavement, emancipation, Reconstruction, the Jim Crow era, and the Civil Rights Movement to the current day.

The narratives are organized into four thematic sections: Ancestors: Creating the Parallel World; Ancestors and Narrators: Lifting as They Climbed; Ancestors and Narrators: Toiling, Striving, Reaching toward the Sky; and Ancestors and Narrators: Frontlines of the Civil Rights Generation. Each section focuses on a significant theme that emerged while analyzing the narratives.

The Narratives by Themes

Theme One: Ancestors: Creating the Parallel World

This first section highlights early ancestors migrating to and staying in Tuskegee. Many of these ancestors helped Washington build a parallel world for Black opportunity and achievement in the Jim Crow South. The narratives show how, in the late 1800s and early 1900s, Black people were drawn like magnets to the school and community Washington was building in Tuskegee. However, the narratives in this section illustrate that the monumental achievement of building Tuskegee into one of the most influential Black communities in the South was not solely the achievement of Washington but of a community of Black professionals and laborers alike.

These narratives of migration to Tuskegee reveal unexpected answers to the broader question of why families stayed. Furthermore, they represent an understudied aspect of Black history—intra-South migration. The ancestors who migrated to Tuskegee embraced the Hampton-Tuskegee model of self-help and industrial education and utilized their newly acquired education and skills to benefit Tuskegee Normal and their families.

Theme Two: Ancestors and Narrators: Lifting as They Climbed

The narratives in this second section detail how ancestors used their newly acquired educations to uplift the surrounding rural, impoverished communities of the Black Belt. Many ancestors who received their teacher training at Tuskegee Institute were recruited to teach in rural schools in Macon County and nearby communities, some of which were Rosenwald Schools. Tuskegee Institute, founded in part to train teachers for newly emancipated Black people, never lost its basic mission to educate teachers. These teachers played a singular role in cultivating the parallel world of Tuskegee and surrounding areas. Tuskegee Institute's mission to "lift the veil of ignorance" from Black people, most of whom were not long out of slavery, and to improve their social, health, and economic conditions depended on the production of generations of Black teachers.[64]

These Black teachers, trained at Tuskegee, often taught in trying conditions. Schools for Black children in small rural areas most often lacked running water, indoor toilets, and electric or gas heating. While these middle-class Black teachers taught in conditions quite different from those they lived in and the ones their children went to school in, they remained dedicated and always wanted the best for their rural students.

Educational outreach remained a significant mission for Tuskegee Institute during the emergence of the Civil Rights Movement in the 1960s, and the children of the struggle picked up the mantle. During this era, several of the narrators worked in the Tuskegee Institute Summer Education Program (TISEP), which was later transformed into the year-round Tuskegee Institute Community Education Program (TICEP).[65] The massive grant, supported by the US Office of Economic Opportunity and the federal Student Work-Study program, was written by

Tuskegee's dean of students, Percival "Bert" Bertrand Phillips. The grant enrolled over five thousand Black elementary and high school pupils in several Alabama counties and hired over nine hundred student workers during its existence. The program served as a valuable source of summer income and internships for Tuskegee students, as well as students from some predominantly White colleges and universities, such as St. Olaf College in Minnesota.[66] The main goal of the program was to improve the educational preparedness of Black students in rural counties surrounding Tuskegee in wake of Alabama's legal changes regarding school desegregation. Continuing Tuskegee Institute's mission to train educators to uplift the race educationally, these programs demonstrate the critical role education has played in Black people's fights for freedom.

Theme Three: Ancestors and Narrators: Toiling, Striving, Reaching toward the Sky

The title of this section is taken from a line in the Tuskegee Institute High School song, "Toiling, striving, never ceasing, reaching toward the sky." This theme emphasizes the importance of the Tuskegee tradition of honoring hard work, perseverance, and having lofty goals. Specifically, the narratives in this section detail the role an emphasis on education played in intergenerational experiences of upward mobility. Although Tuskegee is often associated with Black professionals and the Black middle class, the parents of the narrators in this section and six other narrators lacked academic degrees. Nonetheless, they reared their children to value educational achievement. While all of the narrators whose parents had college degrees went to college, two-thirds of the narrators whose parents did not have college degrees went to college. Narrators also reported high rates of college going and skills training among the grandchildren and great-grandchildren of both groups. This intergenerational commitment to educational attainment reflects the broader values of the parallel world created by the Tuskegee Institute environment.

Theme Four: Ancestors and Narrators: Frontlines of the Civil Rights Generation

The final section explores one of the most ubiquitous themes found in the study—ancestors' and narrators' persistent resistance to the practices and effects of White supremacy. From everyday forms of resistance to the bold actions of the civil rights generation, resistance to Jim Crow is detailed in every narrative.[67] Furthermore, every narrative addresses the ways the Civil Rights Movement shaped their lives as well as their connection to the movement. Both narrators and their ancestors participated in some of the less and the most notable civil rights activism in the country during the 1950s and 1960s. Some were involved in proactive volunteerism such as shopping for elderly neighbors who did not have transportation to shop in other cities during the Tuskegee Boycott of local White businesses. Donald writes about his grandmother volunteering him to help elderly neighbors with their groceries. Others tutored rural Black youth in preparation for mandated school integration. Other narrators assisted with voter registration. Redmond recounted taking a bus very early one Saturday morning with other students to travel from Tuskegee to Mississippi to help with voter registration. Others participated in marches to protest Jim Crow practices generally and specifically the killing of Sammy Younge Jr.[68] Lastly, those families whose narratives are featured in this section were active participants in historic legal cases that changed the South forever.

While still children, some of the narrators in this section sacrificed much for freedom and justice. They suffered through bomb threats to their homes, the burning of their school, threatening and harassing phone calls to their mothers, and violent, hateful, and profane language directed toward them from angry White crowds. Still children themselves, they suffered from the stress of being escorted daily by FBI and secret service agents at school and on school buses. After over sixty years, the momentousness of these narrators' actions remains almost incomprehensible.

The narratives in this section also tell the stories of how these ancestors were willing to pay the ultimate price for freedom—putting their children in serious and dangerous situations to obtain freedom and justice not only for their children but all Americans. Here, in this section, we witness the ancestors of the four narrators—Lee, Wyatt, Sullins, and Billes, along with civil rights attorney Fred Gray—wage a momentous legal war of resistance against the sordid system of segregation to acquire justice for the masses of Black Americans "who stayed" and returned.

In summary, the first-person narratives featured in this book grew out of deep friendships and emotional ties forged among the 1964 graduating class of Tuskegee Institute High School during a turbulent time in American history. Threading through the narratives is the influence of Tuskegee Institute and its role as an educational institution, economic engine, and cultural center. Consequently, not only do these narratives provide an alternative understanding of Black migratory decisions but they also illuminate the role Black schools, especially HBCUs, played in the development and growth of Black communities across the South.

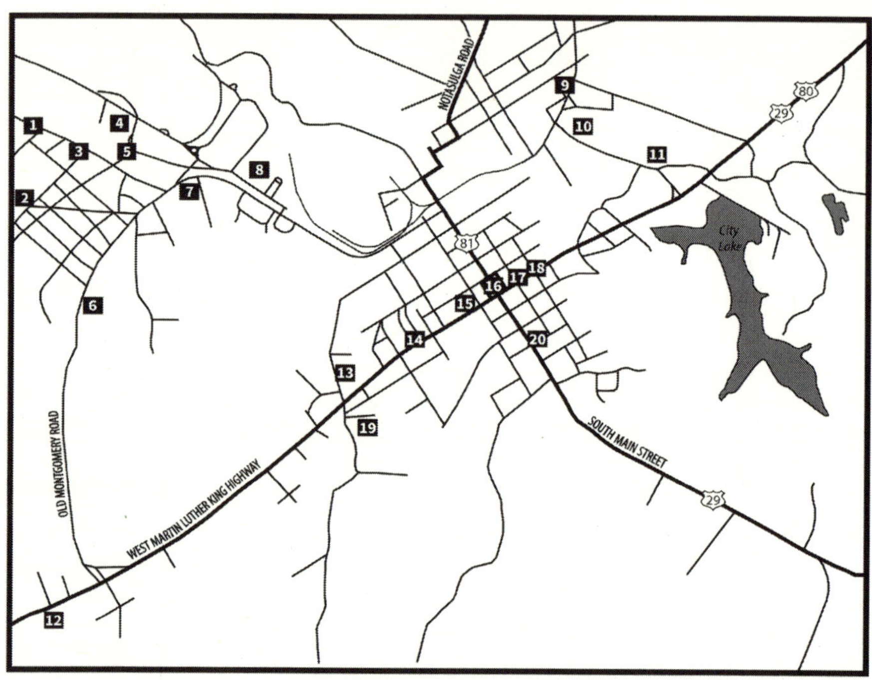

City of Tuskegee

1. Tuskegee Institute High School
2. Greenwood Missionary Baptist Church
3. Masonic Hall
4. Chambliss Children's House
5. Reid's Chicken Coop
6. St. Joseph Catholic School
7. Lewis Adams School
8. Tuskegee Institute (University)
9. Bethel Baptist Church
10. Mt. Olive Missionary Baptist Church
11. Washington Public School
12. Green Fork community
13. Butler Chapel AME Church
14. Reid's Phillips 66 Gas
15. Dairy Queen
16. Tuskegee Confederate Monument
17. Standard Oil Gas
18. Greyhound bus terminal
19. Zion Hill community
20. Tuskegee High School

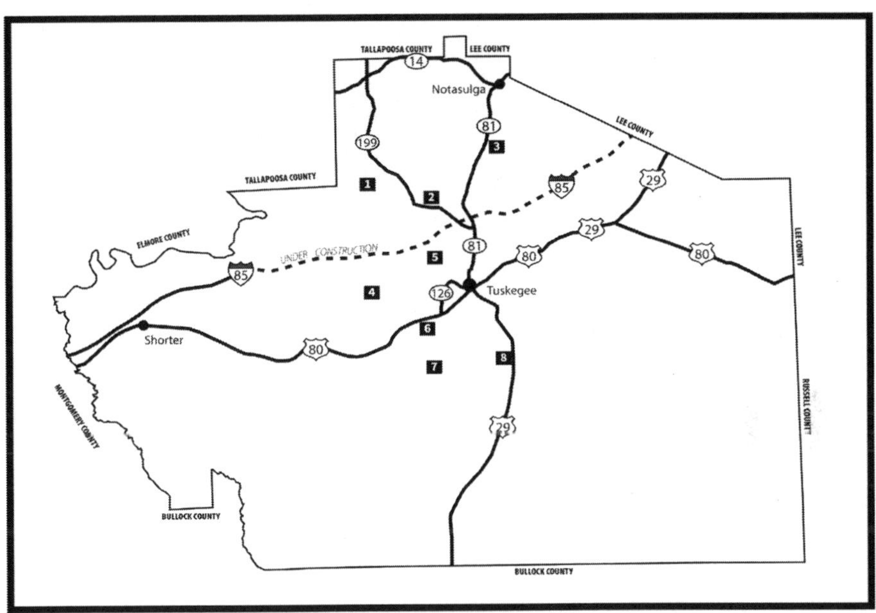

Macon County

1. Moton Field
2. Chehaw train station
3. Shiloh Missionary Baptist and School Historic Site
4. Shady Grove Missionary Baptist Church
5. VA Hospital
6. Greater St. Mark Missionary Baptist Church
7. Heritage Hill community
8. Macon Academy

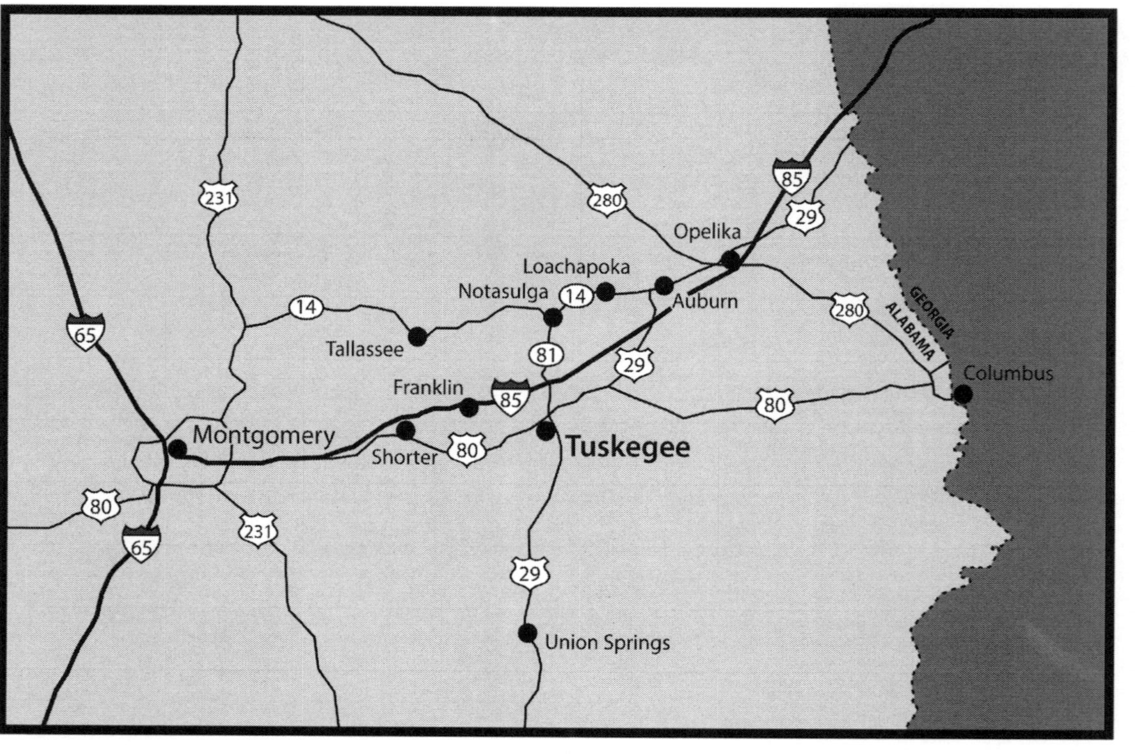

Tuskegee and Environs

I

ANCESTORS

Creating the Parallel World

CHAPTER 1

Raymond Adams

Editors' Note: Before Booker T. Washington was offered and accepted the position of founding principal at Tuskegee Normal School, and approximately fifteen years after the Emancipation Proclamation, Raymond Adams's great-great-grandfather Lewis Adams had a vision of what Black Americans in Tuskegee and Macon County could become. The son of his White master and enslaved mother, Lewis was born in the area and learned trades as well as three foreign languages from the books of his White brothers and sisters. After the end of slavery, he moved to the city of Tuskegee, set up a successful business, and became a leader in the Black community. He knew his community needed a school and engaged in political maneuvering to get it. He stayed in Tuskegee to assist Washington in establishing "the school." He was Washington's social and political advisor, introducing him to the White establishment in the area. He also accompanied Washington to foreign countries as his translator. It can be said that Lewis was the major person who came to Tuskegee and stayed to help create a parallel world for the Black community that served as an antidote to the surrounding Jim Crow society. Ray's narrative also highlights Christianity's role in his family, from his great-great-grandfather and the early days of the school to his present-day family. Building upon Adams's momentous efforts to help his people by founding a college are Ray's especially poignant descriptions of strong family support for education among Black people. He describes how those family members who had migrated North sent money and clothes to family back South, secured summer jobs up North for nieces and nephews attending college in the South, and how his parents sent care packages filled with "welfare" food items to help him through college.

I AM THE GREAT-GREAT-GRANDSON OF LEWIS Adams, the man who had the initial idea for the establishment of a school for Black Americans in Tuskegee. Booker T. Washington is known as the founder of Tuskegee University because he was the first principal. My great-great-grandfather was the person who worked with local and state politicians to establish the school. The story of his involvement in establishing Tuskegee Normal is interesting. He was indeed a Renaissance man. What I know about my great-great-grandfather is a combination of family history passed down through generations and what I've read about him.[1]

Adams, born in 1842, was known as a powerful man with a profound dream. His mother was enslaved, and his father was a plantation owner named Jesse Adams. He grew up in the main house. Although he could not attend classes with his White brothers and sisters, he studied mathematics, English, French, German, and Spanish. He also learned the trades of blacksmithing, tin smithing, harness making, and shoemaking.

After the Civil War, he married Sallie Green with whom he had sixteen children. His White father gave them a house. Adams applied his trades and earned a good living by training Black assistants and hiring them out to local businesses. Family lore or fact has it that by the late 1870s, almost every household in Macon County had a pot, pan, shoe, or tin roof made by Adams.

Maybe one of the reasons that Christianity and learning run so deep in our family stems from Adams's love for school and church. Our family has always heard that he loved learning and teaching. He used his Sunday School class to teach the children at the Butler Chapel AME Zion Church not only religion but also reading, writing, and arithmetic.

Family lore has it that Adams always sought opportunities to educate his people. White children in Tuskegee attended local schools; Black children often had to travel far distances for education. In 1879, an opportunity arose that would change the course of history for Adams, Tuskegee, and Black people in the area. Wilbur F. Foster, a White Confederate soldier and politician, was running for reelection to the Alabama

Ray Adams's great-great-grandfather, Lewis Adams, founder of Tuskegee Normal, now Tuskegee University. Frances Benjamin Johnson Collection, Library of Congress.

Senate, and Arthur L. Brooks, editor of Tuskegee's newspaper, the *Macon Republican*, was running for reelection to the Alabama House of Representatives. Both men had reason to believe they might not win. During Reconstruction, Black men were eligible to vote. The White politicians saw an opportunity to take advantage of this situation. Adams knew that Black people outnumbered White people in Macon County three to one. Brooks and Foster approached Adams for his support in garnering the

Black vote. Adams agreed to help them, and they asked what they could do for him in return. Family lore has it that they offered him a house, a mule, and then money at various times, but Adams refused each offer. It is said that he told Brooks and Foster that he wanted nothing for himself but that his people needed a school.

Brooks and Foster both won their seats with support from the Black community in Macon County. With their help, the legislature appropriated $2,000 a year for the training of Black teachers. The new college Adams had hoped and bargained for was called Tuskegee Normal and Industrial Institute and was administered by three commissioners—two White people and Adams. They needed an administrator. From the beginning, Adams had collaborated with his White friend George Washington Campbell, a local banker and former enslaver who lived across the street from Butler Chapel AME Zion Church. Campbell suggested to Adams that they contact General Samuel Armstrong, the founder of Hampton Institute in Virginia, for advice. Armstrong recommended Booker T. Washington, a Hampton graduate, as the founding principal.

When Washington accepted the position, Adams worked side by side with him, introducing him to the community and helping him develop plans for the new college. In Washington's autobiography, *Up from Slavery*, he wrote the following about Adams, "I have always felt that Mr. Adams, in a large degree, derived his unusual power of mind from the training given his hands in the process of mastering well three trades during the days of slavery."[2] It might be that Adams's academic and technical brilliance that had led to his economic success also influenced Washington's educational philosophy for the new college by placing a heavy emphasis on the trades in the curriculum.

My great-great-grandfather taught classes for many years at the college. When Washington traveled to Europe to raise awareness and funds for the college, Adams went along as his translator for Spanish, French, and German. He died from a stroke in Sunday School at Butler Chapel AME Zion Church, April 30, 1905, singing the hymn "Whosoever Will Let Him Come." He was sixty-two years of age. Had he not understood the need for higher education for Black people, the need to form alliances with White people, and the potential strength of the Black vote, there might never have been a Tuskegee University.

My brother, Reverend Charles M. Adams wrote, "There was one main ingredient that was paramount about the success of Lewis Adams and that was his personal relationship with Jesus Christ. Undoubtedly there were times when he wanted to give up, but through it all, he continued to walk by faith and not by sight."

My father, Raymond Thweatt Adams, a great-grandson of Lewis Adams, was born in Tuskegee, Alabama. He married my mother, Pearl Taylor, from Opelika, Alabama, in 1943. They had three children and stayed in the South to raise our family and to make a living. Because of deeply rooted family ties, our parents did not leave for opportunities in the North or West. However, we did have uncles and aunts on both sides of the family who moved North to the New England area, mainly to Massachusetts and Connecticut. They got factory jobs and did well raising their families. Although my mother's siblings often encouraged her to come North with her family, I have no recollection of my parents' voicing regrets about staying in the South, although there probably were some. They were obviously impacted by segregation, but they mostly focused on their love and passion for their Christian faith and family. In addition, my father had a government job, and I am sure he did not want to jeopardize it. My mother was also a very reserved person, so she wouldn't have been involved in any protest, although she was aware of it. Despite any challenges they faced, they handled most situations with quiet grace.

I attended St. Joseph Catholic School for kindergarten and then Lewis Adams Elementary School, which was also founded by my great-great-grandfather. At a certain time of the year, probably his birthday, a special assembly would be held to recognize his descendants. My sister, cousins, and I would be asked to stand to be recognized. As a kid, I did not really understand who Adams was or why we were honoring him. I do remember a cousin Lily Wilson, who taught me in the fifth grade, and a cousin principal Mrs. Carter. I remember the administrators having a sense of pride and honor at these celebrations for my great-great-grandfather. As I grew older, I began to understand his contributions to the Tuskegee community. Maybe one of the reasons my parents decided to stay in the South was because of our closeness to the history of the Tuskegee community.

My father worked at the Tuskegee Veterans Administration Hospital for most of his career. He was a clerk typist, an unusual job for a man at that time. My mother spent most of her career at John Andrew Hospital on Tuskegee Institute's campus. As far as I know, my parents were not involved in the Civil Rights Movement. I do not remember those conversations. It might also be that they did not want us to be involved. They were very reserved church folk trying to make a living for their family. I knew the Civil Rights Movement was going on, but like my parents, I did not participate in any of those activities. That just was not our focus. We were more focused on religious issues.

I attended Tuskegee Institute High School and graduated in 1964. I was an average student. One of the things I remember most about high school was the tradition of the older boys cutting a T in each freshman boy's hair at the beginning of the school term. I guess I remember it because I was so nervous about it that I thought about not going to school. But I had to go to school, and I did get a T cut in my hair.

My parents expected all three of us to get a higher education. My brother and I went to college, and my sister went to trade school in Birmingham. With my mother working on the campus, it was an opportunity for us to go to Tuskegee Institute at a reduced rate. As it turned out, I did not attend Tuskegee Institute. I applied and took the entrance exam, but I didn't pass. When the time came for me to retake the test at Tuskegee, I had received acceptance to Tennessee State. I majored in business administration and again was not involved in campus activities because I had to work so much to help pay for my education.

I worked in a downtown Nashville restaurant near the Grand Ole Opry. My hours were from ten o'clock at night until two o'clock in the morning, and then in the morning, I had an eight o'clock class. I worked in what was called Printers Alley. There were many restaurants there, and I was a waiter in several of them. Things were very tough economically at that time. Sometimes we would get hungry late at night in the dormitory. My parents would send care packages with whatever it was that they were able to send. I remember they would send me this big block of welfare cheese that I shared with other students. They also sent me potted meat, Vienna sausages, and saltine crackers. They sent me some of whatever they were eating at home. It never failed to touch my heart that they were taking off their table to send to me. That is something to think about.

That was their way of supporting me and making sure their dreams for me going to college came true. It was a sacrifice that many Black parents were making for their children at that time. They did not have lots of money to send, but they sent care packages with the government cheese that they probably could have used themselves.

While I did not participate in civil rights activities in a significant way while at Tennessee State because of my work and academic schedule, I do remember this was the time of Stokely Carmichael and Angela Davis. I remember there were marches on and surrounding the campus. I remember when Dr. Martin Luther King Jr. was assassinated. We joined students from Fisk and Meharry and marched on Centennial Boulevard. Centennial Boulevard was a very busy street running through campus. That main street running through the center of campus led to the prison. I remember on the night of King's murder that many students were out on the sidewalk throwing bricks at any White person that passed by. Using violence was their way of expressing their anger and protesting what had just happened.

I finished all my coursework at Tennessee State in December but returned the following May to walk at graduation. Between completing my coursework and graduation, I came home and worked as a teacher's aide in a rural school in Macon County. At the time, my family did not have a car. After a few paychecks, I was able to buy a 1960 blue Volkswagen Beetle. It was a five-speed, and I couldn't drive a stick shift. The salesman brought it home and showed me a few pointers. Later, I managed to drive the car to pick my brother up from a basketball game. That was a funny scenario, but I had bought my first car!

After graduation ceremonies in May, I was on my way to Boston where I began my professional career. Because of the Civil Rights Movement, many corporations were looking to hire Black people. Consequently, I got my first job as a business administration major with General Electric. It did not matter to me that they were looking for Black people. I just wanted a job. Over the next few years, I moved around to several companies, primarily to make higher salaries. I worked in New York, Indiana, Michigan, and Illinois.

I got married on Christmas of 1975 and went to work for a health care foundation that was establishing a government review program for hospitals in Indiana. I worked in the health care policy and administration sector for several years, using some time to do an MPA at Indiana University. That is when I got the opportunity to return to the South. I finished my career here in the South as a health care district administrator with responsibility for a rural geographic area with four hospitals and as a fundraiser for the United Way of West Palm Beach County. Near the end of my career, I was also fortunate to form my nonprofit.

While growing up, I would say that we knew that Black and White issues existed, mainly because of segregation. We almost never experienced any of that direct racism on a personal basis because we were sheltered from it by Tuskegee and our families. Our day-to-day contact with White people was limited.

I remember one summer when I was in college, my uncle got me a job in a factory in Massachusetts where he worked. He did not tell them that I was a college student and would return to college at the end of the summer. One day my supervisor called me into the office to offer me the tool and die job. I told him that I'd be going back to university at the end of the summer. He was shocked and disappointed.

I was hoping the situation would not get my uncle in trouble because he was a longtime welder and had his retirement benefits set up. Like many Black people who had gone North, my uncle did what he could to help the rest of us who were still in the South with our dreams. Northern relatives were known for sending money and clothes "back home," as well as finding summer jobs for their siblings' children who were in college.

In Massachusetts, my relatives lived in an integrated neighborhood. I noticed there weren't any obvious White or Black issues, as it would have been in the South. There seemed to be more opportunities to make decent money. They went to the same stores and parks and through the same doors. Some of my relatives had not experienced the kind of segregation and racism that occurred in the South. They had not been in Alabama when the Klan occasionally rode through the Tuskegee neighborhood on Montgomery Road or had cross burnings somewhere nearby. While it was unbelievable to me initially, I realized that that was their reality. Later, I learned that racism could come in different forms, such as a lack of promotions and lower salaries. I can remember my older brother telling me that while at work in Massachusetts one summer, somebody called him the N-word and he responded by saying, "Where is he? I have never seen one. Where is he?" That was funny.

The Civil Rights Movement has paved the way for younger generations of Black people to experience life in a much more open and honest way. Young Black people have such a rich history of Black achievement to emulate and be proud of. I just got back from a family reunion where all the branches of the Adams family came together. We've been having it for several years now, and this year, it was held in New Orleans. We usually talk about Lewis Adams and the history he made. His offspring have done well and continue to make contributions to society.

Regarding the future, I would say to young Black people that it is so important to be informed so they can respond more from a global perspective and with kindness. I include the global perspective piece because the world is about more than just Black and White issues. It is about learning to be more inclusive of all people, whether a person is White, Black, or green. A more global perspective puts you in a better position to see different points of view. When one is narrowly focused, you don't know what you don't know.

CHAPTER 2

Carolyn Earline Foster Bivins

Editors' Note: Carolyn Earline Foster Bivins's great-grandparents heard about the founding of "the school" in Tuskegee and migrated there by mule and wagon to a homesite a few blocks from it. The new school was located in a lean-to building at Butler Chapel AME Zion Church. Her family, the Hastings, readily adopted the skills-based education being offered at the school. They learned building trades and assisted Booker T. Washington in erecting many of the early campus buildings. While Bivins's great-grandparents and their children mostly became skilled laborers and teachers of the trades at Tuskegee, their grandchildren and later progeny almost without fail received academic degrees at Tuskegee or other colleges throughout the North and South. This family's continuing emphasis on education—private elementary schools and early adoption of sending their children to other parts of the South or North to college—can be traced from its early Tuskegee settlers to the present. Bivins's narrative not only demonstrates the early allegiance to the Hampton-Tuskegee educational philosophy, but it also clearly shows how well Washington's philosophy worked in creating upward mobility through succeeding generations.

When I researched the history of my family for this narrative, I became aware of the close connection my parents and grandparents had to the building and establishment of Tuskegee University. Based on information passed down through pictures, oral family narratives, and Bible records, I was able to reflect on the struggle that took place to establish a location and facility for Black people to be educated in the South. My family and many Black people in Alabama benefited from this effort. I remember stories about my grandmother Alice Sims who was born in 1881 in a small town in Macon County called Society Hill, Alabama, located seventeen miles from Tuskegee. According to our family Bible, her parents, Governor and Ellen Sims, felt the need to load their wagon with their two young children and all their earthly belongings to start a new beginning. They moved their family of four to Tuskegee with hopes of a brighter future for their children. My grandmother Alice's birth in 1881 was the same year that the Tuskegee Normal and Industrial Institute was founded. My great-grandparents quickly became involved. Great-grandfather Sims helped with the restoration and construction of some of the first buildings at the school.

My grandmother Alice and my grandfather Sylvester Hastings met as teenagers in Tuskegee and later married. He was a carpenter by trade and built them a home right down the hill (Zion Hill) from Butler Chapel Church.

The Hastings children attended Chambliss Children's House, the private laboratory school on the campus of the Tuskegee Normal and Industrial Institute. My mother, Elinor, was the fourth of seven children; the fifth child, Buster, died at the age of nine or ten. All seven Hastings children loved school. The six living children earned diplomas and degrees in their chosen fields of study. The girls became teachers, and the boys became brickmasons, educators, and carpenters. Grandfather Hastings became a member of the Masonic Lodge and a Shriner in Tuskegee, and Grandmother Hastings was the secretary for the Order of the Eastern Star.[1]

When my mother and her siblings attended school at Tuskegee Normal and Industrial Institute, students were required to "board" in the campus dormitories. They were also required to have hands-on work experience. They worked on the campus farm and in the dairy, built bricks, and performed other trades on campus to pay their tuition. Dr. Booker T. Washington believed in teaching students to use their heads, hearts, and hands. The girls learned to sew and made their uniforms. They had to wash and press their skirts and blouses until they stood nice and crisp from the starch they used. In *Up from Slavery*, Washington wrote that when teaching his first class of thirty students, the shanty was so

Carolyn Foster Bivins's grandfather, Sylvester Hastings, wishful master of the Masons, with children. Courtesy of Carolyn Foster Bivins.

dilapidated and leaky that sometimes someone would need to hold an umbrella over him as he taught his class. It seemed to be an impossible task to achieve what was needed to educate the people. At this point, he felt the best way to achieve his goal was to teach the community how to use their hands to acquire an education. It was a concept that did not go well with the students since they were more interested in a book education. To convince them, he headed to the woods with an ax and began clearing the woods to plant a garden to grow food for the school. When they saw him do this the students followed. This was the beginning of

Washington's efforts to help his students provide the school with what was needed to progress: food and shelter.

In those days, there was an emphasis on keeping the facilities and oneself tidy and clean. My mom said they heated the irons for smoothing their clothing on the hearth or potbellied stoves. She spoke often of how proud the students felt and how beautiful they were as they marched to required chapel services in their starched uniforms on Sunday mornings and evening vesper services. Grandmother Alice told me that in the early days at Tuskegee, the school only went as far as the seventh or eighth grade. Upon completion of these grades, students were expected to go out and teach in surrounding communities.

When my mother was a student at Tuskegee Institute, she joined the famed Tuskegee Institute Choir under the direction of the internationally renowned composer Dr. William L. Dawson. The choir traveled around the country to raise money to support the school by giving concerts at Carnegie Hall, Radio City Music Hall, on Broadway, and other famous places. My mother sang soprano and had perfect pitch. Once when the Tuskegee Institute Choir traveled to New York City, my mother's voice was the "sounding tone" you heard when the Radio City station came on the air.

My mother and her two sisters majored in home economics education. One of her sisters, my aunt Geraldine Hastings, graduated from Tuskegee Institute and became a member of the home economics faculty and taught classes there for two years. She later received her master's degree from the University of Pennsylvania and a PhD from Cornell University. She ultimately became the head of the Home Economics Department at Grambling State University in Louisiana. She held that position for over thirty years. My aunt Christine Hastings also graduated from Tuskegee Institute, taught school, and later married. She and her husband became evangelists and traveled throughout the United States.

During the 1950s, my uncles Ben and Lawrence Hastings were selected by Tuskegee Institute to travel to Nigeria and Indonesia to teach what they knew about making bricks and building homes and other facilities. Through the pictures they brought back from their travels, the children in the Hastings family saw a view of the world. We also received amazing souvenirs that they brought back for us.

Carolyn Foster Bivins's mother, Elinor Hastings (*front row, first from right*), the lady with the golden voice, with the Tuskegee Institute Choir and renowned composer Dr. W. L. Dawson. Courtesy of the Tuskegee University Archives, Tuskegee University.

My father was born into a Catholic family in New Orleans in 1910. His father was a carpenter/contractor, and his mother was a seamstress. His father, James Thomas Foster, along with his sons, built their home. His mother sewed for some of the richest White and well-to-do "mulatto" women in New Orleans. Many times, ladies would come to Caroliner and ask her to make a dress like the one on display in a fashionable shop in downtown New Orleans on Canal St. She never left her home to see the dress but would send my dad downtown to sketch the outfit. My father had an eye for important details of the clothing (number of buttons, collar or no collar, sleeve length, zipper or no zipper, etc.) and would make a complete detailed sketch of the outfit. My grandmother never used a pattern yet was able to create a replica of the desired garment. Her patrons were incredibly pleased and paid her well for her skills.

On Sunday mornings, Caroliner would line up her eight children and proudly walk with them to Mass at the designated Black Catholic church located several blocks away from their home. My father was the oldest male child and was the last one in line so he could watch out for his younger siblings and make sure they never wandered off. As a young boy, he would sometimes sneak into Mass at some of the White churches they passed along the way. He would also sneak sips of water from the "Whites Only" water fountains. On several occasions, the White priests would pull him out of their congregations and take him home. It was fun to him when he was younger, but as he got older, the priests felt he was threatening, disrespectful, and a menace. He would also skip school. His parents became fearful for his life and decided to send him to Tuskegee Institute to live with his mother's sister, Martha Lewis Reed. My dad was about sixteen years old when he first came to live in Tuskegee.

Martha Lewis Reed, my great-aunt, was on the staff at John A. Andrew Hospital on the campus of Tuskegee Institute. She worked as a rehabilitation nurse and physical therapist in the Infantile Paralysis Wing of the hospital. I once saw a picture of Great-Aunt Martha in the George Washington Carver Museum at Tuskegee Institute. She was fair-skinned and had dark hair. She could have easily passed for White, but she chose to work for many years helping the Black patients at the John A. Andrew Hospital.

After my parents married, they had a long-distance marriage because "life happened." When my mother graduated from college in 1936, her first teaching job was in Anderson, South Carolina. World War II broke out in 1941, and my dad joined the navy. Shortly after joining the navy, he shipped out. He had the opportunity to travel to many places, including Europe, Chicago, and Hawaii.

My parents did not think they could have children, but ten years later, in 1946, I was a BIG SURPRISE! They eventually had four children: Carolyn Earline, Cynthia Gayle, James Earl Jr., and Mignon Vanessa. I cannot remember my parents ever discussing moving North or West to escape the South. I would guess that they wanted to be close to family and considered Tuskegee home.

Carolyn Foster Bivins's parents (*front row*), James E. Foster and Elinor Hastings Foster, with children and grandchildren. Courtesy of Carolyn Foster Bivins.

I, along with two of my siblings, attended kindergarten through eighth grade at St. Joseph Catholic School. The youngest of us, Mignon Vanessa, attended elementary school at Chambliss Children's House. My mother felt that at least one of her children should attend her old alma mater, and Mignon did.

My mother loved to sing, and she often joined church choirs in the community where she was boarding in teaching jobs away from Tuskegee. I read a newspaper article from Anderson, South Carolina, where she was the featured singer at churches. The people gave rave reviews about her beautiful soprano voice. It is amazing to me that she and all her siblings had musical talent, but her youngest child, Mignon, was the only one of us to be musically inclined.

My mother also taught in Georgia and Russell County, Alabama. I can remember my mother boarding the Greyhound bus on Sunday afternoons and traveling to the county where she worked all week. We would meet her bus on Friday evenings when she would return home to Tuskegee. I was very young, but I was conscious of the great sacrifices my mother made working away from home. We were still living with Grandmother Alice.

My family lived with Grandmother Alice in the original home my grandfather built for his family. It was a big three-story framed home with a basement. It was heated by a coal furnace. I remember the coal truck backing to a small chute-like window in the basement, and tons and tons of coal would come tumbling down the chute. In the wintertime, it was my dad's job to shovel the coal into the furnace to keep the house warm.

My mother eventually got a job in Macon County teaching at Cotton Valley Elementary School located on Highway 29 near Union Springs. She was a classroom teacher and the designated music/choir director. She directed all the plays and musicals at the school and played the piano for all assembly programs. I loved attending the musical programs the school had at night. To me, it was just like attending a big Broadway production.

My mother also taught at Macon County Training School and retired from teaching at Washington Public School. She had a total of over fifty years of service. Long before she retired, she carpooled with teachers who taught at her school. She never learned to drive, so she had to pay the teachers to let her ride with them. She had to pay the male teacher more than she paid the women teachers to ride. I asked her why she paid him more, and she said it was because he was the head of his household and needed more money. I did not think it was fair. In her spare time, my mother performed with the Chandrises, a gospel group in Tuskegee directed by Beatrice Hyde Ashley. Our Tuskegee Institute High School counselor, Jeannette Branch, was also a member of the group. The Chandrises performed at local churches and neighboring communities.

One summer when I was five or six years old and school was out, my mother took me with her to Carnegie Hall, the music building on the Tuskegee Institute campus. She took voice lessons there, and I joined the children's rhythm band. I played the triangles and the cymbals. Every Thursday at ten o'clock in the morning during the summer, the campus would close, and everyone was requested to attend the weekly performances. Different groups from throughout the campus took turns entertaining and performing on the stage at Logan Hall. It was so much fun to participate. I remember once my mother had a solo. She held the note so long that I thought she would die if she did not stop and take a breath. It was scary and exciting to be a part of something so magnificent.

The Hastings continued to achieve. The younger two sons bought land next door to the ancestral home on Zion Hill. Winston, the oldest son, went North to seek his fortune and never came back to the South. The two younger sons, Lawrence and Ben, continued advancing in their careers, marrying, and building their own homes side by side next to the big family house where I lived with my widowed grandmother, parents, and three siblings.

I remember the first telephone number we had when we lived with my grandmother. The telephone number was simply 2-6-0. We lifted the telephone receiver and told the operator who we wanted to call, and she connected us with the party. Giving the operator three little numbers connected us to the whole wide world at that time. "Hastings on Zion Hill": those were the magical words I said when people asked me who I was or where I lived. Everybody in Tuskegee knew that location and who we were.

Our families became more self-reliant based on the philosophy espoused by Washington and George Washington Carver. They all planted gardens and raised chickens, cows, and pigs. When pig slaughtering time came, neighbors came from everywhere to help. It was a day-long process, but everyone who came to help was gifted with fresh packages of pork to take home. The remainder was salted down and later smoked to preserve it. The same thing happened when a cow was slaughtered. Grandmother Alice had a garden, raised chickens, and made apple, pear, and plum jelly and preserves. The Foster children helped my grandmother gather eggs from the chicken coop and pick fruit from the fruit trees during summers.

In the early 1950s, my first cousins Inez, Alicia, and Christine came of age, and my uncle sent each of them away to college to a new and different world. We all went down to Chehaw train station to see them board the trains and be whisked off to Hampton Institute in Virginia, Lincoln University in Missouri, Howard University in Washington, DC, and other places.[2] When my cousins came home from their respective colleges at the end of each year, they all looked different, talked with sophistication, and even walked differently. I wanted that same "scholarly air" for myself and my future children.

When my uncle Ben Hasting's daughters finished school at their respective colleges "up north," they got their master's and doctorate degrees. They found jobs in the bigger cities. My cousin Inez Hastings became a pharmacist in Brooklyn, New York. My cousin Alicia taught at Howard's medical school and eventually opened her own medical practice. Christine taught special education in Denver, Colorado. After retirement, Inez and Christine both returned to Tuskegee to care for their elderly father.

Uncle Lawrence Hasting's children did well also. Cousin Alzetta became a high school counselor and later a high school administrator. Cousin Helena became an elementary school teacher in Atlanta, Georgia. Lawrence Jr. is the only one of my cousins who stayed home and attended Tuskegee Institute. After graduation, he began working for IBM Corporation.

I can remember my grandmother ordering groceries over the telephone. She would make her grocery list, then call Mrs. Fair at the White-owned Wilburns' grocery store in downtown Tuskegee, located on the corner of Highway 80 and Tuskegee Square. They only hired light-skinned Black people or White people to be clerks in the store. One of the reasons for the Tuskegee Boycott of downtown businesses was that the White store owners refused to hire Black people as clerks. There were Black janitors, but no Black clerks to run the cash registers. Mrs. Marie Williams was eventually hired and became the first Black cashier at Price's Jewelry store in downtown Tuskegee. My family had a running account at Wilburns' that never seemed to decrease, although they paid on it once a month. Sometimes, a man named Red would deliver our groceries. When I went to high school, that same man named Red married Mrs. Marge Cravens, one of our Tuskegee Institute High School teachers. I thought that was a strange connection. That was my first time knowing of an older woman marrying a younger man.

In Tuskegee, civil rights mass meetings were held in local churches to discuss voting rights and gerrymandering around the city that excluded Black people from voting. I can remember going with my parents to Butler Chapel AME Zion Church, my mother's family church, for one of the mass meetings during the midfifties. There was standing room only inside, spilling over with people standing patiently outside looking through windows trying to hear the plans and discussions of the next moves that would be made. One could feel the electricity and excitement in the air. One night, Dr. Martin Luther King Jr. was the main speaker. We got home that night and saw the church and the speakers on Montgomery's WSFA TV's ten o'clock news. After the mass meetings, Tuskegee's Black citizens boycotted the White stores in downtown Tuskegee.

It was at that time, in 1957, that I discovered that there was another world outside of Tuskegee city limits. We had been sheltered from the real Black and White world issues while living in protected all-Black neighborhoods in Tuskegee. On most Saturdays during the Tuskegee Boycott, my family drove to neighboring cities and towns to shop for groceries and other necessities. It was utterly fascinating for me to visit surrounding Alabama towns like Auburn, Montgomery, Opelika, Union Springs, and Columbus, Georgia. Venturing out beyond Tuskegee, I began to witness racial hatred and notice the signs that said, "Whites Only" and "Colored Only." Most of the children in Tuskegee were very sheltered; a beautiful Black world had been created around us—Black schools, Black music teachers, Black doctors and dentists, Black cultural events, and Black neighborhoods.

When we became teens and ventured out of our community, many experiences taught me that the quiet, peaceful, respectful world I had been used to did not exist in other places. I remember seeing "Whites Only" signs on gas stations we passed as we traveled to Montgomery on Highway 80 through Shorter, Alabama. I came to realize that their "Whites Only" gas station was the very last place we would ever want to have to go if we ran out of gas or needed to use the restroom.

On one of our trips to Montgomery, I remember visiting the Kress 5 & 10 Cent Store in downtown Montgomery. The restroom area and water fountain for Black people were located downstairs at the very back of the store. The water fountain was dingy looking, while the "Whites Only" water fountain looked clean and well polished. I decided I was going to "test" the "Whites Only" fountain. I bravely walked back up the stairs and positioned myself to drink. Before I could bend to sip from the fountain, a voice hollered out to me and said, "Get away from there, n****r!" Embarrassed about getting caught, I quickly ran back down the steps. There were no repercussions except my embarrassment and anger.

On another occasion, I remember going shopping at a well-known clothing store in Columbus, Georgia, when I was a young teen. The store had a room in the back for trying on clothes. It was small and crowded, and my sisters and I had to take turns changing. We were happy to at least be able to try on clothing until one of us decided to venture out and realized that there were four other unoccupied dressing rooms available closer to the front of the store. We stepped out and attempted to use them instead of being crowded in the back. Unfortunately, we were ushered back to the one crowded dressing room in the back of the store that had been reserved for Black customers.

Another incident continually comes to my mind time after time. After many decades I can still feel my humiliation and that of my parents and other parents on the bus. My mother belonged to the Women's Social Club in Tuskegee, which often chartered buses that exposed our families to places we would ordinarily not visit on our own. We went to cultural events, amusement parks, and beaches. Mr. Henry Hooten Sr., our classmate Nancy Hooten Garrison's father, was often our bus driver and tour guide. He once took us South to a beach in Pensacola, Florida. He parked the bus on a sugar-white sandy and sunny Pensacola beach.

We immediately heard people shouting that we were at the wrong beach! They said that our beach was down the road. They said, "Get out of here, n****rs!" Mr. Hooten quickly got directions and drove down the road to Johnson Beach, the "Colored Only" designated beach. Even though it was a bright sunshiny day, that beach did not have sugar-white sands nor was it well kept like the first one. These incidents always left me feeling scared, nervous, threatened, and often angry, but usually, there was little that could be done except to comply or run away. We all knew that horrible, violent, or lethal things could happen if one insisted on one's rights in the wrong situation. Many of our parents and other adults had mastered the art of responding to racist incidents while maintaining their dignity and safety. However, they left no room for the perpetrator to misunderstand their displeasure. I always felt much safer when I was with a group or with adults from my family or community when such racist incidents happened. A Black person could be easily killed or disappear, and no investigation would be conducted.

In March 1965, my family watched the Selma to Montgomery march on TV. It was one of many civil rights protests that took place in the South in the 1960s to advocate for voting rights and to protest violence against Black people. The day was later known as Bloody Sunday, as six hundred peaceful marchers were assaulted on the Edmund Pettus Bridge by Alabama State Troopers. Among those beaten was civil rights leader John Lewis.

My great-aunt Martha, now in her eighties, was watching the TV as well. As she watched, she stated she would love to be in Montgomery to greet the marchers when they got to the steps of the capitol. Without hesitation, we jumped in my dad's car and drove to Montgomery to participate. Hundreds of people lined Dexter Avenue. We were able to walk among them in anticipation of the arrival of the marchers, but they didn't show up that day. Later we learned that the marchers were resting on the grounds of St. Jude Catholic Church after their long walk. However, it was very exciting to be there. We safely traveled back to Tuskegee.

On January 3, 1966, word passed that Samuel "Sammy" Younge was dead. It was horrible, shocking news. He was a civil rights activist, a member of SNCC, the Student Nonviolent Coordinating Committee, a navy veteran, and a student at Tuskegee Institute. Students gathered quickly and decided we would protest. It seems that in a matter of minutes, students organized a grand march in the middle of the night from campus to the downtown site where he was murdered. Hundreds of students got out of their beds and joined the march to protest the White man's senseless killing of Sammy just because he wanted to use the restroom. In retrospect, we were sitting ducks for the KKK or anyone who wanted to do us harm in the dark. This march demonstrated the love we had for one of our own and that we were dedicated to the struggle. Our hearts were broken. We were angry and so very sad that hatred and prejudice could have such a horrible consequence for one of our classmates in our small Tuskegee community.

While in college at Tuskegee, I also worked for the Tuskegee Institute Community Education Program (TICEP), a large federal educational outreach grant that had been written by Dr. P. B Phillips, our dean of students. I enjoyed traveling to the various cities and counties surrounding Tuskegee. My job, making and delivering lunches, allowed me to meet other people with diverse ways of thinking and existing. I was excited to see a world that was different from Tuskegee where I had lived my whole life.

After graduating from Tuskegee, I could not wait to spread my wings and fly. I went to Atlanta to live with my cousin Helena. My first dream job was working with Atlanta Gas Light Company as a home economist in business. The job allowed a Black college-educated girl from a small town to drive a company car in the big city. I thought I was living life; I demonstrated how to use and care for gas appliances in private homes, middle and high school home economics classes, and in appliance stores as well. I had worked there for two years when I met my husband. He was from Atlanta and had a degree in engineering from Savannah State College.

We moved to Schenectady, New York, for better job opportunities. Later, I returned to Alabama with a healthy, beautiful baby girl named Adrienne Michele. This was a time in history that was very difficult for a divorced woman with a child. I also feel truly fortunate to have had a home place and a community of people who stayed through the struggle of Jim Crow. Many of them provided the support I needed for a new beginning. I began a career with Auburn University's Alabama Cooperative

Extension System. I was employed by this system for forty-five years. I worked my way through the system and retired as a regional science extension agent responsible for providing human nutrition, diet, and health programs in eight southwest counties in Alabama.

I survived the pain and pleasure of watching my daughter grow and thrive, and thrive she did. She participated in about every competition and activity in 4-H, the Alabama Extension youth program. Adrienne attended Alabama A&M University, AAMU, in Normal, Alabama, and received a bachelor's degree and a master's degree in elementary and early childhood education. She is an excellent teacher in the Huntsville city schools system. Adrienne and her husband, Casey Henry, have two sons, Casey Elijah and Michael Jamison, who attend AAMU, both majoring in mechanical engineering. They are both in the AAMU Marching Maroon and White Band. The thing that is so profound about my grandsons is that they are following in the footsteps of my great-grandfather Governor Sims and my grandfather Sylvester Hastings, who helped with the construction of Tuskegee University; their grandfather James R. Bivins, an electrical engineer who designed truck engines with Ford Motor Company in Dearborn, Michigan; and their father, Casey, who is also a mechanical engineer and the owner of a heating and air conditioning business. Our ancestors are always with us.

I thoroughly enjoyed my work at the extension system because I was helping people of all ages, races, and religions live healthier lives. I enjoyed being able to travel all over the United States, meeting other health professionals, while keeping current in my field.

Although I have excelled in my career, it has not always been without experiences of prejudice and discrimination. For example, early in my professional career in the South, one company I worked with had a general holiday party for everybody. Then the next day, they had a private cocktail party for White employees only.

When I first started working in Brewton in southwest Alabama, I was the first Black college graduate to ever work in the Escambia County Court House. This was November 1, 1974. The county extension coordinator was extremely nervous about having me there. He said, "I have never been around educated Black people before. I am just used to my maid and my yard people." When people from the Washington, DC,

Equal Employment Opportunity Commission came to check to see how things were going for me, he had a heart attack. He retired after that.

I was blessed to be mentored by Peggy Bracken, the White county extension agent woman in the office. When we hosted meetings together, I later found out that other White people would say, "Don't bother Carolyn. She is Peggy's girl." They always thought I was her assistant, the helper or maid, instead of her colleague, her equal.

These situations did not bother me much because I never forgot who I was. I realized I was Black in a White environment. White people on the job often wondered if they could talk openly in front of me. I just knew if I pretended that I wasn't listening, I could hear what they were saying and discover what they really thought. I knew how to code switch. Sometimes, I would talk a certain way in front of White people and then a different way when I was in a Black environment, so I knew how to play the game to survive.

Another reason that many of these prejudicial and discriminatory situations did not bother me is that I had grown up in Tuskegee and had life experiences that gave me confidence. From kindergarten, I had been taught by White nuns at St. Joseph Catholic School to excel, to always do my best, and to strive for excellence. As long as I can remember, I have been taught to have self-confidence. People with self-confidence were all around me when I was growing up. In my neighborhood, there were important people who just acted what we considered normal. Normal was excelling, dignified, and self-confident. For instance, Dr. William L. Dawson, the famous composer, put me in his car and took me downtown one day and bought me a doll. Lionel Richie's mother taught me in summer school. I have always felt I was as good as everyone else. There were some differences shown in the community when it came to skin color. Sometimes lighter-skinned people were provided with more opportunities than darker-skinned people inside and outside our community. This was typical in the Jim Crow system. However, I was raised to believe in my worth based on the self-sufficiency system taught at Tuskegee Institute.

I consider my career with the Alabama Extension System to be part of the Civil Rights Movement. Tuskegee Institute was instrumental in the development of the extension system during the 1890s. By 1990, extension work was being taught by one thousand Tuskegee graduates in twenty-eight states, Cuba, Jamaica, Puerto Rico, Barbados, and the continent of Africa. Tuskegee Institute's success in educating people that began in 1881, the year my grandmother Alice was born, is little known for the huge contribution it has made in extension services around the world. The amazing power of educating Black people is the foundation of many achievements in the world today. It is a never-ending story that has been an amazing journey for me and my ancestors. For those who stayed and those who left, they will find that what they went looking for was already inside of them, passed down through their ancestors. I hope that my effort to be fair to everyone gave Black people the opportunity to be proud of me and my accomplishments and that I set an example for young people to look at me and say, I can do that. To continue the struggle, I would like to leave this quote from Dr. Mae Jemison, the first Black female astronaut, to all young people, especially Black youth. "Don't let anyone rob you of your imagination, your creativity, or your curiosity. It's our place in the world; it's your life. Go on and do all you can with it and make it the life you want to live."

CHAPTER 3

Milton Donald

Editors' Note: Milton Donald's grandmother and her family migrated from Mississippi to Tuskegee to take advantage of the health care she could access there for her husband who was an injured World War I veteran. She had heard of the new hospital that the president of Tuskegee Institute, Dr. Robert Moton, the NAACP, and US President Harding had secured for Black American veterans. She took seriously the Washingtonian values of hard work, education, and helping others in the community. Although she did not have a college degree, she valued education highly for the young people in her family and the community. Milton writes that education was always a top priority for his grandmother's household. She used her home to board Tuskegee students who could not afford housing elsewhere. Milton shared a letter written to his grandmother by the famed scientist Dr. George Washington Carver. In it, Dr. Carver thanked her for referring a young man to him presumably for academic advice or maybe to work with him in his laboratory. Milton's narrative also includes a heart-wrenching racial experience that illuminates the dangers that could and often did beset young Black American men in the South in those days. The incident is a reminder that despite the pervasiveness of racism in the South at the time and the ever present potential for losing one's life, something beautiful continued to happen in the Black community in terms of their support for the continuing progress of the race. Milton's grandmother's work with the youth of the Tuskegee community is a vivid example and represents the depth of informal community support for hard work, education, and the importance of giving back for the betterment of the community.

I WAS RAISED PRIMARILY BY MY grandmother Ollie V. Donald. Education was most important to her. In 1923, she moved from Mississippi to Tuskegee with her children including my mother, Mayme Donald after my grandfather Phillip Donald Sr. was transferred to the VA Hospital in Tuskegee. The airbase, Tuskegee Institute, and the VA hospital collectively provided better employment opportunities for Black people than most other places at the time. Those factors, along with the fact that my grandmother had established herself as a part of the Tuskegee community by the time of my grandfather's death, led to her making Tuskegee our home.

My grandmother subscribed to the *Montgomery Advertiser*, which she read each day diligently. She encouraged us to read it as well. She made the major sacrifice of purchasing the *World Book Encyclopedia* set instead of having us rely on the cheaper encyclopedia sets offered in grocery stores. The answer to many questions we asked her as children was, "Look it up in the encyclopedia." She saw education as a means of our surviving and prospering in the Jim Crow South and the world.

My grandmother encouraged members of our family and friends to register to vote. Even though Black people outnumbered White people in Tuskegee and in Macon County, we lacked political power. She assisted many of her peers to prepare for the literacy test that was used to deny many Black people the right to vote. She also helped many people who struggled to pay the required poll tax.

My grandmother's oldest child learned brickmasonry and was able to find suitable employment opportunities locally. Her second child died in her early twenties before I was born. I do not remember hearing much about my deceased Aunt Lorraine, other than that she died in a hospital in Birmingham, Alabama.

My grandmother's third child worked at the old Tuskegee Airbase, which made her a member of the Tuskegee Airmen. She was also married to a Tuskegee Airman. She spent most of her career working in the laundry at the VA Hospital. My grandmother's fourth child and her youngest son worked as a nurse's aide at the VA, as did my grandmother and my aunt's husband.

Of my grandmother's five offspring, my mother was the only one to relocate to the North. My mother moved to New York City to seek employment opportunities when I was relatively young. I do not recall what caused her to return. However, I do remember hearing her tell someone that she was so happy to get off the train at the nearby Chehaw train station that she kissed the ground. I did not understand this as a child, but the statement has stuck with me throughout the years.

I do not recall any of my relatives expressing regret for their decisions to remain in the South. I remember many of the warnings they shared with us about surviving in our environment. We were always expected to be on our best behavior, especially when we were around White people. We were expected to avoid contact with White people, and Black males were especially warned to avoid White females, whenever possible. We were warned to allow White people to check out ahead of us at downtown stores. The clerks would probably have enforced this rule even if we forgot.

In addition to waiting for White people to be cashed out first at stores, I have vivid memories of separate water fountains and toilets. I remember that the toilets we were forced to use never seemed to be properly clean and were often out of order. Public toilets were usually at gas stations since we were not allowed in the cafes and restaurants. The Torch was a truck stop on Highway 80, which has since moved to exit 42 off Interstate 85 going toward Auburn, Alabama. They served good fish, shrimp, and chicken platters, which we could buy through a window in the back of the restaurant.

The Jim Crow South of my youth included totally segregated schools, swimming pools, and seating in the local movie theater. I attended segregated schools all the way from first grade through graduation from high school. Swimming opportunities were initially at Logan Hall on the Tuskegee Institute campus and later at Abbott Park. The swimming pool owned and maintained by the city of Tuskegee allowed White people only.

In hindsight, the segregated theater was hilarious. Black and White people were basically in the same large, divided area where we watched the same screen. We purchased treats from the same concession stand, just with White people on one side and Black people on the other. The separate bathroom rule was still in effect. The movie experience in Tuskegee was slightly different from the movie theater experience I had while visiting relatives in a small Mississippi town during the same period. In Mississippi, White people used the main level and Black people sat in the balcony. Everything else was pretty much the same.

We were reminded by our parents to use a title when addressing White people. Most parents were not comfortable with their children being out at night alone; my grandmother certainly was not. Heeding these warnings became second nature and resulted in very few negative interactions with local White people. Ironically, the warnings or reminders we were given were pretty much identical to the behavior we were expected to exhibit toward all adults. The emphasis on not attracting negative attention from adults, especially from White people, was not missed. Nevertheless, the sense of pride as Black people in Tuskegee prepared us for that first Crusade for Citizenship meeting held in Butler Chapel AME Zion Church on June 25, 1957.

This is when we saw the men in our families and other men throughout Macon County put themselves on the line on behalf of all of us. Even as a ten-year-old, I fully appreciated the significance of the event. I had also heard the whispers about the potential of trouble from the local White Citizens Council, the Ku Klux Klan, and other hostile White people. The sense of danger was confirmed when I saw two of my uncles cleaning their matching 32-caliber pistols, weapons I did not even know they owned until that day.

The meeting was held without incident and became the precursor to the boycott of local White merchants. The Tuskegee Boycott required determination and resolve on the part of local Black people, but it also required major cooperation by Black people assisting each other. People who did not have transportation were offered rides to merchants in adjacent cities by families who had cars. People who received assistance from my family often received help in carrying their groceries by yours truly. My grandmother volunteered me. Many of the families who volunteered to give rides to others had participated in giving rides to people in Montgomery during the famous Montgomery Bus Boycott a few years earlier.

Young people began to dominate the Civil Rights Movement by the time I entered high school in 1960, the year of the Greensboro sit-in. I remember only one march I participated in while in high school. I don't recall the specifics very well. The most memorable thing about this march was a statement made by an elderly White woman who was literally being propped up by others around her. As we marched through Tuskegee Square, she stated, "I have never seen so many blackbirds in my whole life." Her statement amused rather than threatened me.

While this narrative is focused on growing up in the segregated South, I hope the reader does not get the impression that all was "peaches and cream" in the North. I marched more in New York City than I did in Alabama. We protested White Castle's practice of hiring only White people as carhops. We protested at construction sites due to their hiring practices. One of my cousins volunteered to be arrested for lying down with others to block trucks from entering and exiting the site.

When I graduated from high school, the woman who would become my wife was carrying my daughter. The responsibility of my impending fatherhood caused me to switch my focus from college to employment. I thought the easiest route for me was to return to New York to resume the job I had had the previous two summers. So, like many before me, I fell into the category of those who left the South seeking better employment opportunities.

I did not learn about the worst thing to ever happen to a family member until I was in high school. My grandmother's first child went by the name Lamon B. Donald. I remember asking my uncle what the B in his name stood for, and he responded that his middle name was Brown. I had never heard of Brown as a first or middle name, but I did not dwell on it. Some years later when my uncle was seeking proof of his age for Social Security purposes, the family received shocking news.

You must understand that birth records for Black children in rural Mississippi during the early 1900s were quite sketchy. After months of searching, my grandmother was able to locate an elderly woman in Mississippi who had worked as a midwife. The affidavit signed by the midwife included a statement indicating that she remembered the teenage girl who married a man by the name of Brown. She went on to state that a White man had killed Brown and that the widow left town with her infant son. Her affidavit included the year this occurred, and the government fortunately accepted it as adequate proof of my uncle's age for Social Security purposes.

We were shocked to hear this and even more shocked that our grandmother had never mentioned it. When pressed as to why she had never shared it with us before, her response was simply, "It was nothing to talk about." We wisely left it alone.

My children and grandchildren have heard many of my "Tuskegee stories." I have always wanted them to appreciate their family's history. I always wanted them to understand that the environment my generation and generations before me grew up in was an essential part of that history. Fortunately, my descendants were interested in hearing about the family history and opened the door for me to share answers to the questions they asked of me.

I shared how used books were delivered to us at the all-Black Lewis Adams Elementary School in Tuskegee. A Black woman who worked for the board of education delivered our books in her vehicle. I think her name was Mrs. Lightfoot, but I may be wrong about that. She was a heavy-set, fair-complexioned woman with a sweet smile. Some of us boys were "volunteered" to retrieve the books from her car. We never gave much thought to the fact that the books were used. We received the books from the White school when they received new books.

I shared with my family the impact of seeing history books that glossed over the whole issue of slavery in America and how horribly wrong Native Americans were treated in this country. Enslaved Black people dancing around a campfire was the only image of Black people I remember in one of our history books. The caption was intended to make the reader believe that the enslaved people were happy and content. I balance this by sharing one of the many advantages our segregated system offered.

Our competent, concerned, and committed Black teachers went well beyond what was required of them. We were exposed to history and literature beyond what was approved by the state of Alabama. We were fortunate to have access to the Hollis Burke Frissell Library on the campus of Tuskegee Institute (currently Tuskegee University). The library was well stocked and even had a children's section. We were encouraged to use this library as much as possible.

Some teachers assigned book reports and other assignments that required us to seek out books beyond those provided by the state of Alabama. I even remember teachers checking books out for children who lived in rural areas and had difficulties accessing the library. I appreciate how our teachers responded to the state's deficient standards for Black students. They ensured that we were exposed to educational information, materials, and practices that made us intellectually competitive when we did have the opportunity to go to school with White people.

Regardless of the US Constitution's Fifteenth Amendment's guarantee of the right to vote, Jim Crow laws made it illegal initially and subsequently difficult for Black people to become registered voters. This was especially true in areas like Tuskegee and Macon County, where the ratio of Black people to White people was approximately seven to one. The White people in control relied on poll taxes, which were not abolished until 1966, and a literacy test to prevent Black people from registering. My high school civics class was encouraged to assist adults in our families and our communities who were preparing for the literacy test.

To add insult to injury, the person who had the job of registering people had the habit of ignoring lines of Black citizens, while he sat in his office and just watched them stand there waiting. White citizens could simply walk past the Black people standing in line and proceed to register. We also learned that White people who could not read were having the questions read to them. Any response they gave was accepted, and they were able to register to vote. On the other hand, Black people could be deemed to have failed the test for any reason the registrar chose to give.

I shared with my family an amusing story that involved a bus ride from Tuskegee to New York City at the beginning of the summer of 1964. Notwithstanding that the Supreme Court had banned segregation in public education by its ruling in *Brown v. Board of Education of Topeka*, 347 U.S. 483 (1954), there was still segregation of cafes and restaurants at Greyhound bus terminals. They were not integrated until 1964, following the court's ruling in *Heart of Atlanta Motel, Inc. v. United States*, 379 U.S. 241 (1964), and Title II of the 1964 Civil Rights Act.

I was traveling with two other guys from Tuskegee when we stopped in Washington, DC. We proudly strolled into the bus station cafeteria only to find that we were not impressed with the food. I remember one of my companions saying, "They knew we were coming, why haven't they fixed anything we like?" It was customary to see Black people boarding Greyhound buses with shoeboxes in their hands before the Civil Rights Act of 1964. The shoeboxes usually contained sandwiches, fried chicken, chips, cookies, and soft drinks. We knew we were not assured that we would find a place to buy anything at the bus stops along the way.

The closest I came to having a seriously negative incident involving racial relations in Macon County occurred one night as I was returning home from visiting a friend who lived on the other side of town. I avoided going through the Tuskegee town square but still found myself encountering a few White men and a boy about my size and age.

Upon seeing me alone at nine or ten at night, they called me over to them. Resisting the urge to run, I approached them. They asked a series of questions such as my name, where I was going, and where I was coming from. Then they tried urging the White boy and me to duke it out. I immediately realized that this would be a fight I dare not win. As I was grappling with how to survive the impending fight, it became clear the White boy wanted no part of fighting me. I do not know whether he realized that this was a fight he would surely win. The men finally accepted that the boy would not initiate an altercation, and God knows I was not going to. One of the men turned to me and said, "Git on boy," and I got on.

My legs were trembling so bad I was afraid I would fall over if I attempted to walk. So I trotted across the street and around a corner. My trot became a sprint once I was out of their sight. They probably laughed at the sound of my feet striking the sidewalk as I sped toward Tuskegee's campus. My usual route home would have been to take Franklin Road to Washington Avenue to Adams Street to my home on Anderson Avenue. I changed my route that night. I went through the campus and came out at the Franklin Gate. I then took side streets until I reached Adams Street. I did not relax until I was in my grandmother's house.

I also explain to my children and grandchildren my perception of the difference between growing up in Tuskegee and other areas of the South during the 1950s and 1960s. Even as a preteen, I could see a difference in the attitude and behavior of my adult relatives whenever we traveled to areas outside of Tuskegee. A subtle level of tension could be felt when they interacted with White people in other areas that was not present when they interacted with White people in Tuskegee. For us kids, it meant being on our best behavior and staying close to our parents or whatever adult was accompanying us. While accompanying the adults on shopping trips to Montgomery, Birmingham, or Atlanta was still exciting, that subtle tension always tempered the excitement.

None of my family members who opted to remain in the South have ever shown any indication that they regret their choice. Ollivette L. Donald Core, my sister and only sibling, opted to stay. After obtaining a degree from Alabama State University, she opted to "pay it forward" by serving as a teacher for the Macon County School District. She has been active with the Friends of Tuskegee Airmen National Historic Site and volunteered to work with the US Park Service staff at the site. She continues to contribute to the cause through her service on local boards for the town of Franklin, Alabama, where she resides. She also serves the Tuskegee/Macon County area by participating with Alpha Kappa Alpha Sorority and St. Joseph Catholic Church.

My grandmother continued to support young people seeking educational pursuits. Her house in the Greenwood community was located about one-half mile from Tuskegee Institute's campus. Many Tuskegee Institute students seeking off-campus housing resided in the Greenwood community. My grandmother provided low-cost housing to many of them. I met several members of the Tuskegee Institute women's basketball team during a visit to Tuskegee during the early 1980s when a few members of the team resided at my grandmother's house. We lovingly referred to my grandmother as "Dear." Dear was limited in what she could do to further aid in the struggle for civil rights and equality, but she continued to do whatever she could regarding the pursuit of education by Black people. Her support of the education of young people in our community is immortalized by her efforts to arrange a meeting between a young man in the community, one whom she presumably thought had promise, and the famous Tuskegee Institute scientist Dr. George Washington Carver. Dr. Carver, known for his kindness and generosity, rewarded her efforts by writing her a letter that has been passed down in our family.

TUSKEGEE NORMAL AND INDUSTRIAL INSTITUTE

FOR THE TRAINING OF COLORED YOUNG MEN AND WOMEN

RESEARCH AND EXPERIMENT STATION

George W. Carver, Director

TUSKEGEE INSTITUTE, ALABAMA

12-12-'34

My dear Mrs. McDonald

My dear friend, Mr. Stevenson has told me so much about you and your boy that I am anxious to see if I can help him.

I can see him any time Fri. Afternoon up to 4:30. If you come before 2:30 come to the laboratory at the Agrl. Bldg., After that to Rockefeller Hall. Room No. 1.

I thank you also for your kindly expressions relative to work that I am trying to do.

Very sincerely yours.

G. W. Carver.

P.S.
Mr. Ollie Stevenson is one of the finest men I have ever met.

Letter from George Washington Carver to Milton Donald's grandmother, Ollie V. Donald. Courtesy of the Milton Donald Family.

Her support of education no doubt contributed to my determination to attend college. I started at John Jay College of Criminal Justice in New York City. All the distractions caused by living in the city and working as a corrections officer led me to return to my roots to succeed in school. My grandmother was my biggest cheerleader as I worked at any job I could get as I completed my undergraduate program and acquired a BS degree in management from Tuskegee. She was also a motivating factor in my decision to attend law school. It was worth everything it took to get her from Tuskegee, Alabama, to Madison, Wisconsin, to attend my graduation from the University of Wisconsin Law School. As I accepted my law degree, the look on her face is something I will forever cherish.

Milton Donald's grandmother, Ollie V. Donald, at his graduation from the University of Wisconsin Law School. Courtesy of the Milton Donald Family.

Milton Donald, an avid supporter of *The Children of the Struggle* project, in his law school regalia. Courtesy of the Milton Donald Family.

I appreciate my southern upbringing, which instilled positive traits and characteristics in me. However, growing up in Tuskegee made that experience more memorable. We were exposed to many world-renowned people in our everyday lives. Imagine walking down the street and seeing Dr. William L. Dawson after one had just seen his name listed as the composer of several songs in one's church hymnal.[1] Imagine a small-town boy knowing that one of the teachers at his high school, Alice Coachman

Davis, was an Olympic medalist.[2] How many young boys from small-town America were fortunate enough to have a world-renowned scientist as their Boy Scout leader. Those of us who belonged to Troup 70 of the Boy Scouts of America had Dr. James H. M. Henderson, the noted physiologist who performed plant experiments with Dr. Carver, as our scout troop master.[3]

The level of success we saw from everyday people in our communities in the little town of Tuskegee gave us confidence that "it can be done!" and that excellence was expected of us. Thus, it is no surprise that we have peers who have excelled in various areas. We had athletes like Zeke Moore, who went on to play for the NFL's Houston Oilers, and others who went on to play professional sports or become coaches. We grew up with awesome musical talents such as Lionel Richie and the Commodores and Viola Billups (Pearly Gates) of the Flirtations.[4]

In the world of business, we had the Joyner brothers: Albert, who owned and operated multiple McDonald's franchises in Alabama and Mississippi, and the "Sky Jock" himself, Tom of the Tom Joyner Morning Show. We grew up with peers who would become notable in government as well. Myron Thompson has been elevated to the US Appeals Court. The late Patti Grace Jones Smith (one of the students who integrated the all-white Tuskegee public school in 1963) did extensive work for NASA after having served with distinction in the US Department of Transportation.

We had many peers who pursued careers in education. We can point to peers who served in various capacities in education. Dr. Robert Moore of the University of Miami and Dr. Sonjia Parker Redmond of California State University are just two examples of our peers who have excelled in education.

Tuskegee calls itself the "Pride of the Swift Growing South." Most of my peers and I made that pride a part of who we were as we entered adulthood. Having grown up around people who had not only been successful but people who had excelled gave us the courage to live up to the words in our high school song, "toiling, striving, never ceasing, reaching toward the sky." Reaching high enabled us to succeed. As my grandmother and our other ancestors adopted Booker T. Washington's values of hard work, education, and giving back, we have been able to have great careers and make the country less discriminatory along the way.

While I have held numerous jobs during my life, my chosen professions are still my work as a tax preparer, something I have done for well over fifty years, and environmental protection. My upbringing really prepared me for my tenure as part of the team charged with enforcing compliance with federal and state environmental protection regulations. Joining an office as the only Black lawyer out of fifteen attorneys was not an issue for me. My upbringing convinced me that I could compete with anyone. Admittedly, I could still hear the voices in my head reminding me that I had to be better than everyone else and that any job worth doing deserved to be done well.

The attitude and level of professionalism I brought to my position as a staff attorney in the Wisconsin Department of Natural Resources led to my being asked to serve as director of the department's Bureau of Environmental Analysis and Review. The appreciation I developed for the environment while growing up in the South contributed to my embrace of nature. My desire to protect it led to my success as bureau director.

After surviving seventy-five trips around the sun and having lived in various parts of America, I am convinced that the lessons we learned in the South were just as applicable in the North and Midwest. I am also convinced that many obstacles placed before us during my childhood and in prior times to impede progress are the things that still need to be in the forefront of the Black struggle.

Two of the issues we fought to address in the past that still demand our attention are voter rights and education. Attempts to restrict voter rights and access to the ballot are being made in many states. At the same time, conservatives continue to drag their feet on passage of the John Lewis Voting Rights Advancement Act of 2023 pending in the 118th US Congress. Some of the restrictions adopted by various states recently are detrimental to voting equity.

Consider one of the restrictions adopted by the state of Georgia. It is now a crime to give any food or drink, including water, to any person standing in line waiting to vote.[5] To fully appreciate the impact of this and similar restrictions you need to understand that it is traditional to experience long lines during voting in predominantly minority areas. People have been forced to wait for three to five hours or longer to vote. Delays are caused by equipment breakdowns, insufficient number of ballots, and inadequate staffing. It sure sounds like the antics used in the "Old South" to me.

Taking another example from Georgia, look at the election of the current governor, Brian Kemp.[6] Kemp was secretary of state when he ran for governor. He was projected to lose against Stacey Abrams, a dynamic Black female attorney.[7] Stacey, very much like President Obama had done early in his career, had spent years working with various community groups promoting voter registration, voter education, and voter participation. Some accuse Kemp of using his authority as secretary of state to negate several hundred thousand ballots from heavily minority, Democratic districts to assure his victory. Again, if true, this seemingly open and obvious abuse of the electoral process is quite reminiscent of the "Old South."

In the area of education, we must continue to support and strengthen our historically Black colleges and universities (HBCUs). HBCUs provide higher education opportunities to many Black students who would face obstacles being admitted to, paying for, or having the support to succeed at many major predominantly White colleges and universities. HBCUs are often not supported as much as other colleges and universities by state legislatures who provide funds to public educational institutions. We must be involved in these funding decisions and be prepared to bring discrepancies to light.

While pushing for greater access to higher education we must be mindful that Booker T. Washington's educational philosophy included the trades, which were an excellent pathway to the middle class. We must inform our young people that even today, tradespeople can be as financially successful as many college graduates.

Of all the things I want my children and grandchildren to remember as it relates to continuing the struggle is to remain informed, inspired, and involved. They need to stay informed to know what is going on around them. I encourage them to know who their elected officials are and what they stand for. They need to be informed about issues affecting their lives in their communities, their counties, their state, and their country.

Being informed should lead them to be inspired. If my wife, Karen, and I have been successful in instilling positive values, love, and integrity in them, the information they receive should inspire them to act. This will lead to them being involved. I want my offspring to remember that as great and committed as our leaders were, people such as Martin Luther King, Ralph Abernathy, Stokely Carmichael, Rosa Parks, John Lewis, and so many others are not the ones who made our movement successful. I want my children and grandchildren to understand that change was brought about by the involvement of the masses—millions of nameless or unfamous people like their great-grandmother Dear who rose up and got involved.

Their involvement can be as passive as providing financial support to organizations, events, and initiatives that advance the struggle or more active as becoming an organizer or even running for office. The struggle depends on many people fulfilling many different roles. I would be happy with my descendants being involved at any level if it benefits the struggle.

My classmates and our generation tried to build on what our ancestors and others had done. As we come to the end of our role in the struggle, we must pass the torch to future generations. I am convinced that if they follow the advice to stay informed, inspired, and involved, that struggle will be in very good hands.

CHAPTER 4

Nancy Hooten Garrison

Editors' Note: Nancy Hooten Garrison's family came to Tuskegee and took advantage of the educational opportunities offered by the school. Her parents joined the teams of Black recreational therapists at the Veterans Administration Hospital and teachers in rural elementary schools in Macon County and throughout the South. Her uncles became builders of new housing subdivisions with brick homes for first-time Black homebuyers for Tuskegee's growing Black middle class—some of whom had never lived in homes with inside plumbing. Nancy's parents were instrumental in helping to build and support the social milieu of the parallel world by organizing youth activities. Her family stayed in Tuskegee because they had good-paying jobs and believed in the mission of the Tuskegee Institute. Many members of her family worked in the field of education and helped bring education to rural areas in Macon County and beyond. With their degrees from Tuskegee, members of her family were sent by Booker T. Washington to establish two educational institutes, Snow Hill Institute in Wilcox County, Alabama, and Laurinburg Institute in North Carolina. Her family continues to be a family of educators, having helped to create parallel worlds for Black people in Tuskegee and the rural South into the mid-1900s.

After World War II, veterans took advantage of the GI Bill to obtain their education and to get good jobs. Tuskegee Institute opened its doors to Black veterans, and the federal government built housing close to the campus for their young families. My father, Henry Hooten Sr., entered Tuskegee Institute in the summer of 1946. He played football and worked in Logan Hall, the campus sports and entertainment facility at the time. He studied year-round to graduate in three years in 1949. My mother, Lillian Carter, was a teacher and found teaching jobs in Macon County to maintain the family during that time.

Early on, we moved into a small apartment in the Veterans' Projects. When my dad graduated, he got a job as a recreational therapist at the large Veterans Administration Hospital. My uncle lived with us while he attended Tuskegee Institute. My uncle got his diploma as a master brickmason and built many dormitories, classrooms, and business offices on campus.

Nancy Hooten Garrison's father, Henry Hooten Sr., treated patients at the VA hospital, including his son, Herman, who developed polio. Herman became one of the first Black football players at the University of Notre Dame. Courtesy of Nancy Hooten Garrison.

During the Jim Crow era, many banks in the South did not want to lend money to Black people to buy cars or homes, even if they had good educations and good jobs. One bank president thought this was not right. Mr. Parker at the Alabama Exchange Bank made loans to anyone he felt was able to repay the loan. This was not always good for him and his family in their relations with most other White citizens, but he had strong principles and did what was right.

With a loan from Mr. Parker's bank, my family bought our first car and started building our home around 1950. My uncle's business boomed. His company was building homes all over Macon County. He built most of the houses on Colvert Street where we were building our home. Tuskegee was growing with the veterans staying after graduating from Tuskegee. The White citizens feared that Black people would vote and put them out of power since White people controlled all of city and county government positions.

Nancy Hooten Garrison's parents, Lillian Carter and Henry Hooten Sr., with paternal grandmother, Rebecca Lee Hooten, at home in a subdivision built by Tuskegee Institute's 1940s/1950s building trades program graduates. Courtesy of Nancy Hooten Garrison.

As a result, gerrymandering began. With the assistance of the Alabama State Legislature, the Tuskegee City Council redrew the city limits so that only four Black families were able to vote for city elections. Tuskegee Institute professor Dr. Charles G. Gomillion, attorney Fred Gray, and several other Black citizens formed a group to fight discrimination.

The group called themselves the Tuskegee Civic Association (TCA). The TCA met on Sunday evenings to plan strategies. In 1957, they called for a boycott of White businesses in Tuskegee because of the gerrymandering. In 1960, the *Gomillion v. Lightfoot* case was filed against the city of Tuskegee.[1] We boycotted downtown White businesses that participated in the voter suppression efforts. We went to other towns to shop. Some Black businessmen opened a grocery store that was burned. Burning homes and businesses was a common terror tactic used during Jim Crow by the Ku Klux Klan (KKK). One night we heard our neighbors yelling, "The chapel is on fire! The chapel is on fire!" I remember neighbors congregating in the street as they tried to get a glimpse of the smoke billowing into the sky.

It was suspected, but never proven, that the KKK burned down what some would say was the heart of Tuskegee Institute's campus, the beautiful Tuskegee Institute Chapel. Some say it was caused by an electrical failure or lightening. The chapel had been designed by famous Black architect Robert R. Taylor, the first Black student to graduate from the Massachusetts Institute of Technology and the first accredited Black American architect.[2] It was said to have been one of the most beautiful college campus chapels in the United States at the time.

The burning of the Tuskegee Institute Chapel sent shockwaves throughout Tuskegee and surrounding rural areas because the chapel was the spiritual and cultural heart of the campus and, to some degree, the surrounding community. On Sunday mornings, all students were required to "go to chapel" and to evening vespers. Sunday vespers included messages from Dr. Booker T. Washington and later from the school's leader at the time. In later years, vespers changed into current events speakers and cultural performances for the students. Many community people also attended Sunday morning services and vespers at the revered chapel. The chapel contained extraordinary stained-glass windows that told the story of Black people's struggle through Negro spirituals. The stained-glass windows were reproduced and installed in the new campus chapel and continue to draw thousands of visitors each year.

During the Tuskegee Boycott, Black citizens worked together. Even the children were involved in the movement. Being around eleven years of age at the time, I remember making shopping lists for elderly neighbors and delivering their groceries to them. Black people came together as a wonderful community working for a common goal. These hands-on civics lessons taught young folk the importance of voting. We would keep working for our rights as we grew up.

My family has been blessed to know about our ancestors back to the enslaved Mike and Phoebe. The story has been told for generations. Two cousins have researched and written books about them.[3] At every family reunion, the story is told by our family historians. We have had reunions every two years for over fifty years. Even the young children of our family can tell the story of our ancestors. I am sixth generation from Mike and Phoebe.

Mike and Phoebe were owned by different enslavers in South Carolina in the late 1700s. Mike was loaned out to numerous plantations since he was a skilled blacksmith. Mike and Phoebe met, fell in love, jumped the broom, and started a family. The wedding was on Christmas Day of 1812. Enslaved people from nearby plantations attended.

In 1820, enslaver Rump decided to move his plantation to Alabama where the soil was rich and the crops would thrive. He wanted to purchase Mike from his enslaver and take him with him, but this was not possible since Mike was so valuable to his owner. Phoebe, pregnant with my ancestor Patty, and her seven children moved with her enslaver to Dallas County, Alabama. Mike stayed in South Carolina.

Mike was able to work for pay at various plantations in his off time. Four years later, he had earned the $1,500 needed to buy his freedom. He headed to the Black Belt of Alabama to join his family. Mike was welcomed by his family and the other enslaved people in the area. Enslaver Rump hired him to work as a freedman. Mike and Phoebe eventually had eleven children. All of them lived on the Rump plantation until freedom came at the end of the Civil War. When they were freed, the children decided they would not take the name of their master but honored Mike by taking the surname Carmichael.

Education was important to our ancestors, and many of them became educated in the years that followed. My great uncle William James Edwards went to Tuskegee and studied under Washington. When he graduated, he went back to Wilcox County, Alabama, to start a school for Black people. It was called Snow Hill Institute. Uncle Edwards was part of the Tuskegee Program. Washington established it to send graduates to found schools in the Deep South to educate other Black people in areas in need of schools. My great uncle Emanuel McDuffie started the Laurinburg Institute in North Carolina. Most of the faculty at both schools were descendants of Mike and Phoebe. Both schools still exist in some form.[4]

The contributions of Snow Hill Institute and Laurinburg Institute to the Black community were enormous. They taught landownership, civic values, and family values, along with academic classes. My grandfather Frank Jesse Carter went to Snow Hill to study farming. Every summer the students from Snow Hill went to Tuskegee to take advanced classes such as organic farming from Dr. George Washington Carver. When Grandfather Frank graduated from Snow Hill Institute, he moved to Escambia County, Florida, to start farming. During the Jim Crow era, Black people were not able to purchase land in Escambia, so his White grandfather bought the land for him. He married my grandmother Nancy Louisa Johnson who was a teacher at Snow Hill, and they moved to Pensacola to raise their family.

Nancy Hooten Garrison's maternal grandfather, Frank Jesse Carter, whose White grandfather bought land for his farm in Pensacola, Florida, at a time when Black people were not allowed to purchase land in the county. Courtesy of Nancy Hooten Garrison.

Nancy Louisa and Frank raised six children to adulthood. The three girls all became teachers and educated other Black people throughout the South. Grandfather Frank was the first school bus driver for Black children in Pensacola. He started taking his children, their cousins, and neighbors to school in his truck, then the county gave him a bus. He had a large 150-acre farm. He raised pecans, veggies, hogs, fruit, and other crops to sell to the military and large companies such as Green Giant and Del Monte. I spent my summers on the farm following my grandfather around and enjoying every minute of the experience.

Our family has attended various historically Black universities, including Hampton, Tuskegee, Morehouse, Spelman, Alabama State, Alabama A&M, and Howard, and they have also attended numerous other predominantly White universities, including the University of Texas. Through the years, Mike and Phoebe have produced doctors, lawyers, teachers, dentists, businesspeople, movie directors, artists, actors, therapists, social workers, and military professionals. Several of their progeny worked for voter registration campaigns during the 1960s. Most of us have stayed in the South working for civil rights and trying to make the world a better place.

My cousin Vivian Malone integrated the University of Alabama in 1963. Her younger sister, Sharon, is a medical doctor and is married to Eric Holder, the former US attorney general under President Obama. Spike Lee and Malcolm Lee are relatives creating movies that make a difference. My brother Michael Henry Hooten was the first Black National Merit Scholar from the state of Alabama in 1962. My brother Herman Hooten was one of the first Black people from Alabama to play football for the University of Notre Dame. Many of the descendants have done much and continue to do much for our country and the advancement of all people. In our family, we are taught that Mike and Phoebe left us a rich heritage that we are very proud of. The Mike and Phoebe legacy combined with the rich educational, employment, and social environment that was being created in Tuskegee created a sense that we had greatness to live up to.

Our parents did not ask if we wanted to go to college. They asked where we wanted to go. It was understood we would get a college education. I had scholarships to Howard, Fisk, Tuskegee, Hampton, and Auburn for the fall of 1964.

Auburn University sent representatives to some of the top students in our class before high school graduation to talk to us. They were planning to integrate the university in the fall to comply with the new *Lee v. Macon County* court edict requiring all Alabama public schools to integrate. Auburn was offering tuition, books, and supplies but would not be providing dormitories for Black students. They wanted Black students who would drive back and forth to campus every day. They were not prepared to allow them to live in the dorms with the White students.

Auburn's scholarship was the largest scholarship I had been offered, but I was unsure if this was what I wanted to do. I called my grandfather Frank in Florida to get his advice. He informed me that Pensacola Junior College was planning to integrate that summer of 1964. Some college administrators had gone to Black churches in the Pensacola area to recruit students. No one accepted, so Granddaddy asked me to try it. The school was paying all expenses, except ten dollars, and the summer program was not that long. I would get college credit for the class.

So I headed to Pensacola after graduation from high school. My uncle let me drive his car, and he drove Granddaddy's station wagon. I was excited. I enrolled and effectively integrated Pensacola Junior College in the summer of 1964. The class was interesting, the students were friendly, and I was invited to the president's home for all types of events. The students wanted to sit next to me in class and asked all sorts of questions about being Black. They invited me to go to the beach with them on the weekends. I did inform them that the beaches were not yet integrated.

One Saturday, I drove my aunt to the mall to shop. We saw three of the young ladies from the class. I waved. They acted like they did not know me. That is when I decided that Auburn University would not be my choice and that I would attend an HBCU: Hampton! My grandfather was a very wise man!

In September, I headed to Hampton Institute in Hampton, Virginia. There, I joined the NAACP and worked to get out the vote. On election day, female students in the NAACP went to homes to babysit, while the boys drove people to the polls. I felt like I was doing my part in the Civil Rights Movement as I had been trained to do by my family and community in Tuskegee.

During the summer of 1965, I went home and worked with TISEP, the Tuskegee Institute Summer Education Program. Students hired to work in the program initially lived on campus during training for what we would be doing in the field for eleven weeks. The federal grant paid college students, including White students from the University of Michigan and some other northern colleges, to tutor rural Black students in academic courses. My group went to the infamous Lowndes County to tutor Black students to prepare them for forced integration in the fall. The planned integration was a result of our classmates' school desegregation lawsuit, *Lee, et al. v. Macon County Board of Education*, which made segregated schools illegal in Alabama.[5] At the time, Lowndes County was noted for having some of the most dehumanizing oppression and violent practices toward Black people in the country.

TISEP students normally lived with families in the county in which they tutored and taught in Black churches since most counties would not let us use the schools. Some students worked in the counties where they were from and lived at home. There were only three Black homes in our area that had city water or telephones. So we used the outhouses and collected rainwater for our host to do laundry and water her plants. Mrs. McCall was my host, and she was wonderful! She had three grandchildren living with her, plus the three girls in our group. She was a fantastic cook and had dinner ready when we walked in from tutoring all day. She always baked a delicious cake each week.

Our young pupils were great and excited about going to the integrated county schools in the fall. It was a joy to work with them. The program brought lunch for us to the church every day. We felt we were doing something great for humanity. Again, I felt that I was contributing to the Civil Rights Movement. At age eighteen we were very naive. We did not know how dangerous it was. The White people in Lowndes County did not want us there. We got bomb threats, were harassed when walking to and from the church, were called n****r, and were told to go back to Tuskegee. It was quite an education.

Civil rights workers, mostly Student Nonviolent Coordinating Committee young people, were in Lowndes County registering people to vote. They were often arrested and thrown into jail. We walked by the jail every day. The young civil rights workers would yell out of the windows asking us to call the feds for them. One day they were not there, so we continued to walk. When we got to the little store in the neighborhood, there was a crowd in front. We saw two men lying on the ground. They had been shot. Jonathan Daniels, a young White Harvard-educated seminarian, died before he got to the hospital in Montgomery.[6]

The car arrived from Tuskegee to pick us up. To report what had happened, we had the car take us to the Montgomery Airport to call the FBI. Before going to Lowndes, the university had arranged for the FBI to give us their telephone numbers in case we needed to call them. We had the driver stop at the airport because we did not trust the local folk in Lowndes County.

When we got back to campus, we met Dean Phillips, the program director. The university had to decide if we would go back to teach in Lowndes County on Monday. My parents were upset and wanted us to stay in Tuskegee. They had seen the news before we got back to campus. My mother said that is when she got her grey hair.

Of course, we went back, but the university made a deal with Avis to let two of us drive a rental car, even though we were only eighteen years old. The administrators felt we would be safer driving back and forth to the church to work during the week. We all grew up a great deal that summer.

I went back to Hampton in the fall, studied hard, did well, pledged AKA, and fell in love. In May 1966, representatives from NASA came to campus looking for math and science majors to work at the Space Center at Langley Air Force Base in Hampton. I was selected. We were trained in operating the IBM computers and in utilizing Basic and Fortran computer languages. I cannot remember for sure, but I might have been trained by some of the Black women mathematicians at Langley who were memorialized in the movie, *Hidden Figures.*

Mickey and I got married in June 1966 in Tuskegee. I went to NASA the following week, and he went to New York to take a class at Rutgers and to work. My education at NASA was great. Mickey graduated from Hampton in December 1966 as a commissioned officer, second lieutenant in the army. We moved to California the next year. I got a job at Space Ordinance Systems operating their computers and doing data reduction. The company made flares for the F-111 jets in Vietnam.

Twenty-three years in the military took us to Saugus, California;

Fort Bliss, Texas; White Sands Missile Range, New Mexico; Fort Bragg, North Carolina; Fort Benning, Georgia; Germany; Huntsville, Alabama; and Vietnam for him. We met wonderful people at each place. Being the only Black officer in many places was difficult sometimes, but it was a good life for the two girls and ourselves.

We moved back to Fort Bliss and bought a home in 1980. I worked with the Neighborhood Watch Program, worked in a craft store, and served as a permanent substitute at one of the high schools. I also started my own silk flower business where I decorated homes, banks, and hotels for Christmas. We were block captains for our street for thirty-five years. I was on three police chiefs' advisory boards. We advocated for and obtained many resources that made our community safer.

El Paso is one of the safest cities of its size in the country. It is on the Mexican border with mountains and desert. After Mickey retired, he taught twenty years in Texas and seven years in New Mexico. Now, we are enjoying the retirement life. We still work with our church and neighborhood watch. Mickey is a high school referee official for football and basketball and a member of Omega Psi Phi fraternity. We register people to vote and fight for civil rights. This is our legacy.

My folks stayed in Tuskegee because it gave them the opportunity to get good educations and good jobs, buy property, build homes, raise their families, and be near their relatives. They raised their families to appreciate education and their heritage and to give back to their communities.

My mother called our family Rainbow Connection. We are Christian, Jewish, Muslim, Latter Day Saints, Catholic, and Protestant, all believing in a supreme being. Some of the enslaved ancestors practiced their Muslim faith in secret in the fields and slave quarters. They taught their children and other enslaved people the religion of their homeland.

My grandmother and her brothers and sisters were all educators. My mother and her sisters and sisters-in-law were all teachers. Even the children, their spouses, and grandkids are educators from college professors to elementary school teachers. When we attend our family reunions, all are recognized for their contributions to society, much of which started in Tuskegee.

Those of us who grew up in Tuskegee were blessed to learn our history, appreciate the struggle, and give back to the community and the nation. Just living in Tuskegee was an education in Black history. We taught our children and grandchildren their history by bringing them back to Tuskegee whenever we could. Tuskegee University, the Carver Museum, the Tuskegee Airmen Center, and Black churches are all important teaching centers. Many Black people who did not attend HBCUs were not taught Black history. We must tell our grandchildren living in a diverse nation to learn about their heritage, appreciate their family's contributions, and do all they can to live up to their legacy. We all must do what we can to make this nation a better place by voting!

The Civil Rights Movement has made it possible for all of us to succeed, but the fight is far from over. Trump showed us this nation is filled with White supremacists who hate people who do not look like them and wish them harm. We must fight racism and fight voter suppression and continue the fight for civil rights for all. If you wish, run for office, donate to causes that fight for our rights, and speak the truth to all who will listen. This is our duty, and we need to make sure our children, grandchildren, and future generations know they also have a duty.

CHAPTER 5

Douglas Mayberry

Editors' Note: Douglas Mayberry writes about his professor father, Dr. Bennie Douglas Mayberry, and his major contributions to the building of a parallel world in Tuskegee. Dr. Mayberry's grant-writing skills were renowned in Tuskegee. He continued Booker T. Washington's legacy of securing funds for buildings and programs for the school and programmatic and building funds for the city of Tuskegee. Douglas writes that some of his father's grant-writing successes secured 1960s antipoverty program funds for low-income citizens of Macon County—continuing Tuskegee's outreach to the community and rural areas. He states that along with his father's hard work and success came his parents' embrace of the Black middle-class values infamously cited by E. Franklin Frazier—consumerism, recognition seeking, and competition.[1]

It might be said that most of the class of 1964 adopted their ancestors' values and learned to balance what some might describe as both their possible positive and negative effects. However, while benefiting from his parents' largesse and fame as a teenager in Tuskegee, Douglas later eschewed what he deemed the consumerist culture of Tuskegee's Black elite. He suggests that upward mobility, along with his family's dysfunction, produced some downsides for him. As an adult, he turned toward criminal ventures to earn the prestige and lifestyle he had been given as a child. This resulted in twenty-seven years in prison.

After serving some twenty-seven years behind the walls of federal prisons and having to live in a complex reality of federal inmate life, I made it! Free now for over five years, I have finally arrived at that point where I can enjoy the goodness and respect of God's love and appreciate and respect the beauty of being part of a loving family and community.

I was born Douglas Gene Mayberry on August 18, 1946, at 6:50 a.m. CST in Tuskegee Institute's John A. Andrew Hospital. Dr. Mitchell was the staff pediatrician. My father, Dr. Bennie Douglas Mayberry, was a professor at Tuskegee Institute. He was born November 7, 1911, and was thirty-five years old at my birth. Selena Irene Williams Mayberry, my mother, having earned her master's degree in education, had been a teacher at Alabama A&M College. She was born July 5, 1915, and was thirty-one years old at the time of my birth.

I was raised as a big, spoiled brat. My parents were not deeply involved in my development to become a cultured human being. I was wild and crazy with little discipline. I grew up with the simple illusion that I was "all that," but I was none of that!

To this day, I hate that Tuskegee served as the cultural arena for my upbringing and youthful development. I was raised in a Black bourgeois family. My family's emphasis was on getting money and spending it primarily to show off. It was all about clothes, shoes, job titles, where you lived, or what you drove. This was the lifestyle I developed while growing up as a child in Tuskegee's Black upper class, and I carried such behavior fully into my young adult years.

My mother came from a rich family in Birmingham, Alabama. She was one of thirteen siblings. My father came from an extremely poor family in Tallassee, Alabama, and had thirteen siblings. His dad was a teacher, and his mama was a midwife.

Eugene Williams, my maternal grandfather, was involved in real estate in Birmingham. It is said that he bought a home for each of his children, an unusual occurrence for a Black man at that time. However, his success cost him his life. The story is that the Jim Crow White people became jealous of his success and killed him on train tracks there in Birmingham. Later, my mother's mother, Grandmother Irene, died almost a year after her last child was born. Grandmother Irene's death left my mother pretty much adrift at the tender age of fifteen. It is reported that it was a sad period when our extended family members began snatching the kids up one by one just to get portions of my grandfather Eugene's wealth. As for my mother, she was sent to Tuskegee Institute. She eventually got a master's degree in education and began her teaching career.

My parents met at Tuskegee Institute. My dad was twenty-six, and my mother was around twenty-two years old. As a student enrolled in the field of agriculture, my dad's job on campus was to clean the horse barn. My mother's money helped to finance Daddy being awarded his doctorate from Michigan State University. My daddy could not find housing for our family because of the prevailing racist housing practices in East Lansing, Michigan, and they moved back to Tuskegee.

A hotel became available in Tuskegee, and my mother bought it for my father to manage along with his teaching. A subsequent parental dispute, with accusations about the hotel's clientele, led my mother to decide never to work again and demanded that my father take care of their son financially. And he agreed! Thereafter, Daddy would go to work, and Mama would get his checks to manage the household. Daddy was OK with it as he did not know about managing money, whereas my mom had grown up with money. I never had to want for any material things.

After returning to Tuskegee, I never remember my parents mentioning leaving Tuskegee and the South again. It was what they knew. Daddy had experienced racism firsthand in the North, and he had a good job that provided a comfortable middle-class living for our family.

Daddy taught in the Agriculture Department at Tuskegee Institute. He became a renowned agronomy researcher, professor, and mentor at Tuskegee Institute.[2] He went from teaching to being head of the department. In that role, his responsibility was to write educational programs to get money for his department and the community. The academic community realized my daddy's talent for writing and getting programs funded. Interestingly, my son and I both have had success in writing as well. As a result of my father's talent, Tuskegee got the City Hall building, the Model Cities Program, the Holiday Inn, the dog racing track, Tuskegee's industrial park, the airport expansion, and the Community Action Program. I guess you could say that these programs were my father's contribution to the community as they helped thousands of poor people in the area. Some of the programs that were funded were part of the federal government's antipoverty programs of the 1960s and 1970s.

As a result of the time my father spent teaching, researching, and writing, I felt I did not have a father as he was never at home. As a child, I would wake up at six thirty in the morning, and Daddy would be gone. He would go to his office or his friend's house. My question was always, "Why was he going to someone else's house dealing with their family so early in the mornings. In the meantime, I ain't got no daddy." I did not know what was happening, but at the time, I knew that my mother was mad. I was alone most of the time. I did have a half-sister, and Daddy had a closer relationship with her than he had with me. Relatives in the North thought she was too smart to be going to segregated schools in Alabama, so eventually my parents sent her to Washington, DC, to live with relatives to finish her education.

Here I was, ten years old, and all that angry mother energy was falling on this boy, so I would do her deeds. I don't know if that's what she intended, but that was the bottom line. Whatever my request, foolish as it was or may have been, or whatever my lack of responsibility, I would get whatever I wanted, whenever I wanted it.

It was never presented to me to have a moment's doubt that I could not have whatever I wanted. Whenever Mama or I called, Daddy would immediately respond and bring whatever I wanted. Other than a few times at Christmas or Thanksgiving, we never sat down to eat as a family. I felt that my dad's position became, "I don't want to raise no brat! I grew up a poor man. I don't know nothing about this! Let his mama raise him as she will and wants." He went off about town and up to his office and other activities such as his womanizing required. I rarely saw him. I never saw him hold hands with my mother. I never saw him hug her. I cannot even ever remember being hugged by either my mother or my father. There was no "I love you, Dougie" or "what are you doing, Dougie?" or "what are you planning on, Dougie?" None of that. It was "How much you need, boy? Here." My father would give me some money and run off with speed. That is the attitude I picked up on when I went to Howard University.

I had just turned seventeen when I finished Tuskegee Institute High School and went to Howard University. I was in the class of 1964, but I graduated early with the class of 1963 by going to summer school. I went straight into remedial classes at Howard. You see, in high school, I was

Dr. Mayberry's son. Sometimes I did not go to class or do the work, but I still passed. My arrogant attitude was because of who my daddy was!

Everybody knew who he was. He used to showboat me. He would put a suit on me and take me to one of his presentations, and he would say, "Oh, that is my son here in the audience." I didn't know what to do, so I would smile, sit down like a good little boy, and then he would drop me back at the house. I really do not fault my father because I do not think he knew any better. He didn't have the experience of being a father.

I do not fault my mother because she really got her money too early in her life. I do fault the culture they raised me in. They were unaware of the effects that the culture they were raising me in was having on me. The Black culture in Tuskegee at the time was high on recognition and competition—competition for the best homes, the best cars, the best clothes, the highest degrees, and the best jobs. This straight materialism existed not only among our parents, "those who stayed," but among their children as well. All that history was just to say it took me five and a half years to do a four-year degree in accounting at Howard University just because I thought I did not have to study in high school because of whose son I was.

While at Howard University, I was in the Reserve Officers Training Corps (ROTC) program. I was a cadet lieutenant colonel overseeing two hundred cadets under my command. Of course, this was a student position, and I was under the command of the military instructors on campus.

After graduation and before doing my mandatory military service, I worked for the Federal Aviation Administration as an accountant for a short period. I was the only Black person working there. They gave me no assignments, so I used to sit there and draw. Of course, I eventually quit that job, and my parents set me up in an apartment. They sent me a check every month, and I would blow it. They were paying all the bills. I didn't know anything about saving.

Finally, I decided to do my required ROTC two-year stint as a lieutenant working directly with the commanding general of five thousand soldiers at Fort Lewis, Washington, where I learned to write grants. As the only Black lieutenant in the entire Fort Lewis Army Camp of some five thousand men, they made me director of drug research, flying me up and down the West Coast to instruct officers about the effects of drugs on the soldiers returning from overseas in the early 1970s. I had to deal with a lot of racism being the only Black person in such a position. My attitude as I had been taught while growing up was to ignore the racism. I would say, "Damn you ignorant ass White folks. I got money too!" Being in the military was not an experience in leadership for me; that was for the White folks during that time. The work was better described as a class in abject racism—if you can imagine being the only Black officer, working under the direct command of the commanding general, among a cadre of White officers who wished to have your position.

At this point in my life, my rebellious nature came out! After my military service and unsuccessful job experience, I relied on Pops to help me find another job. He (and I) put myself in a situation where I basically became a reflection of him. I became a grants writer for my daddy's department at the university and was paid $8,000 a year. I was about twenty-five years old.

In that position, I wrote a grant like the community drug education grant I had written in the military at Fort Lewis, Washington, and it was funded for $1.8 million for three years. The money came in. Because of the poor employment situation in Tuskegee at the time, I had talked to many of my people in the community and had begun to identify which ones I wanted to bring onto the project if it were funded. Unknowing to me, my father and his colleagues decided they were going to do something different with the money and decided not to allow me to hire my friends. I got very angry and confronted them. Instead of Pops backing me, he and his friends played me. I had written the drug education program grant, and it had been funded to serve Black residents in twelve counties surrounding and including Macon County. Even the salary they had promised me was lowered. I was angry. Being arrogant, rebellious, and irresponsible, I quit! I didn't know what I was doing.

After the altercation with my dad and his colleagues, I ran home to Mama. I told her that Daddy had taken the money. She said, "Told you, once a dog, always a dog. Now come on in this house. What do you want, boy?" I told her there was a pizza shop for sale and it cost $5,000. My mother called my father, and minutes later, he arrived with a check for $5,000 for me to open a pizza place. I was still angry because I had written the grant for $1.8 million dollars and all I was getting was $5,000.

The pizza parlor, located next door to Lionel Richie's house, opened, and it did very well. I was making about $200 a day because it was close to campus, and many students and friends came in. At that time, it was doing better than many other businesses in the area. However, less than six months later, the pizza parlor was closed because the taxes were not paid. I was depending on my father's accountant to pay the taxes, but they were not paid. I was at the point of total frustration. I rebelled and bounced around from New York to New Orleans to Mexico and ended up in Los Angeles. In Los Angeles, I was driving around in a Mercedes, but I did not have any money. The person I had been traveling with left town without telling me. I was stuck. When I was stuck, I didn't know what to do. I still had this attitude that I was Dr. Mayberry's son. When the money was gone, I was just trying to survive.

One day, I was driving around Las Vegas in my Mercedes with no job. A woman invited me to stay with her in LA. Of course, having no other place to stay, I agreed. Later that week, one of her friends borrowed my car, ran over a curb, and busted the airbags. He said he had no money but that he knew how to get money to fix the car, and he needed my help.

He introduced me to cooking PCP. I was not familiar with this kind of stuff. I saw an opportunity to get some money though, not looking at any illegal aspects. I just needed money, and that is why I approached it blindly. I began to make lots of money cooking PCP—enough money to even help other people buy cars, pay house notes, and give money to their grandmas and other family members.

I had no understanding of how to manage and save money and then get out of the game. I just knew that if I got broke, I could roll over and have $30,000 in my pocket. But I didn't know what to do with it. I was being foolish with it. The bottom line is after three years of this madness in Los Angeles, the FBI came and indicated that I had the reputation of being one of the best cookers of PCP in the United States. People in the business recognized my leadership ability and considered me a threat. This situation brought to me the realization that I was smart, but it did not help me realize how foolish I was. I did not understand that I didn't have a command of the culture I was working in, and as a result, I couldn't be successful. Today, people in the business would kill me for doing what I was doing, but at that time, they called the police. That is what happened in my case. They called the police.

When I first went into where they were cooking, I saw the money that was being made. The next time we went, I memorized everything about the way it was being cooked—at what degrees, what power levels, and how often and at what stages to make the mixtures. I memorized all that in my head because I didn't want them to know I was stealing. I went out and applied what I had learned and made lots of money. I had no idea of the environment in which I was working. The short is that I went to jail. They gave me the maximum of five years, and I did five years.

After cooking PCP for several years in the Los Angeles area and doing five years in prison for it, I met some people and went to New York with them. The man was in education, and his wife worked in media. They let me move into their house, and they bought another one. After a few months, they asked for rent. My attitude was you asked me to come up here and help you develop this organization and get an opening in the Black community. Now you want to charge me rent? So, after four and a half unsuccessful years in New York, I was back in Tuskegee, and it was scary, of course. I thought, " I ain't got nothing to do. Ain't got no jobs, and Daddy's future programs don't include me." I didn't like going down there to that city at all.

I came home to Tuskegee to develop a drug organization in the Macon County, Alabama, area. The last time I was in Tuskegee, I had been the publicly respected son of a publicly respected Tuskegee University faculty member. This time, I came home a felon. Regardless, I decided to make and sell drugs at a level that would not draw too much attention. However, as in dealing with PCP and the people involved in the life, I was eventually arrested.

I ended up in the court of Judge Myron Thompson, one of our younger Tuskegee Institute High School classmates who had gone to Yale. Myron was later appointed the youngest ever federal district judge by President Carter. My parents had wanted me to go to Harvard. I was looking at Myron, and he was looking at me. At that time, I was thinking how he had sold out to the White man. In my head, I was also thinking about what he might be thinking of me. Maybe he was thinking, "Look at this n****r and what he has done with his life."

My father had paid the attorney $15,000. That time I was acquitted of the charges and because of winning that little case, I was really messed up in my thinking that I could do anything. I continued in the business, but I decided I would stop the PCP business because they gave people too much prison time for that. I decided to go into the weed business instead and just sell it to people I knew. I was arrogant and stupid.

My new direction just required getting on the phone and making calls to people that I knew. I was doing quite well. But unknown to me, I was making all the other local dealers jealous. They would come out to my house and tell me what my prices should be. I would tell them that they could not tell me what to do. They were coming hard at me. One day, one of them came over there to kill me. He shot me in the back. He shot at me several more times, but now, I am sure it was the angels that pushed me out of the way. I could feel the bullets coming past my head. I knew the cop down there, and we were going over the scene. You could see how the bullets were coming straight down toward me, but still, most of them missed. I went to the hospital, but they didn't take the bullet out. The nurse cleaned the wound and everything and instructed my wife on how to continue to do that. The bottom line was since they didn't kill me, I continued in the business until I had done another twenty-two years in prison.

I have been asked why I did not get out of the business after my five years in prison or after the shooting incident in Tuskegee. I didn't get out because I did not know any other alternatives that would produce such lucrative gains. The real problem was that I never considered the consequences on both me and all the druggies involved. I was arrogant and stupid.

All of this is to say that because I was raised as an arrogant self-indulgent kid and young adult, I didn't know how to have proper relationships with the various complexities of people and the complexities of life. I was raised alone. Even now, I am happier alone, not being bothered with anybody else and their problems.

My personal and spiritual growth began in prison when I was introduced to *The Urantia Papers*.[3] I have been reading and researching them for over forty years. I did much of that studying while I was in the joint. While in the El Reno federal prison, I was the lead business inmate for the prison business manager. I got close to a German guy who also was an inmate and worked there. He was a good talker, and we hit it off as good friends. At the time, he was a follower of *The Urantia Book*, a two-thousand-page book of spiritual, philosophical, scientific, and religious teachings. At the time, I was the imam of the prison Muslim community. So, he thought I would be interested in it. He arranged a meeting with me and some leaders of the organization. Thus, a whole new chapter in my living began to evolve.

It was between 1978 and 1981 when I began meeting with some of the lead teachers of Urantia. A Ms. Berkeley, a retired accountant and international chair of the Urantia Foundation came to the prison to see me. As time passed, more people came through to help me acquire a deeper understanding. Some of them were Jewish. They came to see me on Sundays and would sit down and read a few chapters and discuss them, but it was not penetrating my psyche. It was just knowledge to me.

I was trying to form a special point of view. I wanted to know about our humanity, our origin, and how we got to this point. I started questioning everything about myself. Urantia ideology is about evolution, how it gives you spiritual and mental capacities, and how immaterial energies flow. The ideology specifically lays out how God created us for Him to function, and in our case, we must learn how to be as Him. I have learned that God controls the environment, not only me but my environment. I think God moved me around in different environments during my life, and he showed me my errors by the arrests I accumulated. Understanding and growth become two-way communication with God based on what is in the environment. At some point, He said I was moving forward.

In terms of my relationship to Urantia, I did not know anything about spirituality when I was growing up and as a young adult. It is now my life. I must share what I have learned on the level of the person having very little or no foundation to grow from. I didn't want to be held up in Urantia by White folks as an example. I rebelled because they wanted me to be the token up in the organization, but they never knew everything it took for me to get to where I am now. I do not want to be like a little show dog and answer their questions so they can show me off. With my rebellious nature, I decided to do a blog independently and acquire the understanding that I now have without being involved with those who wanted me to take on a subjugated role in their group. I just told them that I was joining God instead of them.

According to Urantia philosophy, some humans evolve to the spirit level and will tell you some things that are recommendations and some things that are duties to reach growth and understanding. The spirits can have direct communication with you. It's so funny, but I can communicate with the spirits. For example, I wake up in the morning and have a clear mind. I am glad to get up. When I sit down at a computer, it hits me. All I do is type what comes to me. It is me talking about God. I just post it on the blog. I have done nothing willingly to bring anybody to the blog or the philosophy because my position was and continues to be: I was instructed by the spirit of truth. I learn as I am typing because it is not me writing and instructing. It is as if God is saying this is what I want you to write and this is the way I want you to write it. I don't have to figure all that stuff out. God figures it out, and I only put it in the blog. After I get the message, it does take some time to work on the wording and structure, but I get all that instruction too.

What I am trying to say is that all my rebellion has led me to realize I need God. All the issues I have been involved in were God's way of telling me He is the best to guide me. In my past life, my focus was not on taking in ideas. Maybe what a person is doing every day is not what God is instructing them to do. He is saying that He is trying to raise the whole humanity of this planet to a higher level of spiritual understanding, and He needs some help.

In my past life, I had to hustle. Now I get everything I need because I am doing God's bidding. I am trying to pass that on to those who want to listen and know that they do not have to hustle as well. I have learned that doing this bit in life is so much easier. There is no need for further hustle. What God was doing with me was evolving His planet, and it ain't over yet.

My son was up here yesterday. He said something to me that I thought was out of place. I did what my father should have done with me. I told my son, "I am still your dad, and you are my son. We can squabble all day because you know I am arrogant. You are selfish and I am selfish, and we can play those roles all day. You know I love you, but you ain't going to talk to me anyway you like. At the end of the day, I am your father, and it is my responsibility to instruct you." I had to do with him what my dad did not do with me. I had to sit him down and talk to him. I said to him, "You are going to get a job, pay these bills, and you're going to make sure your mama's straight."

I became the roadkill of my parents' unhappy life. It turned me into a very arrogant and selfish person. I understand now from God's point of view that He does not want me to hold all that old business up in my head. During my life, I was trying so hard to get rid of it. Now, I get to use that computer, but I am still trying to get rid of all that old business in my head. That old business still fights me sometimes.

My blog currently has thousands of viewers from over two hundred countries. It is primarily read and researched by those seeking to find some specific answer to some specific question related to a specific spiritual truth.[4]

And it all had its very beginning at Tuskegee Institute in the little town of Tuskegee, Alabama.

CHAPTER 6

Annie Jean Baker Reed

Editors' Note: Annie Jean Baker Reed grew up hearing stories of how her great-grandfather was known as one of Booker T. Washington's "humble friends." While Washington ushered in an era of Black upward mobility built on what some would refer to as middle-class values and actions, he was always "reaching back" toward those who could benefit from his major mission: to improve the educational and health status of all Black Americans. He was also a pragmatist and a brilliant politician and knew how to develop friendships with both the rich and the poor. While Annie Jean's great-grandfather, Henry Clay Baker, was an uneducated man, he did have something to offer Washington—land for building a rural Rosenwald school and interesting conversation.

Although from different stations in life, Mr. Baker, an uneducated farmer, and college president Washington enjoyed each other's company and took time to be with and learn from each other, sharing information about religious music and farming. Washington might also have recognized Baker's brilliance at "pulling himself up by his bootstraps." Annie Jean describes the family lore of how White people had taken her great-grandfather's land, but he had relocated to the Tuskegee area and had become a landowner of significant worth. We do not know why he stayed in the South if the family lore is true, but we do know that his relationship with Washington contributed something valuable to Washington as he was creating the parallel world.

My father said that my great-grandfather was friends with Booker T. Washington. He said that five men in Hickory Grove were called

Washington's "Humble Friends," and my great-grandfather was one of them. "Humble Friends" is a term that is not used these days. It is about people from different stations in life being friends.[1] My great-grandfather was an uneducated farmer and Dr. Washington was president of a university, but they were still friends. According to my father, Washington would walk or ride his horse from Tuskegee University toward Hickory Grove, and my great-grandfather would come from Hickory Grove to meet him. My father said that they would sit outside under a tree. As the story goes, my great-grandfather would start singing old spiritual or slave songs, and Washington would write the words down. They would sit there and sing the songs together. My father said they would also talk about planting and crops since my great-grandfather had a large farm.

Annie Jean Baker Reed's great-grandfather, Henry Clay Baker, born in 1870, one of Booker T. Washington's Humble Friends. Photography by P. H. Polk. Courtesy of the Tuskegee University Archives, Tuskegee University.

Some of Mr. Washington's humble friends (*See page 136*)

Annie Jean Baker Reed's great-grandfather, Henry Clay Baker (*second from left*), as shown in Emmett J. Scott's book, *Booker T. Washington: Builder of a Civilization*, which included photography by P. H.. Polk. Courtesy of the Tuskegee University Archives, Tuskegee University.

My dad said that my great-grandfather's people were from North Carolina. The enslaver that brought them down to Alabama was named Baker, so that's how my great-grandfather got the Baker name.

My father and grandfather were born in Macon County, Alabama. My great-grandfather Henry Clay Baker once owned 250 acres of land in Tallassee, which is about forty miles from Tuskegee. We were never told how he obtained that much land. I do remember family members saying that White people came in and took his land in Tallassee, so he came to Tuskegee. Here, he bought about 150 acres of land in the area that is called Hickory Grove. The family helped to build the Hickory Grove Baptist Church, which was burned. The family has said that White folks burned it down. I was never told the circumstances. The church is gone, but the cemetery is still there. People are still being buried in the cemetery in the Hickory Grove community.

My father, Murray Hampton Baker Sr., and my mother, Annie Lee

Brown, met in Tuskegee. They had two children: my brother, Murray Jr., and me. My daddy grew up on those 150 acres in Hickory Grove. My father had a sister, but she had polio and died at an early age. Daddy said that he and my grandfather had all the land they needed to have a good life. They built a big house up there and had a big farm. My grandfather also helped to build the Rosenwald school in Hickory Grove, which, at the time, went to the seventh grade.[2]

My great-grandfather, grandfather, and father never considered leaving the South because they owned so much land. Most of my relatives stayed in the South. My great-grandfather's land was divided among his four children when he died. Some of the grandchildren and great-grandchildren still live on the land. Some land has been sold over the years to help family members with living expenses. I now own my daddy's land and the house I grew up in.

My mother did not work outside the home until later in her life. She cleaned, cooked, and sewed all my clothes including my prom gowns. When I went to the tenth grade, she went to work at Tuskegee Institute (University) in housekeeping. My dad did not get a degree from Tuskegee Institute. He was a blue-collar worker there. He also drove school buses for the Macon County Board of Education and worked at the Chicken Coop restaurant in downtown Tuskegee. My parents participated in the Civil Rights Movement. I can remember them going to some of the marches.

Things were hard here in Tuskegee for some Black people when Preston Hornsby was the sheriff. He had a lot of power in Macon County. When he met you during the day, he would always say, "Don't forget to vote for me. Don't forget to vote for me." He wanted to stay in office. Everyone thought he was in contact with the Ku Klux Klan, but nobody could ever prove it. Everybody thought that, but he would still ask for the Black vote. Many people, Black and White, owed him money because they borrowed money from him or bought used cars from him on credit. Sometimes you would hear someone say, "Well, my cousin is missing, and we haven't seen him in weeks." Sometimes I would hear adults say something like, "They probably threw him in Eufaula Creek." During the '50s and '60s, some people thought people in the sheriff's department might have known something about those missing Black men. Nothing was ever proven about people in the department, and most of the time, nothing was ever proven about the missing Black men. For some reason, the law did not ever mess with my father. I think it was because my father had White relatives here in the area. Many of our White relatives are here in Macon County, and I am still in contact with some of them.

My mother's mother was Molly Brown. She worked all her life for White people here in Macon County. She cooked for them and took care of their children. She did pick some cotton too to help make ends meet. They treated her well. They would give her clothes for her girls, that is, for my mom and her sister. I never heard my grandmother speak badly about White folk, although she had to work very hard for them.

I spent much more time with my dad growing up than I did with my momma. That is how I was able to hear things about what people were suspecting about the sheriff's department in Macon County. On the other hand, my son did not get a chance to spend much time with me. My son was killed here. He was seventeen. He would be fifty-four years old now. A Black guy who was not from Tuskegee shot him with a .357 Magnum right between the eyes. We never got a reason for it. My son was a student at Tuskegee Institute High School at the time. The other students at his high school took it so hard. On the day of the funeral, there was no one at school. School buses were used to take students to the funeral. Some students walked from their neighborhoods to the funeral. The students all said that they never had a friend like my son. For reasons I will never understand, the killer was never prosecuted.

My son's death has affected the rest of my life drastically. Some days, it feels like it just happened. So I understand it when someone loses a child to violence. I tried to get through it by praying. It took me three months to go back to work as a counselor at the high school after he died. When I went back to work, I often had to go home because I could still see my son walking down the halls.

I went to Alabama State College in Montgomery, Alabama, about thirty miles from Tuskegee. I could have gone to Tuskegee Institute for half price since my mother worked there, but Alabama State was where I had always wanted to go. It was during the Civil Rights Movement. In 1965, I was a freshman at Alabama State. One of my classmates from Tuskegee Institute High and I were roommates. We lived in Bibb Graves Hall. Bibb Graves was a governor of Alabama who was also head of the

Ku Klux Klan at one time. Several universities that had buildings named for him have changed the names of those buildings. One Friday evening, suddenly, the doors to our hallway opened. Some of the girls were in the shower. Some were changing clothes for the evening. Several male students came into our dorm and said that we had to go with them because Martin Luther King Jr. was in town, and we should get ready for the march and protest.

We tried to march. A large group of us went down Jackson Street and up the hill. By the time we got off campus, a pack of large dogs that looked like German shepherds ran after us. There were columns and columns of White Alabama State Troopers and White police officers on big Clydesdale-type horses. The dogs and horses ran us back to the campus. We ran, we ran, we ran, we ran! Some students were able to climb trees to avoid the dogs. I still remember to this day that a male student managed to get on the top of a lady's house. I still do not know how he did it, but if he had not done so, those dogs would have eaten his legs up. Once we had gotten back to Jackson Street, the troopers and police started pulling back and calling the dogs back because they couldn't come on the Alabama State campus.

Dr. Bronson was my advisor at Alabama State College. He and my father were best friends. They grew up together. Because I was involved in the march and someone reported me as being one of the leaders, my name kept coming up to the administration to be expelled from Alabama State. Dr. Bronson knew I was not a leader, and he removed my name. My dad was quite upset. He asked me what I was doing down there in Montgomery. I told him that King was in town, and I wanted to march with him. Although my dad was in support of the movement and had marched himself, he wanted me to get my education. He told me that King was not my daddy and that he was not paying my tuition. He told me to stay out of the marches and to go to class!

I did leave Alabama State. I think I just lost interest in school. I wasn't pregnant or anything like that. I went North to Philadelphia to live with a sister, my mother's daughter from another marriage, for the summer. I liked Philly. Philly was nice. I had never seen Philly before. We had good times and went shopping at places like John Wanamaker's, Blum's, and all the expensive stores in Philadelphia. It was about having fun. I got a job working at Wanamaker's, but it wasn't what I wanted. I tried to get hired on with the school system, but it was too far away. I had to take the train and go here and go there. So, I just eventually came home and got a job at Macon County Hospital. That's where another one of my grandmothers was working. She always looked after me when I was growing up. When she got older, I took care of her because she did not want anyone to take care of her but me. She would always say, "I want my granddaughter to feed me."

I worked doing nursing for a while at the hospital where my grandmother worked. I attended nursing school during that time until I just could not go any further with it, so I went to what I was used to doing and that was typing. I passed the Board of Education typing test and started to work at the senior high school. I worked there for twenty-two years, mostly as an administrative assistant. I worked at the Board of Education for four years. Lastly, I transferred and worked with juveniles with problems who had to go to court. We were having serious problems with kids who never showed up to school and were consequently ordered to appear in court with their parents. I had to go with the parents and kids before Judge Ford. He was our classmate Doris Dinkins's husband. I had to explain to the parents that according to Alabama state law, parents are responsible for their children getting to school and being obedient in school. At that time, parents could be fined $600 for the child not attending school and/or continuously being disobedient to school teachers or administrators.

After I retired from my twenty-six years at Tuskegee Institute High School and the Macon County Board of Education, my daughter graduated from the University of Alabama. I then came to work here at Tuskegee University as an administrative assistant in the Math Department. I had intended to sell my house and move to Atlanta after I retired, but my parents got sick, and I stayed here in Tuskegee to take care of them. I took care of them until they passed. My dad told me exactly how he wanted to be buried: on a Wednesday at eleven o'clock, in a blue casket and in his blue suit, next to my son. I did everything just like he wanted.

My dad and I had a special bond. He was my heart, and my children were his heart, especially my son. My relationship with my father was one that you do not see much these days between girls and dads. Some girls these days do not even know their fathers. Every girl needs to have a relationship with her father. You learn a lot from a man's perspective. My daddy taught me about my body. He took time. He brought me out here to Tuskegee Institute to work with him sometimes. Over seventy years ago, when I was five or six, he fixed my food and braided my hair.

I have let my daughter know about our family history, and how her great-grandparents tried to make a good life for us in Macon County even though there was prejudice and discrimination. She knows about how her great-great-grandfather was a special friend to Washington and helped him with the building of a Rosenwald school and by just being his friend when he was trying to build up Tuskegee. I have told her about how my generation tried to march for civil rights and make things better for her and her generation. I did not have a chance with my son because I lost him so early, but my daughter knows how I have tried to help students along the way. She knows I care about student success. Students know I care because they come to me with their problems. They might talk to me about personal relationship issues or serious issues like wanting to hurt themselves. I do what I can and then refer them to the professionals on campus.

My life's work has been with young people. Even though my father was not an educated man, he was a wise and kind man. Members of my church know I am writing my story and wanted to make sure I said something about what a kind and gentle man he was. I have tried to pass on some of the wisdom and kindness my father gave to me to the young people who have crossed my path so they can have good lives and help others along the way like Washington and people of his generation did. That is how we as Black people have managed in this country, valuing family, and helping others along the way.

II

ANCESTORS AND NARRATORS

Lifting as They Climbed

CHAPTER 7

Margaret Meadows Jones

Editors' Note: Margaret Meadows Jones's father was able to secure employment at the Veterans Administration Hospital where he helped Black veterans with their journeys back to health and sometimes back to their families. Margaret's mother joined the cadre of Tuskegee-educated teachers who not only taught in the Black schools in Tuskegee but also in rural Alabama and other states throughout the South. Margaret's mother began her career in Georgia. She talks about her parents staying in the South because it was home, they wanted to be near family, and they had good jobs. She also writes about her parents' support of the Civil Rights Movement and sees some of her work and volunteerism as a continuation of her parents' work.

To the best of my memory, my parents never considered leaving the South (Tuskegee) because it was home for them and they had good jobs. My maternal grandmother, Lecie Mitchell, was born in Macon County, Alabama. My maternal grandfather, Dock Trawick, was born in Henry County, Alabama. Family lore has it that he was invited by Dr. Booker T. Washington to teach at Tuskegee Normal and Industrial Institute. It was Dr. Washington's practice at that time to invite people with special skills and knowledge to work at the school. We do not know what subjects he taught and could not find information about him in the archives, so information about him comes from oral history that has been passed down through the generations.

My father, John Meadows, was a World War I veteran. The newly built Veterans Hospital became a source of employment for him. My father supervised the veterans who worked on the grounds of the hospital. My mom, Maybelle Trawick Meadows, was an educator and began her teaching career in Naylor, Georgia, and some other counties surrounding Macon County. It was not always easy for her to find teaching positions close to home. When I was a child, both my parents had very good jobs to support themselves and their three children.

Margaret Meadows Jones's parents, John Meadows, a Veteran Administration Hospital employee, and Maybelle Trawick, a teacher in rural Macon and nearby counties. Courtesy of Margaret Meadows Jones.

Some older Black people in the area, like my grandmother, survived during those times mainly by farming. Many of them sold their fruits, vegetables, and handmade goods such as quilts and crocheted and carved items every Saturday at the Curb Farmer's Market. People used to come from all over to the market to buy fresh produce that the Black farmers surrounding Tuskegee would bring to market. The market was good for everybody. It helped the farmers supplement their farm income, which sometimes could be meager depending on the weather or how much acreage they had for planting cash crops. The presence of the market helped people in the city of Tuskegee to be able to eat fresh produce. Many of the farmers had benefited from Dr. George Washington Carver and his students going out into the rural areas to teach them about soil chemistry and crop rotation. The market also helped improve relationships between the mostly uneducated or undereducated rural people and the more well-off and more educated city residents.

Margaret Meadows Jones's maternal grandmother, Lecie Mitchell, sold vegetables at Tuskegee's once-flourishing Saturday Market. Courtesy of Margaret Meadow Jones.

Living in Tuskegee was quite manageable for Black people during my grandmother's time because the city was largely populated by Black people. White people may have had more prominent businesses or held governmental positions, but Black people had built a community supporting each other. It included Black lawyers, doctors, nurses, teachers, grocers, and building tradespeople. Black people sometimes shopped at White establishments, which helped them stay in business. White businesses depended on Black trade to stay in business as proved by the effects of a later boycott during the Civil Rights Movement.

The legal system that supported the mistreatment and hindered progress for the Black community was problematic. The legal system dictated how Black people should act in their relationships with White people. The Jim Crow justice system dictated that Black people take subservient positions to White people and made living life outside of the Black community difficult. One never could be sure what might happen when there was contact with White people in those days.

During the early 1960s, my parents were very active with the Tuskegee Civic Association (TCA).[1] This organization was formed mostly due to White people redistricting Tuskegee, which excluded most of the Black voters from the city limits. The TCA organized Black citizens to boycott all White-owned businesses, and a lawsuit ensued. My parents regularly attended these meetings. I do not remember if they held any positions. Dr. Gomillion, one of my Tuskegee Institute sociology professors, led the TCA.

My parents had the same interest as Dr. Gomillion and others, which was to better the conditions for Black people living in Macon County, Alabama, and the South in general. Due to the mistreatment of Black people in their day-to-day living and the segregation laws that supported this disrespect and mistreatment, the TCA called for a boycott of Tuskegee businesses. I did not know of anyone during this time who had a lack of interest in the Tuskegee Boycott or who became discouraged. It seemed that the entire Black community that I knew of was involved and strongly supported the boycott. Black people who had vehicles traveled to Auburn or Montgomery for their shopping needs and often assisted others that did not have transportation. Many White businesses suffered financially and eventually closed.

As I think back to the days of segregation and boycotting, I am happy that my parents participated in the movement. It made the South a better place for them to live as well as their family, and the entire community. They stayed in the South to fight for what they felt was the right thing to do. In fighting for their rights where they were, they did not have to move. Like my parents, I never thought about leaving the South. I always wanted to be near my family.

If I had grandchildren, I would tell them of the discrimination, verbal abuse, violence, and the denial of the right to vote that existed throughout the South when I was growing up. However, being raised in Tuskegee, Alabama, was quite different. As stated earlier, Tuskegee was largely populated by Black people; therefore, I don't remember any direct abuse from the White community. I do remember the separate bathrooms, separate water fountains, and separate seating areas at the Macon Theatre in downtown Tuskegee. So, while we were spared the normal day-to-day direct racism that most other Black people faced in the South at that time, we still realized what awaited us in the broader community and society. We knew that we had no real political power in the city and state. We also realized that we were not being awarded the appropriate city and state revenue for the schools and organizations in the Black community.

After high school, there was no question about what I was going to do. I knew I was expected to complete my education by going to college. There was no question about what college I would attend. I wanted to attend Tennessee State in Nashville. It seemed to be the "go-to" school at that time, so I wanted to go there too. However, my parents spoke differently. Mom and Dad said it would be less expensive to stay at home and attend Tuskegee Institute. While in college, I attended rallies and participated in the marches to express my feelings and to hopefully make a change for the better. During 1964 to 1968, when I was in college at Tuskegee Institute, there were marches and rallies all the time. We marched in Tuskegee when Sammy Younge was killed, and we participated in marches in Montgomery.

My first career choice was business. Being a business major meant having to take several math classes, but I was not a good math student. As a result, I felt it was best to choose another career. My sister majored in social work, so I investigated social work and became interested, and social work it was.

One of the first jobs I had in Tuskegee was working for the Job Corps. It was an antipoverty program designed to provide low-income young people with skills that would help them live productive lives. As in the past, Tuskegee University was always looking for ways they could help the community. As a result, they housed the Job Corps program on campus thinking that the environment and contact with college students would be inspirational for the Job Corps students. The program was administered on campus for a few years but eventually moved to the community. I do not know why the program was moved, but not all efforts to help the community work out as planned.

I enjoyed working with the Job Corps students. I provided social as well as academic support. It was very rewarding work. Some Job Corps students were very successful and became college students at the university. Some of the young people had too many issues to overcome and ended up leaving the program.

I also worked at the Magnolia Haven Nursing Home in Tuskegee as a social worker for a few years. However, most of my career was with the state of Alabama where I worked as an Equal Employment Officer in the Department of Transportation. That was rewarding work as I felt I was continuing the civil rights work that I grew up watching my community engage in. I retired in 2018.

Looking back over the years, many people have helped to build a foundation for us to work from: Booker T. Washington, an American educator, built a university; Sojourner Truth, an American abolitionist, spoke out for civil and women's rights; Rosa Parks, an American civil rights activist, refused to give up her seat on a bus to a White man; John Lewis, an American politician, marched early on to end legalized segregation and worked the halls of Congress to ensure that Black people and other people of color continue to have the right to vote. Each of these accomplishments would have been considered getting into "good trouble" by Representative John Lewis. Due to the "good trouble" these individuals made in history, I, along with other family members, was free to earn degrees, earn good incomes, own property, and pass down wealth to future generations.

Living in the Jim Crow South and seeing the mistreatment of Black people in years past and today, I became interested in joining the Macon County Democratic Club. I wanted to become more knowledgeable about politics and to assist in making things better. Some activities I currently participate in are fundraising, screening candidates running for office, and assisting with voter registration. This is my way of helping to improve things for Black people. Participating in the Democratic Party is my way of continuing what my parents started in their support of the TCA and its activities.

I may not have been able to make as big a mark as some of the people just mentioned, but I have tried to build on the foundation they have built for us. Regarding the current political and socioeconomic situation for Black people, my advice to my son and my community is that the struggle must continue. Some progress has been made over the years, but the color of one's skin far too often remains a deciding factor in the political and socioeconomic arena of Black versus White people in this country.

At the age of fifty-one, my son knows of the struggle that took place in the 1960s and has often stated that some of the same issues still exist today. This is so true. A large percentage of Black people experience a lack of proper health care, lack of educational attainment, and lack of equal or adequate income. We must continue the struggle to finish all that is yet to be done.

CHAPTER 8

Barbara White Atkinson-Liggins

Editors' Note: Barbara tells a fascinating story of how successive generations of her family progressed from being domestic servants to now having four generations of college-educated professionals, one of whom is a lawyer fighting for voting rights in a southern state. Her family held close to their faith and taught their children to value education, hard work, doing one's best, financial management, and the importance of close family ties. Barbara's parents received their education from Tuskegee University, obtained good jobs, and participated in segments of the parallel social world of Tuskegee, such as their involvement with the Freemasons, the Eastern Stars, and the Missionary Society. They also exposed their children to this parallel world through piano lessons, recitals, and road trips to the beach.

Furthermore, Barbara's description of her mother's dedication to her rural pupils whom she taught in a wooden schoolhouse without electricity and running water exemplifies the ideals of lifting as we climb. She writes about how proud she was of her mother, how much her mother loved her work with the rural school children, and how the children returned their love, respect, and appreciation when they happened to meet in downtown Tuskegee. Barbara's parents also demonstrated the value of "lifting as we climb." to their children while they resisted Jim Crow assaults and stood up for their rights with dignity in the presence of their children.

I WAS BORN INTO A FAMILY of ordinary people with extraordinary attributes, which allowed them to thrive despite the odds that were stacked against them. Each generation became educationally, economically, and socially stronger, even in the Jim Crow South.

My father, Clima White Sr., a traditional head of the household, was mainly responsible for the economic well-being of the family. He worked at the Veterans Administration Hospital in Tuskegee during my entire childhood and into early adulthood. He was a very proud and fearless Black man. So many of my memories of him involve an unyielding demand for respect in the segregated South. I will never forget an occasion, during one of our road trips, when a White man referred to my father as "uncle," a common term many White people used to diminish Black people as subservient. Wrong move. I remember my father confronted this White man and, using expletives, he let the man know that he was not his uncle and not to refer to him as such. This made all of us observing this encounter—my siblings, my mother, my grandmother, and me—extremely nervous. In those times, cussing a White man out, or simply standing up for yourself, might have incited deadly rage in White folks. By the 1940s, thousands of Black people had been lynched or beaten in the South for simply demanding mutual respect. It is reported that more than three hundred Black people had been lynched in Alabama alone.[1] When my father took a stand, we did not know what would happen. By the grace of God, nothing happened.

My mother, Bertha Bascomb White, was the quietly strong buffer in the house who kept the household running smoothly. Modest, unpretentious, a nurturer, and a caregiver, Mother Dear (as we called her) was our motivator and cheerleader who always encouraged the pursuit of education. A gifted writer, she prepared a pamphlet of poems that she had written to share with her children. There were four of us, three girls and one boy. Mother Dear wrote a song that was sent to a company to have music applied, which she sang and played on the piano. She just played it for the family; I don't remember her sharing it with anyone else. These were her "outside interests," her "pastimes" that she felt could never develop into a career, so she only shared them with us.

Like my father, Mother Dear was a proud lady, exhibited by her physical carriage. She was always properly dressed from head to toe with her head held high in all situations. I remember once she was shopping for a church hat in a shop in Tuskegee. She wanted to try the hat on, but the White saleswoman forbade it. Mother Dear did not confront the woman with expletives like my father would have done. She simply put the hat down on the counter and told us girls, "Come on! We will never come back to this place again." And we walked out. In this way, Mother Dear modeled quiet resistance. She knew her value and refused the humiliation and indignities that so many White store owners tried to project onto Black customers. She simply spent her money elsewhere. And we never went back to that shop where she had been forbidden to try on that hat.

Barbara White Atkinson-Liggins's parents, Bertha Bascomb White and Clima White Sr., demonstrated personal resistance to Jim Crow practices to their children. Courtesy of Barbara White Atkinson-Liggins.

Mother Dear and Dad bought a piano when I was about ten years old. I'm sure it was due to my mother's encouragement. For about three years, she arranged for my older sister and me to take piano lessons from Mrs. Sims, a local piano teacher. She also arranged for Mr. Brown, a local taxi driver, to pick us up after school from St. Joseph Catholic School once a week and take us to Mrs. Sims's house for piano lessons. I was an average piano student even after much practice, but I continued to practice hoping to get better. I remember having piano recitals at our house with other students and guests. This was a requirement of Mrs. Sims. Mother Dear's friend Ms. Zetherine, a home economics teacher, made our pink-and-blue satin dresses for the recital. We looked pretty, but we were nervous wrecks. Yet our parents were so proud. They tried to expose us to things that were socially and economically out of their reach when they were growing up.

Piano recital at the childhood home of Barbara White Atkinson-Liggins (*front row, seated first from right*). Courtesy of Barbara White Atkinson-Liggins.

My mother and father ended up in Alabama because that is where their parents were from. My maternal grandmother, Elnora Goode Bascomb, and her family, the Goodes, grew up in Hurtsboro, Alabama, in

Russell County. She was born circa 1895 and moved to Macon County as a young woman; however, her sisters stayed in Russell County. Her brothers also moved to Macon County where my maternal grandfather, Levi Bascomb, and his family lived. Levi was born circa 1894. My maternal grandparents married on February 18, 1915. In the 1920 census, Levi was listed as a fireman. He died in August 1924 when my mother was a young child.

My paternal grandmother, Henrietta Blue White, and her family grew up in Perote, Alabama—an unincorporated community in Bullock County. Grandmother and her siblings moved from Bullock County when they were young. According to a marriage license my paternal grandfather, Kylus White, was twenty-one years old when he married my grandmother Henrietta, who was eighteen.

Both sets of my grandparents were eventually able to buy small lots and build modest houses for their families in Macon County sometime between the 1930s and '40s. For instance, the 1930 census shows Kylus renting on Penny Street. The 1940 census shows him as a homeowner. The 1920 census shows Levi renting, and the 1930 census shows Elnora as a widow and homeowner. Both sets of grandparents were working-class people who made their living doing laundry, cleaning, and cooking for others. It was quite an accomplishment for them as Black people living in the South to be able to buy land and build their own homes in those early days. None of my grandparents had very much schooling, but they all could read and write. They were proud to be independent during the Depression while not having full citizenship privileges. They were able to break through an untenable situation and own property.

My father was an only child and had both of his parents while growing up in Tuskegee. My mother was one of three children growing up without a father. Her two brothers joined the army to help support the family. One brother lied about his age and joined the army before he was eighteen years old. The family was hoping to become more stable after the brothers returned from the service, but shortly after returning, the older brother was killed in an automobile accident. This incident still left the family with a meager income. However, they did have homeownership.

There was a network of kind Black women in Tuskegee and in-laws who helped to support my mother. They realized that my grandmother did not have the support of a husband. In addition, my maternal grandmother, Lil' Mama, did not make much money by taking in laundry. There was one Black lady that my grandmother did laundry for who took an interest in my mother. The lady would buy her clothing, teach her simple tasks and etiquette, and often invite her to stay at her house. My mother appreciated her very much, but she did not like being away from her mother and my grandmother. Mother Dear and Lil' Mama took care of each other. My mother took care of her mother all her life. I never heard either grandmother complain about their circumstances. They lost spouses, a son, and others, but they persevered. My ancestors demonstrated perseverance even when situations seemed hopeless.

My parents probably stayed in Alabama because of their widowed mothers. Both were devoted to taking care of their mothers. They instilled the value of taking care of one's parents into their children.

Both of my parents attended Tuskegee Institute. My father took electrical trade courses and became an electrician. My mother went into education. It took her several years to complete her degree because she would take classes in the summers and work the other months of the year. She graduated in 1950 with a BS degree after having three children and being pregnant with a fourth child.

My father often took us on family road trips throughout Florida, Alabama, and Georgia when we were growing up. He had a book outlining welcoming places where "colored" people who were traveling could patronize and feel safe and comfortable. These hotels, inns, restaurants, and even beaches were most often owned or operated by other Black people. I am not sure, but the book that he carried was probably a publication like *The Green Book*, although I do not remember it being green.[2] In those days, most of the Black people who migrated to the North usually took summer and holiday trips "back home" to visit relatives remaining in the South, and many used *The Green Book* for accommodations to avoid potentially dangerous encounters with White people.

We lived in the South and still used one of the travel books when we traveled. Our entire family would load into our station wagon and get an early start so we could go to Pensacola or Panama City, Florida, to the beach. We would enjoy ourselves and get back on the road to go home before it got too late. It was dangerous for Black people to travel at night in those days, but my father did it anyway for his family. We thought he was fearless. We would take our food, go to the beach, dance to Chubby Checker, do the Twist, laugh, and have fun. He gave us that treat for several years. I do not know how all of us, plus the grandmothers at times, got into that station wagon, but we did.

In addition to having a strong sense of racial pride, my father demanded respect for the females in our household, which included my mother, my two sisters, and myself. He demanded it from everyone including his friends and associates. I remember one example very clearly. While I was growing up, White men selling Brown Service burial insurance would come to the house to collect monthly premium payments. My father insisted that they were never to enter the house and they were not to refer to us as "sis" or call my mother or grandmother by their first names. He insisted on this. We knew he meant it, and so did the salesmen.

My father also insisted that his daughters and son learn to be independent. My parents learned their financial acumen from their parents. My father taught us to always save a portion of the money we made, no matter how large or small our earnings. He told us that we should be independent and not rely on monetary support from others. We have all passed this value on to our children. Critical to his value of having us be independent was his attitude regarding renting. My father told us not to rent, whether it was housing or other things.

As we grew older, I became aware of the Civil Rights Movement. We would hear our parents quietly talking about the "mass meetings" that were being held in Tuskegee during the 1960s. My father would attend these meetings. We, the children, knew something was going on but did not know the details. We knew that things were changing all around us. For instance, we used to go to Montgomery (the capital of Alabama which is approximately thirty-eight miles from Tuskegee) to shop for groceries and other items before the Montgomery Bus Boycott. The Montgomery Bus Boycott began with the arrest of Rosa Parks who refused to give up her public bus seat to a White passenger in December 1955.[3]

Once the Tuskegee Boycott started, we went to Opelika, Alabama, and Columbus, Georgia, sometimes for groceries and other shopping. We did not shop very much in Tuskegee because it was very segregated. I do remember a small Black-owned grocery store owned by Red Richburg where we would go to buy some items. My paternal grandmother bought all her groceries there, and Mr. Richburg would deliver them to her.

Grocery shopping was a family affair because we had to go out of town. We would often take one or two older family friends who did not drive distances with us so that they could also do their shopping. We would buy enough groceries to last two to three weeks. Vegetables, eggs, and some dairy products were bought from neighbors who had farms in the area or from Mr. Richburg's store. We learned very early not to spend our money where we were not treated humanely. There were also two White women who had a shop in Notasulga who would make in-house visits to sell their clothing. Notasulga was a small rural town about ten miles from Tuskegee. Occasionally my mother would buy everyday dresses or a dress for a special occasion from them. This was not a frequent occurrence.

My mother and another teacher, Ms. Terrell, taught in a two-room schoolhouse in Little Texas, Alabama, for many years until the small rural schools were consolidated. Little Texas is in Macon County and lies seven miles west of Tuskegee. I remember my mother meeting Ms. Terrell at St. Joseph Catholic School after we were dropped off in the mornings. Ms. Terrell would drive the two of them to Little Texas. There were several age groups in this small, rural, segregated school, and both women taught three or four grades in each of their classrooms. For example, one room contained children in the first, second, and third grades. In the other room were grades fourth, fifth, and sixth. I remember the potbellied stove used to heat the building, which was often cold during the winter months. Usually, a community member would light the stove before the children and staff arrived so the rooms would not be too cold. Mother Dear and Ms. Terrell were well respected in the community by the Black folks, and they respected them in return. When we were in downtown Tuskegee with my mother and we saw one of her students, they would run to her and hug her. I was proud of my mother.

Mother Dear would take us to school with her sometimes when we had a holiday or if we were out of school. My favorite time to go to school with her was May. They had a maypole ceremony at the school on May 1 because of International Workers' Day. There would be a big celebration in the community with food and games. We did not have that at our Catholic school. Everyone was so welcoming. That was a great time.

I do not remember my mother taking any sick time when she worked there. One reason she did not take sick time is that it would have been a tremendous undertaking for the other teacher to assume her duties. She enjoyed her relationship with the students and that community. It was as if her work with the rural community, and mostly low-income students, was a mission for her. She loved helping them prepare for life and seeing them move on and succeed. She taught for thirty years in Alabama.

My dad worked at the water filtration plant at the Tuskegee Veterans Administration Hospital for about thirty years. When he was ready to retire, he became ill. Because he had never taken sick leave, he had one year of sick leave accrued, which he took before officially retiring.

My father was a Freemason in good standing until his death in 1980. He belonged to the Lewis Adams Lodge No 67, chartered on August 20, 1908. It is reported that the lodge was much more than a place where Masons came to meet. It was a place where Black men could go and not worry about being forced to enter through the backdoor or sit in the balcony. Black Masons were respected as leaders in the community. They were recognized as being upright men and were expected to have good moral character. When one of their members died, the other members were responsible for supporting the family of the deceased as needed. It is thought to be an exclusive group.[4] My mother was active in Greenwood Missionary Baptist Church. Greenwood was one of Tuskegee's area churches that participated in and hosted important civil rights leaders during the Civil Rights Movement. My mother belonged to the Missionary Society. The Missionary Society in Black churches is a very important organization of the church. It is normally a women's group dedicated to the support of the missions of the church such as community outreach. My mother and the other ladies would go into the community and provide food, clothing, education, and some health services to the needy. They had monthly meetings, engaged in Bible study, assessed community needs, and planned fundraising activities to meet some of those needs. The Missionary Society in Black churches was and still is a bridge between church and community.

My parents also were members of other social clubs. My father enjoyed playing bridge and became a Master Bridge player. My mother joined a social club composed of educators later in her life. Our ancestors instilled a strong work ethic and sense of responsibility to the community into their children. What a wonderful legacy they left us. Those social clubs were also essential to mobilizing support for the Civil Rights Movement.

My parents were not the people to lead or be out in front of the movement. They taught us, by example, how to support the movement. My father was an active participant in the mass meetings where strategies were decided about protest marches, boycotts, and voter registration. He would talk to my mother about the discussions and how we could support the strategies. Some of the ways the family supported the movement included economic boycotts in which we refused to patronize outwardly bigoted businesses that required Black people to enter through the backdoors to their establishments. My parents also supported the movement financially, contributing monies that they could afford.

We, in Tuskegee, were blessed because we had Black doctors who were our heroes. We also had John A. Andrew Hospital, a teaching hospital operated by Tuskegee Institute and located on campus. The hospital welcomed Black people in need of care from Macon County and surrounding areas and alleviated the humiliation of having to go through the separate entrances at White-operated facilities. They did not have to experience hostility from White people who treated Black people as lesser human beings or worse at that time.

The Black nursing staff and Black doctors so greatly influenced me that I decided at the age of six, while hospitalized, that I wanted to be like them. I later pursued a career in nursing and received my basic training at John Andrew Hospital on the Tuskegee Institute campus.

Tuskegee Institute and the Tuskegee Veterans Administration (VA) Hospital were central to my social activities growing up in Tuskegee. Since I could not and did not want to attend the segregated movie theater in downtown Tuskegee, I took advantage of social events sponsored by the VA. They offered employees and their families opportunities to use the facilities when it did not interfere with patient care. I remember attending a movie there. They also had a bowling alley. I did not bowl, but it was exciting to watch others. Since I had alternatives, I did not patronize the White-owned social facilities as much as I might have if I did not have the VA and Tuskegee Institute.

Our parents and our teachers stressed education as the major way to navigate the oppressive environment of the South. Although my parents chose not to leave, they never discouraged me and my siblings from leaving the South. I remember them saying that often things "up North" were not as they may seem. Relatives would come from Oakland, California, and Chicago relating how great things were where they were living, but it had little influence on me. I always thought I would leave, but it was based more on my desire to see more of the country rather than the stories my relatives would share during a summer trip.

Growing up in the South, listening to my parents and teachers was a constant reminder that I needed to be serious about education. I needed to strive for more than the mundane, and education would help me to achieve this. My mother bought us encyclopedias so that we would have resources to help us with our studies.

I remember that we had to show report cards to both parents when growing up. My siblings and I had to stand there until they reviewed the report cards. As a reward in high school, my father would give us a weekly allowance ranging from three to five dollars so that we would have spending change. We did not get the money if we had not performed well. Even then, I would save my money to use for something I might consider important, not snacks. My siblings and I knew attending college was our only option. We were expected to go to college. It was going to be difficult financially because the three of us were only separated by one grade and would be in college at the same time. We were expected to get scholarships, loans, or work study to be able to afford or offset some of our college expenses. Our parents would contribute what they could. We also knew that unless we received a scholarship with full benefits to go out of state, we would be attending Tuskegee Institute because we could stay at home and attend classes. I was overjoyed when I was accepted into the Tuskegee Institute School of Nursing.

My acceptance into the School of Nursing allowed me to move out of my family home. I was required to live on campus to be in the nursing program, and this was wonderful. I could have the full campus experience even though it was only three to five miles away from my home. My parents had certain expectations for all their children. It was expected that we would finish in four years because of the costs. That meant no scholarly probation, no dropped courses, and certainly not being expelled; nothing that would prolong our stay. So I was a serious student.

When the Student Nonviolent Coordinating Committee (SNCC) visited Tuskegee Institute in the early 1960s and had active members on campus like Sammy Younge, there was a major effort to mobilize students to participate in marches, voter drives, and education in the community. I participated in local marches in downtown Tuskegee and also went to Montgomery in March 1965 to join Dr. King's group coming from Selma, Alabama. I went because my brother and my boyfriend were going, and they were quite excited. I wanted to be a part of this. So my friend and I joined them on a bus to Montgomery. My parents did not know, and my brother and I didn't tell them until later because they were afraid for our safety.

I remember standing in front of the state capitol in Montgomery. We had received instructions at a local Black church on how to conduct ourselves before going to the capitol. We were to stand without moving and wait to be joined by Dr. King and his followers. We were surrounded by White Alabama State Troopers with weapons on horses. I was scared. After the speeches by Dr. King, we were dismissed. I can remember we ran away desperately from the Alabama State Troopers to get on the bus to go back to Tuskegee. My thoughts were, "I need to get back to school. I have to be back for classes." My parents' admonishments rang in my head. We did make it back safely, and we were so glad we participated in what is now history.

In the summer of 1965, I started working with the Tuskegee Institute Summer Education Program (TISEP). The Tuskegee Institute Summer Education Program employed Black and White college students to offer learning and leadership programs to low-income students in counties surrounding the university. The program fostered personal growth and commitment to helping build an inclusive and just society. At the conclusion of its summer program, the organization took on a year-round focus. Program coordinator Joan Burroughs believed that extending the university's reach was vital to influencing students, schools, and communities and building social, economic, and cultural opportunities for Black communities. During the 1960s, most Tuskegee students and a significant portion of its faculty were highly motivated actors in achieving racial equality, combating economic and social imbalance, and challenging the overarching psychological and insidious injustice inspired by race hatred. That was Tuskegee Institute.

While going through Tuskegee's nursing program from 1964 to 1968, we had our actual hands-on clinical experiences at John A. Andrew Memorial Hospital for the first two years. The entire third year, our group of students went to Baltimore, Maryland. Our dean had to find receptive hospitals located outside the South that would allow Black students to train in their facilities. I recall that a previous Tuskegee Institute nursing class had gone to New York City. So, our class went to Baltimore and trained at the Baltimore City Hospital and trained more extensively at Baltimore Psychiatric Hospital. Part of my senior year was spent in Birmingham, Alabama, at the Public Health Department. I trained there in community health nursing. I have the utmost respect for Dr. Lillian Harvey, the dean of the School of Nursing at the time, and the faculty for ensuring that we got the best training that they could provide during those turbulent times.

Tuskegee Institute School of Nursing faculty constantly told us we were the best and anyone would be lucky to get a Tuskegee nurse. I remember repeating this mantra openly several times during my career. The first time was at my first professional job as a registered nurse at Fort Leonard Wood Army Hospital in Fort Leonard Wood, Missouri, in 1968. I had accompanied my husband to his military assignment as a civilian. The colonel interviewing me acknowledged the excellent reputation of Tuskegee Institute's School of Nursing, and I stated that I could be of value to her department, and I believed it.

Later in life during an interview for admission to Emory University's Graduate School of Nursing, the dean of that program inferred that Tuskegee Institute's School of Nursing had some deficits in its science program and implied that I might have difficulties with Emory's program. Well, I politely corrected her misunderstanding, but I knew this program would not be a good fit for me and did not accept the invitation to enroll.

I have another memory of relaying the mantra that "we were the best and anyone would be lucky to get a Tuskegee nurse." I was interviewing for an internship in nursing administration at the University of Alabama–Birmingham with a hospital chief executive officer. I said to him that I was a Tuskegee nurse, and we were some of the best. I did not get that internship. My department head, who was very candid with me, told me the CEO said I did not meet their corporate image. I was able to get another internship with Mr. Vickerstaff, director of the Birmingham Veterans Administration Medical Center, where I was happy. That mentorship suited me well. I never doubted my preparation. Tuskegee Institute had instilled that in me. This belief and my faith in God propelled me to become one of only eighteen chief nurses of color in the US Department of Veterans Affairs Medical Centers in 1991. At that time there were 172 chief nurses in all the United States.

I was engaged in community outreach and worked in the public rural sector for many years. My sons saw and respected my work in outreach with the Maternal and Infant Care Project in Macon County in the early 1970s; the Federation of Southern Cooperatives, a nonprofit cooperative association of Black farmers and landowners in Epes, Alabama, 1974 to 1978; the Veterans Administration Medical Center, 1978 to 1997; and the Mississippi Medicaid Division of Maternal and Child Health in Jackson, 2001 to 2005.

My sons observed their parents working in public service throughout the years. My younger son utilizes his digital technology knowledge to demonstrate Black excellence in very White, nondiverse digital workplace environments. He believes that we can step out of our traditional roles and dare to be different and do differently. My older son is a civil rights attorney and has been fighting for voting rights for citizens in North Carolina and second chances for previously incarcerated persons for the last seventeen years. He has told me that there is a direct linkage between what his ancestors and parents participated in and what he chose to do in his career.

It is important for my children and grandchildren to know their background and how their ancestors were able to make something sometimes out of nothing. It is important for them to understand the tenacity of their ancestors even in the face of Jim Crow and what is now referred to as the New Jim Crow. Civil rights work is far from over. Gerrymandering continues even after the Tuskegee–initiated US Supreme Court *Gomillion v. Lightfoot* decision found that boundaries created to disenfranchise Black people were illegal. In addition, voter suppression is being "legislated" in states throughout this country. It is true that all of us will not be at the forefront of the Civil Rights Movement today, just as we were not in the past. But all of us have a role to play.

My advice to my children, grandchildren, and any child is to throw the gauntlet down wherever they have a platform. They should not remain silent on injustice. They should demonstrate their value regardless of where their journeys take them and always be true to themselves while displaying integrity, perseverance, tenacity, and worthiness.

CHAPTER 9

Alma Jean Foye Stokes

Editors' Note: Alma Jean Foye Stokes's family still owns the land that her grandfather was so proud to own. He stayed in the South and grew crops on the land to support his family. Alma describes how he used the land to bind his children, grandchildren, and great-grandchildren together at harvest time and special occasions. Generations later, Alma's son owns a cattle farm, and her grandson owns a goat farm that attracts customers from across the nation, continuing her grandfather's legacy of being dedicated to the land.

For as long as she can remember, Stokes's family and church in the Tuskegee area were involved with helping Black veterans at the Veterans Administration Hospital. Her church leaders ensured that when the youth of the church were old enough, they were invited to board a bus sent to the church by the VA on some weekends to brighten the days of injured veterans. It was a major mission of the church and its youth ministry. The youth volunteers would walk patients to the canteen and help them buy their products. They would play cards and board games with them. They took them wrapped presents at Christmastime or other holidays. Many patients lived far away from their families, and they enjoyed having community visitors. Alma still volunteers with various veteran organizations. All her children went to college, and one daughter gives back to the community through a nonprofit for disabled foster children, carrying on the family legacy of "lifting as we climb."

Alma also showed courage as she confronted racism after she left her protected hometown of Tuskegee. Her sense of justice and confidence learned while a youth helped her weather the storms and thrive as a public servant.

GROWING UP IN TUSKEGEE GAVE us a deep sense of our rights as Black people. Most of the people we dealt with every day were Black. After I married and left Tuskegee, interacting with White people was a very different and sometimes complicated thing. It was hard adjusting to living elsewhere because, if you needed a doctor in Tuskegee, you saw a Black doctor. If you needed a dentist, you saw a Black dentist. Coming from a place where everybody was Black and going to an environment where I had to deal with White people all the time took some getting used to. After my husband and I relocated to another small town in Alabama in 1970, I had a disturbing interaction with this White lady. I was out shopping. She asked me something, and I said, "Yes, I want this." She replied, "You are supposed to say yes, ma'am!" I said, "No, you are not my elder nor my mother!"

Another racist incident happened when we lived in Camden, Alabama. My husband built low-cost housing developments for a construction company. He graduated from Tuskegee Institute (University) with a degree in construction engineering in 1964. One day, I went to wash clothes at the laundromat. The "Coloreds Only" laundromat was dirty, so I went to the clean "Whites Only" one.

The owner came out and said, "The man down the street and I have this agreement that Negroes should go to his laundromat." I said, "You do? Well, you and he have that agreement. I do not have that agreement. When I put my quarters in with the other quarters, can you tell which one was put in by a Black lady?" You should have seen his face as he turned around and left! That night, we went to a revival meeting at church. A lady came up to me and announced to the whole group, "Look, this is the lady right here who used Mr .——'s laundromat." My husband, whom everyone called Stokes, jokingly said, "You just integrated something, and you don't realize what you did. You will get us run out of this town or killed." I thought to myself that I grew up in Tuskegee; I had been taught that you could not treat anybody disrespectfully. I said no because I wasn't brought up like that. With all the protesting, court cases, and classmates who had stood up for our rights against George Wallace's efforts to prevent integration, we had learned to stand up for our rights.

My mother's name was Alberta Marshall Peterson. My maternal grandparents, John Peterson (Grandpa Pete) and his wife, Jesse Marshall, were from Shorter, Alabama.

My father, Inell Foye, was from Hardaway, Alabama. My father's parents were John and Emma Slater Foye. Although I do not know specifically where my Foye grandparents were from, I used to hear my family say that the Foye ancestors came from the islands, maybe off the coast of Georgia or the Carolinas. Some say we came from down near Mobile. My father was very dark-skinned with jet-black curly hair. They called us "Geechee" people.[1] I have relatives in the Carolinas, Mississippi, Michigan, Ohio, California, Texas, Tennessee, Georgia, and all over Alabama. Sometimes it is confusing because some of the brothers spell our name Foye, and some spell it, Foy without the "e." Nobody ever explained it. You know that during those times, children were not expected to ask many questions about things.

Alma Foye Stokes as a baby with her parents, Inell Foye, who played on the VA hospital baseball team, and Alberta Peterson. Courtesy of Alma Foye Stokes.

My mother's side of the family did not own property. My paternal grandfather and his brothers owned land in Hardaway, Alabama. While growing up, we would go down to Grandfather Foye's farm. He had many farm animals, including chickens, cows, and horses. He had fruit orchards and grew cotton and all kinds of vegetables. He had a syrup-making factory set up with a mule that went round and round to move a machine that squeezed the juice out of the sugarcane he grew. The juice was then cooked until it turned to syrup. My grandfather had sixteen children. Family names were often repeated. The family has about five or six each of Johns, Inells, Solomons, Samuels, James, and Pearls. With my Grandfather Foye having sixteen children, many relatives are all over the country, and we run into them often through our travels.

Grandpapa Foye was so proud of his land. He loved having his children and grandchildren come and visit. Sometimes, when we visited, there would be about twenty children running around playing games, fishing, and taking rides on the wagon. The Foye grandparents never considered leaving the South. They had a huge farm and a good life and made a good living on the farm. They loved country life and were very proud to be landowners. My parents never considered leaving the South because my father had an excellent job at the Tuskegee Veterans Administration Hospital. My paternal grandparents and parents never regretted not going North. Another reason that most of my family stayed in the South was that they enjoyed being near each other. They got together often on the farm. Those were good times for our family.

When my father returned home from World War II, he worked at the Veterans Administration Hospital. He was in maintenance, but he also did some work on the wards with the patients. The job enabled him to provide a good living for his family of seven. There were five of us children. I have two brothers and two sisters. There are two sets of twins, and I am the only single child. Because of my father's good job at the VA we were able to stay in the South and be near our relatives.

Some of my relatives did leave the South. There was a relative who moved to Indiana and had a popcorn farm. We were amazed to see and find out how popcorn looked on a stalk. My maternal grandparents separated at one point, and my grandmother moved to Chicago to stay with her sons.

Not everything about country life was great. Without an inside bathroom, somebody had to get up, take the pots outside, and empty them in the morning. Somebody had to get up early to take the cows out to pasture. Someone had to draw water from the well for drinking, cooking, and bathing. Everything you needed water for came from the well. We had to help with whatever crop needed harvesting, but it was most often fun because we were all together doing the work. When it was harvesting time in the fall, grandchildren came from all over, especially when it was time to "pick up pecans." We would laugh and tell jokes and just have fun with each other when we were working. It would be a house full. We used to have the best times laughing and, yes, getting into trouble and just being kids.

Alma Foye Stokes (*back row, center*) with her parents and siblings. Photography by P. H. Polk; courtesy of Alma Foye Stokes.

Everybody knew about Jim Crow and racism in Macon County where Tuskegee is located, but most older people in those days did not like to talk to children about racist things that were happening to them. I know some things happened to my parents and grandparents, but they were closed mouthed about a lot of things. My parents never talked about serious race-related matters in front of us. Sometimes I would overhear

Dad say things to my mom after we had gone someplace and had had interactions with White people. He would look at her and ask quietly if she had noticed this or that.

In the Green Fork area of Tuskegee, where I grew up, there was one White store that we went to, but most businesses we frequented were Black owned. Mr. Bill Childs owned the service station and right down the street was the McCaster Neighborhood Store. Bull's supermarket was not too far away. Douglas Mayberry's mother operated the Variety Store. Mr. Ware, our high school math teacher, had a grocery store. The famous Alfred "Chief" Anderson, known as the Father of Black Aviation, and who was the chief flight instructor for the Tuskegee Airmen, owned an appliance store. He was also the pilot who famously took First Lady Eleanor Roosevelt for a ride in his airplane.[2] There were Black barbershops and beauty shops. I remember Newsome's Fish Market. You could smell the fish cooking when you passed by. It was some of the best fish in the world.

The Black businesses provided jobs for adults in the community, but they also provided after-school jobs for the Black teens in Tuskegee. Many of the teens who worked in these businesses were mentored by the owners and received their first employment lessons from them. My mother worked in Allen's store for a while. When I went to the fifty-year belated graduation ceremony for Willie B. Wyatt and Anthony Lee at the school they integrated in Notasulga, I learned that my mom worked at Allen's store at the same time as Anthony Lee when he was a teenager. We would go to the White store sometimes, mostly when we needed to charge things.

I remember when the Tuskegee Boycott began around 1957. I remember my family going to Opelika and Auburn for grocery shopping. My parents participated in the movement by supporting the boycott. Buying in Opelika or Auburn might have been buying from another White man, but we did not buy from the White men in Tuskegee. I remember my daddy also going to the civil rights mass meetings that were held in the various churches in Tuskegee. Although my parents were participating in the movement, I think they did not involve us in conversations because they were trying to protect us.

Much of our civil rights and community work was done through the church. We belonged to Greater Saint Mark Baptist Church where many active church men mentored us. Mr. Colin Graham was the junior choir director. There was Mr. Carter and Mr. Thornton along with other members of our church. Those men added happiness to the lives of the children in the church and community. They took our junior choir to sing for the veterans at the VA every first Sunday. We sang at the VA from when I was a child until I graduated from Tuskegee Institute High School and beyond. On Christmas, we went to the hospital and bagged candy and nuts for the veterans. When we became teenagers, we danced with the veterans on Thursday nights. We walked with them to the canteen if they needed to go to buy items. The VA sent a big bus to pick us up at the church and take us back. I remember our church members, friends, neighbors, and classmates were involved. I cannot remember a time when we were not helping the veterans at the VA. I guess that is why I am still a member of the American Legion Auxiliary.

Oh, growing up in Greater Saint Mark Baptist Church had a great influence on all of us. We had a very active and fun youth group in my church. Every year, the church sponsored a fundraising trip to the beach in Panama City, Florida. I remember when we had Tuskegee Institute High School Baby Tigers' football games. We would stay afterward and walk home together—a whole group of Green Fork people. That was something. Those were the times. We just had good wholesome fun and lots of parental involvement in helping us grow up to be good people.

We lived a kind of ideal life growing up in Tuskegee. At the time, we did not appreciate all the uneducated, educated, and famous people who lived there and helped us grow. For instance, I just considered Tuskegee Airman Chief Anderson to be a regular member of the community. Often, we were living among greatness and did not know it. It was such a special time in our lives!

I must admit that there were some things about Tuskegee during that time that bothered me. There was so much emphasis on high expectations and accomplishments that sometimes it seemed like the people who had accomplished a lot and their children got special attention or privileges. Sometimes it also seemed that people with lighter skin also got special attention and privileges. I know that sometimes in school some of the less fortunate and darker-skinned classmates suffered from teasing from their classmates. I guess we just saw it as how things were sometimes and continued to respond favorably to the majority of our teachers, community leaders, and classmates who were fair-minded and did not have those attitudes.

After high school, I worked half a year helping an elderly lady. Later, I went to Tennessee State University for a year and a half. I came home and met my husband, Frederick Stokes, here in Tuskegee. We moved to Camden, Alabama, then to Plains, Georgia, and finally to Eatonton, Georgia, his hometown. He was building all that time. He died in 2001. I am still in contact with people in the various places where we lived while he was building. I still talk to people in Camden and Plains, just like they are next door. I still value all those contacts we made as a young couple. My husband taught detailed construction architectural drafting for close to thirty years here in his hometown of Eatonton. Yes, Alice Walker was born in Eatonton. Tuskegee Airman Hiram E. Little was also an Eatonton native.

My husband and I are the parents of two girls and one boy. I did not get a chance to finish my education, but my children attended college. Both girls went to Fort Valley State in Georgia. They did not go to Tuskegee because it was a private school, and the tuition was too high. We had three in college at the same time. My oldest daughter lives in Rocky Mountain, North Carolina. She is an animal health technician with the US Department of Agriculture (USDA). My younger daughter founded her own nonprofit to facilitate life transitions for at-risk youth with disabilities and disorders. My son and my oldest grandson are following in their great-grandfather Foye's footsteps by owning Black farms. My son raises beef cattle, and my grandson raises and sells goats for market. My grandson has buyers coming from all over the United States to buy goat meat.

My husband was married before our marriage and had two children. We raised five children together. Most of my time was spent raising the children. I worked in the school system doing various jobs with special-needs children, including driving a bus for them. I was at the school one day, and this fellow who knew my husband said, "Alma, what are you doing?" I told him I was not doing anything at that time. He said, "Well, I have some special-needs children. They have to go to a PE class across town, and I know you will try anything. Take these keys, and take these children where they need to go." I ended up being a special-needs driver. I would take them to the Christian Outreach Center for their work assignments. The children folded clothes and hung them on racks. I liked working with special-needs children.

My husband also built houses in our community on the side; that is, these houses were not associated with his employer. He designed three churches here in Eatonton. I do not know how many houses he designed and constructed, but there were many. When we were staying in Plains, I told my husband that I was going back to school to get my degree. He said OK, but that's when they transferred him to Atlanta. We had his two and our three children, and I just said, OK, this is what I must deal with now. I've got to raise these five kids.

In 2002, I ran for, and was elected to, the Eatonton City Council. I stayed on the council for sixteen years. The man who was running for mayor at the time asked me to run for an open seat. He told me he knew I could do a good job. I told him I would stay for a while, but it ended up being sixteen years.

I would like my children, grandchildren, and great-grandchildren to know that during the time I was on the city council, I did what I thought was best for my community. I was not there to cater to this person or that person. I enjoyed it, but I was also ready to leave it. I want them to know that I will always be there for them and have tried to do my best in life. Most of all, in life, you must take the bitter with the sweet and continue moving forward.

I am grateful for all the caring family, friends, parents, church and community leaders, and teachers we had in Tuskegee. Oh, Lord! They had come from all over the United States. They were smart, hardworking, and dedicated. They had such an impact on all of us. I will never forget Mr. Poole, the assistant principal at Tuskegee Institute High School. I can still hear him saying, "You can run, but you can't hide." Again, we probably did not appreciate it when they were hard on us, but most of us now appreciate the high expectations they had for us and the high standards they held us to. I am grateful for how well they prepared us to go out into the world and be successful and make a difference. They wanted so much for us to always do our best and continue fighting for civil rights, just as they had done.

CHAPTER 10

Harold White

Editors' Note: Harold White has spent most of his life "lifting as he climbed." He was one of the classmates who decided to stay in the South. His major motivations were his feeling that he had not found another place he thought was better than Tuskegee and his love for and dedication to his family. Most of his career has been in the political arena trying to improve social, economic, and educational systems for the masses in the Tuskegee area. He recognizes that current Tuskegee is not the vibrant and thriving place of his youth but realizes there are broader statewide and national sociological and political reasons for the situation that make it difficult to ameliorate.

After the Civil Rights Movement nationally, Black people gained some political power, but economic resources often moved away from the places where the Civil Rights Movement had some success. The movement opened opportunities nationally and internationally for talented Black people and other people of color. Businesses and academic institutions began to compete for their talent, drawing many out of the South. Additionally, powerful anti–civil rights forces in the political arena and the courts have fought and continue to fight against equality in the marketplace, voting rights, and education for people of color. Along with local politics, all these factors have had an impact on the city of Tuskegee.

Tuskegee University remains a successful bright spot of excellence in the Tuskegee landscape, continuing to attract talented faculty and students nationally and internationally and being a major recruiting source for Black talent by corporations and other organizations. Those who return to find the town of Tuskegee diminished in their eyes complain, but Harold invites them to return home and join the continuing struggle.

My parents were very active in the Civil Rights Movement in Tuskegee. Though my father did not finish eighth grade and my mom only had some high school, they were very involved parents and activists. They were avid readers. My father read the newspaper every day. Sometimes he brought a newspaper home from work, and sometimes, he picked one up at a nearby shop. During that time, the *Montgomery Advertiser* published an edition for Black people and another edition for White people. You could distinguish each by the number of stars on the masthead. If I remember correctly, they put two stars on the edition for Black people and one star on the edition for White people. They did not want the Black and White obituaries to appear together. I know about this because I was a paperboy when I was growing up.

Harold White's family. Harold is sitting on the lap of his father, George White, next to his mother, Kerry Sharp White. Photography by P. H. Polk; courtesy of Harold White.

My father's name was George White. His parents were Cowans and Johnsons. I do not know much about the paternal side of my family because they migrated North, mainly to the Washington, DC, area. My mother's name was Kerry Sharp. Her parents, Jim and Jane Sharp, worked primarily in the agricultural sector. My maternal grandfather worked at a grist mill grinding corn into cornmeal. My maternal grandmother was a housewife.

The grist mill where my maternal grandfather worked was owned by a prominent White family in Tuskegee, the Lightfoots. My grandparents were old by the time I was in elementary school. They lived to be about ninety years of age. They did not become involved in the civil rights protests, neither did they talk about racial issues around others, especially the children. Many elderly people had learned to be quiet about White people for their safety and the safety of their families. At one time, they lived in a three-room house on the Lightfoots' property near the grist mill. They later bought their own property. I liked to visit them because they had a wood burning stove and a fireplace. They loved telling stories about raising their children and the funny things they used to do.

Harold White's maternal grandmother, Jane Sharp, holding a grandchild at the grist mill where his grandfather worked. Courtesy of Harold White.

I am sure my maternal grandparents never considered going North. They owned land close to the Little Texas area in Macon County. I never heard them express a desire to leave the South, even when people from the North came home with great big cars and fine clothes. My grandparents would admire the clothes and the cars, but they seemed comfortable with their decision to stay in the South.

My parents were in the medical field. Dad worked in the Urology Clinic at the VA Hospital in Tuskegee as an assistant to a doctor. He became so proficient in his work that doctors would request him when they were working on special cases. He was very proud of his work. He would make sure his uniforms were starched and ironed to perfection. He was very serious about being at work on time and doing his work well.

My mother was a nurse's assistant at John A. Andrew Hospital on Tuskegee Institute's campus. She was also proud of her work. She would tell us about the babies and the deliveries she helped with. She enjoyed working with Dr. Foster, who was one of the main doctors at John Andrew Hospital. Once, he was considered for surgeon general of the United States.

Once, my parents considered leaving the South. My father was offered an opportunity to work at a VA hospital in California. He talked about it with us, and we were all excited about it and thought he should take the job. He considered the possible effects of living in a large city and moving might have on us while we were still in elementary school and decided to stay in the small city of Tuskegee.

My parents' involvement in the movement started with my father. He became president of the Parents Teachers Association (PTA) for Washington Public Junior High School and held that position for several years. As president of the PTA, he became involved with the Tuskegee Civic Association (TCA) and the NAACP. My mother attended meetings with my father. A couple of incidents that happened to my family demonstrate how it was racially for Black people at that time and why so many people in Tuskegee got involved in the movement.

We initially lived on Auburn Street in Tuskegee. The White couple we were renting from were very reluctant to make repairs. Once there was a leak in the roof that we had had to live with for some time. We just had to wait until the owner decided to repair it. He finally gave permission for my father to do so. My father hired a Black man to repair the roof. When the White owner came to inspect the work, he looked under the house so he could take any extra shingles away with him. He could not find them. The Black roofer had assumed that the owner would come looking for any extra shingles and had placed them where he could not find them. He knew it would be almost impossible to convince the owner to buy more shingles to make further repairs if they were needed. Although this seems like a small matter, repairing the roof on a house that was not my father's responsibility would have taken money he did not have or maybe money he was saving for other things for his family. Most White people at that time did not want Black people to have any advantage and often took advantage of their status as landlords or grocery store owners.

My dad eventually purchased some property at the top of Auburn Street near County Road 81. It belonged to a White man named Cocola Thompson. During the process, we discovered there was a clause in the will that had left the property to him stating the property should not be sold to Black people. These "exclusion" clauses kept Black people all over the country from owning property in certain neighborhoods. Thompson sold us the property anyway. My father built a house on that property, and it still stands today.

Another racist incident happened to my mother a few years after I returned home from college. I took her to an appointment at the East Alabama Medical Center in Auburn, Alabama. I was about twenty or twenty-one years of age and still filled with the civil rights spirit. My mom went to the desk and registered. When the White clerk called the names of White people, she addressed them as Mr. or Mrs. When she called my mother, she said, "Kerry." My mother was about to get up. I said, "Hold it; wait a minute." I went up and said to the lady, "Look, that's my mother's name. Do you know her that well?" She said, "No, I don't know her." I said, "Well, her name is Mrs. White. You call those other women Mrs., and I expect you to call her Mrs. as well." When I reported it, I was told they had gotten complaints about her before, which indicated to me that her actions were being supported by a supervisor, in essence the system. My mother did not want me to stir the water too much.

There was an interesting dynamic regarding most Black parents' attitudes about their children's involvement in the Civil Rights Movement at that time. My father did not want us to get overly involved in the movement because he feared for our safety or that we might end up in jail. At the same time, he did not want us to put up with any junk. For instance, The Brown Service Insurance company had White male insurance premium collectors who went door to door throughout the Black community to collect the monthly fifty cents or whatever small amount that was due. These White men had no respect for Black people and were often rude and inappropriate, especially with the Black women of the house. They often used derogative greetings such as auntie, uncle, or deacon. My sister enjoys telling the story about what happened once when I was in high school. One day the Brown Service guy came to the house to collect. When I opened the door, he said, "Is George here?" I said, "Excuse me?" He repeated, "Is George here?" I said, "There's a Mr. White here." He said, "Oh, oh, oh yes, yes, yes, yes," I said, "You mean Mr. White?" "Oh yeah, Mr. White." I slowly got my father to the door. He let the guy in and paid whatever the fee was for the insurance. I asked my father if he had heard what had happened when I answered the door? He said no and asked me to tell him. I said, "Well, he wanted to see somebody named George, and I told him that no George lived here." My father said, "Son, just be careful, you know, just be careful."

I knew our parents wanted us to stand up because we had witnessed them doing so and helping to stir the water, but I also realized that they wanted to keep us safe. My parents' attitude reminded me of my grandparents' silence on race-related issues. Ancestors did not want to talk about them because they knew that trouble was always just under the surface of the water when dealing with White people in Alabama at that time. This was the situation Black people in the movement were trying to change.

Living in a mostly Black town with an abundance of educated Black people probably protected us more from the daily racism and prejudice many Black people experienced in other places. In Tuskegee, interacting with successful Black people daily gave us the courage to try to change things. We had people in every profession you can think of. We had doctors, lawyers, and successful businesspeople who owned car dealerships, grocery stores, clothing stores, appliance stores, and hotels. The university had professors in dozens of fields of expertise.

We had those role models to look up to. It produced a "matter of fact" prideful attitude among us. When we visited other places, sometimes people would look at us and say, "Oh, you are one of those UNs ["uppity n****rs"] from Tuskegee." We heard that from Black and White people out of the area. While that comment primarily came from White people, class issues arose among Black people in Macon County. There were class differences based on where you came from, whether it was the northeastern, southern, or western part of Macon County. Class issues also were influenced by who was more educated, who had more income, and sometimes the color of one's skin.[1]

During that time, people from different geographical areas sometimes competed for resources, and similar attitudes still existed years later. When schools were consolidated in Macon County in the 1980s and 1990s, there were still divisions. There was a proposal on the table to build one major state-of-the-art high school in Tuskegee. People in outlying areas of the county could be heard saying, "You all always want everything in Tuskegee." Remnants of that class system remain and still sometimes complicate political, economic, and cultural decision-making in local government.

I was a shy kid in high school and was not involved in many activities. I liked the choir and was a member for a while. I did not get involved in sports because of a lack of talent. I did not have the talent to play football. I thought I could play basketball, but I did not have talent in that area either. I really wanted to be a part of the drama team, but I had a slight fear that I would not be able to make the team because most of the drama team were from a certain part of town. Looking back, my ideas of possibly being excluded might have come from teenage anxiety. I have learned that if you do not try, you will never know if you can succeed. Being a little shy kid, I didn't want to try and fail. Now, I've tried and failed many times and have had some success as a result.

I decided not to go to Tuskegee Institute after we graduated from high school. I did not know if I was ready for college. I worked at the Tuskegee Institute cafeteria for a while, not as a student, just as a community person. While I was working there, one of my supervisors told me, "Well, yeah, I can see you now. You wanna work here long enough to get an old raggedy car and then you'll be satisfied?" I said, "No, that's not me!" What he said to me made me think and showed the importance of informal mentoring in the Black community. I think the next semester I enrolled at Miles College near Birmingham, Alabama. I was expecting a large campus. When I got there, I saw that little bit of a campus. I said, "Oh no!" I was ready to go back home. I had convinced our classmate Paul Todd to go to Birmingham with me. We were roommates for three years at Miles College. We had many interesting experiences because Miles's students were heavily involved in the Civil Rights Movement as well. We participated in numerous marches and meetings. The president of Miles at the time was Dr. Lucius Pitts. He was well respected in the state and the region.

When I first got to Miles College, it was not accredited. Miles College became accredited primarily through Dr. Pitts's diligent efforts. Once we received the notification that we were accredited, many Miles students went to the Birmingham Airport to greet President Pitts. I still have the newspaper article about the students at the airport! When I first went to Miles, we only had about seven hundred students. When I left four years later, we had about 1,500 students. Of course, we were not competitive in sports when I first went to Miles, maybe basketball. We were everybody's homecoming football opponent because they knew they could beat us. We have made so much progress that the campus is almost unrecognizable to me now. They have built several new buildings and have enhanced the curricular offerings. Miles became the first team to beat Tuskegee at its homecoming in many years. In the last ten years, we have beaten Tuskegee seven times! That used to be unthinkable!

When I graduated from Miles, I went to Texas Southern University on a Peace Corps scholarship. After the Peace Corps scholarship, I went to the Ivory Coast, West Africa, for two years. I taught English as a second language and traveled to several other countries on the African continent. My Peace Corps colleagues and I took a little shuttle bus and traveled to Ghana, Nigeria, and Sierra Leone.

The Ivory Coast is a French-speaking country. I never knew why we had to take French or a foreign language in high school or college. I never mastered the language when I was in college, but the Peace Corps gave us a course in preparation for our work. I did well. I knew how to ask where the toilet was and about the food. The markets were fantastic. You could go to the market and get a chicken to cook for dinner. The shopkeeper would select a live chicken, wring its neck, prepare it for cooking, and wrap it up for you. We had a houseman (called a houseboy then) who cooked and cleaned the house for us.

When I first got to the Ivory Coast, people stared at me. They were not used to seeing Black volunteers in this area. Most of the instructors were White French people because the country was colonized by the French. We made some very good friends there. It was a great experience.

I wanted to stay for an additional two years, but my father got ill just before the end of my tour of duty, and I came home to help my mother. That is when I started working at Tuskegee Institute. They saw that I had taught English as a second language, so they hired me to teach world history, American literature, and English as a second language.

After six years, I decided that teaching as an instructor was more volunteer work than the Peace Corps had been. I was not making any money as an instructor, so I went to work for the Community Action Agency, a major federal antipoverty and community development program during the '70s. I really enjoyed that work. I was a grants writer and the inventory control administrator. I was like a man Friday because whatever they asked I would do it or try to do it. That was like my Peace Corps experience because when you worked in developing countries, they did not ask you if you could do something. If something needed doing you were told to figure it out, even if the task was not your specialty or responsibility.

After Community Action, I worked with the Macon County Racing Commission, which regulates parimutuel wagering on greyhounds and horses. I started as a commission judge. We were responsible for managing grievances that people had about the outcome of a race. The process involved showing photo finishes and having hearings if someone contested the race. Sometimes, those contesting a race would get loud and even violent. Occasionally, even after they saw the photo finish, they would accuse us of doctoring it up. In the end, the regulations indicated that the decisions of judges were final. In its heyday, the racetrack would be packed. Exit 22 off Interstate 85 was always tied up with people coming to play the races.

The track eventually closed. It is said that political issues were involved. State troopers sometimes came to raid the track and intimidate customers. After the track closed, the owner resorted to casino gambling. Major revenue was lost to Macon County. Teachers were heavily impacted because they were receiving almost as much money from racing revenue as they were being paid in regular salary from the state. We do not get any revenue from the casino. The closing of the track is one of those situations that some say was aimed to negatively impact Tuskegee and Macon County.

While a commissioner, I was awarded an international leadership opportunity offered by Auburn University's Leadership Program. The Fellowship Program had an agricultural focus on land development, crops, and livestock. Of the twenty participants selected, there were two Black men. Some of those people were very successful farmers in Alabama. We received an orientation on the people and geographical habitats before we went to New Zealand and Australia.

Believe it or not, some participants brought their racial ignorance and prejudices with them. The tour included visiting aboriginal areas. We had been asked not to take pictures and not to insult them. One of the White guys still took pictures. In another incident involving aborigines, the American group decided they wanted to sing "Dixie" as our entertainment gift to them. Without even talking to each other, the other Black guy and I raised our hands to object. Later, one of the White female program leaders told us that they did not mean to offend us. When we arrived at the center to meet our guests, she announced to the group that they had decided to sing "America" instead. The other Black guy and I had already decided that if they sang "Dixie," we would stand up, turn our backs, and raise our fists.

There was much cultural insensitivity on that trip. We were staying with Australians in their homes. Three or four of us would be assigned with a family. They were having a water shortage, and we were asked not to use much water. Because it was so hot, some of our team members took showers two or three times a day anyway. One family member asked me, "You are here with White people. Is there any discrimination in your country?" I told him that there was still discrimination and that sometimes people can work together and still be prejudiced and discriminate.

I told him that when we were in public and a foreign country, we wanted to project a united front. When we left, each of us had brought souvenirs to give to the families. I gave them T-shirts with pictures of Black people on them. The aborigines said that their ancestors did not appear on postage stamps or any other governmental publications. Things might be different now.

I retired from the Racing Commission after working there for twenty-seven years and then became the director of Community Action. Subsequently, I was also elected to serve on the Macon County School Board for three terms. We were having some embarrassing situations in the district that I thought I could help with when I ran for the board. Board members would argue more than they would get the work done. I ran for office and won. Each term was a six-year term. When it was time for the second and third elections, I did not have opposition. I guess the citizens thought I was doing a decent job. After three terms, I said, that's enough. That's eighteen years.

During that time, we had to close South Macon High School because it had health and safety issues related to sewage. Anytime you start talking about closing a school, the people say no. The people were saying, "Y'all just want everything in Tuskegee." This was one of those situations that still contained some of the attitudes that were leftovers from the class system that people often talked about in Tuskegee and Macon County years earlier. Attitudes were more related to urban-rural educational and income differences than skin color differences. I had a meeting with the community and explained that we did not want to close the school, but the school population had decreased, the facilities were in poor shape, and it was not economically feasible to keep it open. The people finally realized that closing the school was the best thing to do for the students.

My wife, Arnetta Diane, and I have raised one child. She is my niece who will be twenty-four in May. She went to Miles College like I did. She did not want to go to Tuskegee. I guess for the same reasons I did not want to go. We wanted to experience something different. She said Miles College was not too big, not too small, and that she was not going there just because I went there!

I "stayed" in Tuskegee mainly because of wanting to be close to family.

I was able to help both my parents as they aged. I have served as a deacon in my church and served the community through my church. I have dedicated my life to continuing the struggle as my parents had done with the aim of making things better for our people and all people.

To my niece and our young Black people, I tell them to do what John Lewis advised us to do, "If you see something that is not right, not fair, you have a moral obligation to do something about it."[2] Too often, we will not do anything, but we will complain. We must stay involved. I like what a Black woman told Supreme Court Justice Katanji Brown when she saw her walking across Harvard's campus with her head down. She told her to "persevere."[3] That is what Black folk must do to continue to fight for racial and economic justice.

It bothers me when classmates come back to Tuskegee and talk about the town. They talk about how bad things look and they ask, "Why don't you all do this or that." I just want to say, "Why don't you come back and help?" Some of us that "stayed" in Tuskegee and in the South have tried to make improvements. Like the old saying goes, it takes a village not just to raise a child but to make changes. Many people ask why Tuskegee is not the bustling city it used to be. There are several reasons. Some will say that Tuskegee has never been forgiven by White state officials and businesspeople for their massive involvement and wins in the Civil Rights Movement. We see economic development all around Tuskegee that comes up to the Macon County line. And it stops. Development from Auburn, Alabama, home of Auburn University, where the state constantly pours in money, is closing in or strangling Tuskegee. Businesspeople know that Tuskegee has everything that's needed for industry to thrive; they will not invest here. We have the needed natural resources. We have an interstate highway system. We have a university. We have everything that a company or business should be looking for to be successful.

Some blame other issues for the decline of Tuskegee. Some say that the brain trust left Tuskegee to take advantage of opportunities all over the United States and the world that opened after the Civil Rights Movement. Some will say that we have not had the most brilliant and robust city leadership to shepherd us out of the booming 1960s and 1970s. Some also say that we have lost our connection to the university, which historically was the driver of innovation and employment in the area. There is probably some truth in all those explanations.

Regardless, I still think many businesspeople are waiting on an opportunity to move in because they are still buying up land around Tuskegee. When people, who are often Black, move out of the area and neglect their taxes, the land goes into forfeiture, and people from the outside pay the taxes and get the land for very little money. Black people often fall asleep and do not keep their eyes on the big picture. Lastly, Black people with financial resources should use their resources to make investments in the community.

In recent years, good business plans have been created for the city of Tuskegee. Local politics has interfered with some of those efforts. A business development has been built at Exit 38 off of interstate 85. It includes a cafe, convenience store, gas station, and a major service facility for trucking. That is one of the first major new facilities in the city in years.

The strategy of some state officials and agencies not to support Tuskegee has not been so transparent, but it has been rather detrimental. With the emergence of right-wing conservatism in this country, it has become popular to tout conspiracy theories and racial hatred. The strategy is emboldened by many who ignore the needs of people of color, while championing the causes of the rich and powerful.

I think Black people have gotten too comfortable. It is good to revisit and be proud of our history, but it is more important to build on our history. All too often that is not happening, especially in the financial and educational sectors. Those of us who "stayed" sometimes get very frustrated because the city of Tuskegee is not making needed progress approaching the excellence we experienced growing up in Tuskegee.

It is going to take some movers and shakers from outside Tuskegee to come in and make the change. Strong city and county leadership working hand in hand with the university can turn the tide. The impact might not be as great as the one Booker T. Washington, Tuskegee Institute, its faculty, students, the TCA, and the Black community made years ago, but we must try. For example, in the past year, there has been a ray of hope for the future economic development of Tuskegee. A South Korean company, Samkee Corporation, an auto parts company, has brought a $128 million facility and 170 jobs to Tuskegee.[4] It took the combined efforts of the city mayor, the community development agency with Tuskegee University, and state and federal assistance to effect this seemingly monumental economic development in Tuskegee.

I am hopeful about a future revival of this important city.

CHAPTER 11

Carolyn Moss Woodard

Editors' Note: Carolyn Moss Woodard's family epitomized the spirit of "lifting as they climbed." Her maternal grandparents owned a neighborhood store in Montgomery that was the center of civil rights activity. Community members could get information about what was going on and how to participate in the movement. They also obtained information about jobs and other social services. Carolyn's grandparents joined hundreds of small Black-owned barbershops, beauty shops, and neighborhood stores throughout the country that played an important information dissemination role in Black communities during the movement.

Carolyn's paternal grandparents and parents lived in Tuskegee and kept abreast of the news through their new and prized television set. The set allowed them to witness the news of the bombing of the four young Black girls in Birmingham, to know when Martin Luther King Jr. and other civil rights leaders were coming to Tuskegee and Montgomery for rallies at various churches, and to follow the path of the young student Freedom Riders for whom her family bagged lunches of sandwiches, cookies, and apples in their kitchen for the students' journey.

Although she had to sit apart from her fellow White Girl Scout leaders at meetings and take her charges to segregated camps, Carolyn's mother "lifted while climbing" by becoming one of the first Black Girl Scout leaders in the South. She mentored young girls into womanhood, supervised them in camping activities, led them in

Tuskegee Institute homecoming parades, and taught them to stand tall and become the best they could be in life while giving back to others. Carolyn's father became one of the first Black occupational therapists in the country.

Macon County, Alabama, is my birthplace. I grew up in an educational environment with my residence being eight blocks from "the campus," Tuskegee Institute, six blocks from Tuskegee Institute High School, and a few blocks from my elementary school, St. Joseph Catholic School. I walked everywhere!

My paternal grandparents, Alvenia and Hank Moss, were both born in Tuskegee and had a home off Franklin Road. Grandmother Moss was an only child. Grandfather Moss had three brothers, and their family had migrated to Tuskegee from Jacksonville, Florida.

Grandparents Alvenia and Hank had a garden, which to me as a child seemed to cover two blocks. It was full of cabbage, greens, tomatoes, peas, watermelon, and many other vegetables. There was no irrigation system, just God's weather. On the right side of their home, they grew root vegetables, sweet potatoes, and peanuts. I always marveled at my grandmother's practice of pulling vegetables from the ground and placing them to roast in the hot ashes of one of their fireplaces. It was my introduction to roasted vegetables, and they were delicious.

My grandfather had learned many of his farming techniques from the famous Tuskegee Institute scientist Dr. George Washington Carver. He always spoke reverently about Dr. Carver and his work in the community. Dr. Carver was a world-renowned agricultural scientist. Most elementary school children can tell you that he developed 105 products from peanuts and taught farmers that, if they rotate their crops, they will avoid depleting the soil and improve the quality and quantity of their crops. Dr. Carver took his students to communities surrounding Tuskegee Institute to teach Black farmers how to improve their crops.[1] That is how he met my grandfather.

My father commented often about how similar Dr. Carver and my grandfather were. He said that both men were soft-spoken and willingly shared advice with anybody about plants and planting and that they both wore coveralls.

As a young girl, I was always impressed with my grandmother's ability to jar vegetables and fruits. They were displayed beautifully in her kitchen cabinets. She jarred pears, apples, peaches, and figs from her fruit orchard. Blackberry bushes grew wild everywhere.

My grandparents also had a hen coop and several cows. They were self-sustaining. Often, I was unsure about that meat wrapped in brown paper, especially when one or two cows disappeared. I learned how to churn milk into butter and, most excitingly, into ice cream! The family ate well and enjoyed the fruits of my parents' and grandparents' labor.

In addition to providing food year-round, my grandfather proudly worked at the Tuskegee Air Base. To him, this job was the greatest of all time. He beamed as he spoke proudly about the "Negro" soldiers and was very impressed with their handsome uniforms. He often said how happy he was that the soldiers had a base of their own where they could congregate, relax, enjoy their music, and not be harmed by the Ku Klux Klan (KKK). I am not certain of my grandfather's job title, but I know he enjoyed working with machines.

My grandfather warned the soldiers, many of whom had come from the more liberal North and West, about the KKK and their hatred for Black people. My grandfather always made it clear that if we ever got into trouble with White people, we were to make it to his house. He told us that no "law" or KKK was going to step on his property. I must say, I never saw either come to his house.

My maternal grandparents, Hattie Fields Hicks and William Hicks, came from Abbeville, Alabama, and made their home in Montgomery, Alabama. Grandfather Hicks had worked with a White grocery chain owner in Abbeville. The businessman noticed my grandfather's interest and skills in handling various merchants and encouraged him to seek employment in the capital city of Montgomery.

The lure of securing a full-time, higher-paying job and working in the capital city prompted my grandfather to uproot his wife and three children. The family traveled by train to the big city of Montgomery, leaving behind their relatives and most of their material possessions.

Grandfather Hicks obtained a job as a courier. He took various packages and mail to beautiful offices in the capital buildings. He said he saw no Black people sitting behind desks. He maintained a low profile but met very influential people who aided him in the acquisition of his home and neighborhood store.

My grandparents operated the neighborhood store from their home garage. Grandmother handled the daily activities. She also taught piano lessons and often served as a pianist for local church events. The Hicks had vast community support. Their location was the "hub" for Black people for information regarding jobs, housing, and the Civil Rights Movement.

When I was in the eighth grade, one of my visits to see my maternal

Carolyn Moss Woodard's maternal grandparents, William and Hattie Fields Hicks, at their Montgomery garage grocery store, a center for civil rights activity. Courtesy of Carolyn Moss Woodard.

grandparents in Montgomery became a major awareness lesson in segregation, prejudice, and discrimination and how they affected me as a human being. Whenever we went to Montgomery, we would go shopping at Montgomery Fair, a major department store in the South at that time. Going shopping in the big city was a major undertaking. We would dress nicely and were told to use the bathroom before going downtown.

I, like most young Black children at the time, was given rules to follow by my parents and grandparents. Many Black people our age will attest to having heard what I called the "Do Not Do Anything to Get Yourself and the Rest of Us in Trouble Segregation Survival Rules" from their elders who had learned to cope with living in the South. The rules included:

Don't use the White Only water fountain or toilet.

Don't put your foot in the new shoes in the shoe store to try them on for fit before your parents purchase them.

Don't try on a hat in the store, even if you want to see how it looks on you before your parents purchase it.

Don't be loud.

Keep your shopping bag closed to prevent being questioned as a suspected shoplifter.

Don't talk back to White people

Stay as close as possible to an adult.

Don't touch anything in the store.

It was a lot for an excited child to remember and produced much anxiety. I liked seeing the pretty dresses and smelling the beautiful perfume scents permeating the air in the department store. Soon, I became aware that the sales clerks greeted the White girls around my age with open smiles and offers of help, and I heard the words pretty and petite. I noticed that they never greeted me with similar smiles or said nice things to me. Although going shopping in the big city of Montgomery was exciting and everything was so pretty, noticing the differences in the ways the clerks treated me and the White girls made me sad and gave me my first uncomfortable awareness and feelings of prejudice and discrimination.

Since I had noticed that many elderly Black people in the community could not read or write, I was surprised to discover that both sets of my grandparents were literate. I was surprised that their cursive skills were superior to my penmanship. My paternal grandparents always kept up on current events. I observed that they sat in the front room close to the radio in the evenings. My role was to be quiet. They listened to how the United States was viewed in other countries. They would talk about current events such as the war and segregation.

My parents, Minnie Hicks Moss and Alonzo Moss, made a good living for our family. By the time I became an early teenager, they acquired a television. Acquiring a television was a very big deal in our house. My grandparents also purchased a television around the same time. There were rules on times for turning the set on and off, who got to change stations, and even who got to regulate the volume. At that time, a television was a prized possession, and the folks meant for us to take care of it. The acquisition of these televisions connected us visually to civil rights happenings outside of Tuskegee. We were now truly able to see the real effects of racism and segregation on the everyday life of Black people in Alabama.

My first memory of watching the start of the Civil Rights Movement on television was the news showing the amazingly strong voice of Reverend Ralph Abernathy. He was speaking at the First Baptist Church in Montgomery. I realized instantly that our race was under full attack. Protesting by peaceful marching was the prescription. Everyone in the church was encouraged to pass the word and organize peaceful demonstrations.

The following week, my family and I traveled to Montgomery to hear and see Dr. Martin Luther King Jr. for the first time. People were packed into Dexter Avenue Baptist Church. The church was beyond capacity, and the mood was tense. Dr King did not mince his words. He stressed the need for Black people to keep on pushing to obtain our rights. There was jubilant applause. I met Rosa Parks that night. As a child, I had no awareness at that moment of her greatness.

Upon returning to Tuskegee, the movement was in full force. One day, I walked into our kitchen and was delighted to see dozens of cookies and large apples. My father was wrapping cookies in waxed paper. My mother was making a stack of sandwiches. I just knew we were going to a grand celebration. I was quickly informed that my parents were preparing food for the young Freedom Riders. They were staying in Macon County. Some were staying overnight with families, and others were staying on the Tuskegee Institute (University) campus.

It was humbling and inspirational to see those young men dedicated to the cause. They were thankful for the food. They were energized and looking forward to reaching Montgomery. I was so excited that I wanted to make additional sandwiches. At the meeting that night, many residents encouraged them and offered prayers and good wishes for their safety. They knew the young people were on a dangerous mission.

Racism was blatantly displayed everywhere in our state. George Wallace was governor. Racism, prejudice, discrimination, and segregation were supreme. The situation for Black people almost seemed hopeless. In my eleventh grade year, we were saddened to the core by the bombing at the Sixteenth Street Baptist Church in Birmingham, Alabama. Four female children were murdered by the White bombers. Several families from Tuskegee knew the victims of the bombing and went to Birmingham to attend the funerals. This was so upsetting and terrifying to all of us!

From the elderly to the youth, everyone was aware that most White folks did not want us to obtain equal rights. In Macon County, voting district lines were drafted to prevent and limit the strength of Black voters. It was a tense time that we were living in.

My paternal grandfather died in my sophomore year. He always reminded us to "watch the White man." While he did adjust to buying some groceries during his lifetime, he still maintained a small garden and believed in the self-sufficiency principles advocated by Tuskegee University and the Black community. His death was a great loss for the family. He had an activist heart and spirit and did what he could to advance the race in the community.

My father, who was an occupational therapist at the Veterans Administration Hospital in Tuskegee, echoed my grandfather's prediction that Tuskegee was going to be squeezed out by Montgomery and Auburn. He often pointed out that the closure of the Tuskegee Air Base and the undisclosed sale of the property to an unknown White family did not bode well for the future of Tuskegee. There was no public information about the plan for the future of Tuskegee. He further mentioned that the closure of John Andrews Hospital on the Tuskegee University campus and, most of all, the closure of the Greyhound bus station in Tuskegee without Black community input were true signs that equal rights still did not prevail. Tuskegee's future was not in the hands of Black people and it was in peril.

Carolyn Moss Woodard's father, Alonzo Moss (*second from left*), one of the first federally certified Black Veterans Administration occupational therapists. Courtesy of Carolyn Moss Woodward.

In 1959, my mother became the Brownie Scout coordinator for Girl Scouts of America in Macon County, Alabama. She often spoke of attending Brownie Scout coordinator meetings in Montgomery and near Birmingham, where all the women would be dressed in identical designated uniforms. For many years of her attending those meetings, she would tell me how the White coordinators sat on one side of the room and Black coordinators sat on the opposite side of the room.

The Girl Scout units were segregated. Although administrators were superficially respectful and open in demeanor, funding for camp programming was unfair. My mother often made repeated requests for supplies and current information from the national office for her troops. Black scouts were permitted to attend segregated camps. They were allowed to use the sanctioned campsites during a designated two-week period in the summer months. We were kids, and we still learned how to be upstanding citizens of the United States, and we enjoyed ourselves.

Regardless of the discrimination, my mother was proud of her work with young Black girls. She took pleasure in visiting elementary schools throughout Macon County, encouraging seven-year-old students to join the Girl Scouts. A premier showcase of Tuskegee's Girl Scout program, which we all got excited about, was marching in full uniforms in the Tuskegee Institute (University) homecoming parades. After twenty-five years of scouting, my mother was finally able to witness and participate in an integrated and flourishing program in the Black community. My mom did what other parents and leaders in our community did when we were discriminated against and excluded because of our race. She went forward and created something for us, something that added value to and enriched our community. She persevered.

My parents were extremely proud to be residents of Macon County. They believed that having an Alabama license plate emblazoned with "46" for Macon County offered some level of protection from being pulled over by the state troopers.

Carolyn Moss Woodard's mother, Minnie Moss Woodard, one of the first Black Girl Scout troop leaders in the South, led her troop for twenty-five years. Courtesy of Carolyn Moss Woodard.

Neither my parents nor my grandparents ever expressed an interest in leaving Tuskegee. They felt proud of its Black commerce, employment, educational institutions, community, and friendships. They felt totally secure and safe within its area. They made certain we were schooled in the unfairness of the unequal justice system and the intrinsically pervasive racism that existed, not only in the South, but throughout the United States as well.

In 1968, James Forman wrote, *Sammy Younge, Jr.: The First Black College Student to Die in the Black Liberation Movement.*[2] Sammy was one of my high school and college classmates. I admired Sammy for his commitment to fight racism and discrimination. Sammy was very fair-skinned and was often teased about his color. Outside of Tuskegee, many thought he was White because of the fairness of his skin. Even when we were in high school, Sammy spoke up about injustices. He was excited by the student movement leaders caravanning through Tuskegee. He traveled into rural areas throughout Alabama and Mississippi in his iconic Southern Nonviolent Coordinating Committee (SNCC) dress of overalls and boots to register Black people to vote.[3]

Sammy took every opportunity to speak openly to the citizens of Tuskegee to demand change. He often drove between Tuskegee and Montgomery to attend civil rights meetings. He provided his peers with vital information regarding our protests. He led marches to Tuskegee's downtown square. He was truly a student activist. He just wanted fairness and equality. Although he had a kidney health condition, Sammy did not stop advocating for change. I became familiar with SNCC when Sammy was a member. I met Stokely Carmichael, whose wife was an upperclassman at Tuskegee Institute High School. I met Eldridge Cleaver and studied his formulas for gaining equal rights.

The Black Liberation Movement, Black Panthers, and the Southern Christian Leadership Conference were all connected to Sammy's passion for change. As he was demanding to use the bathroom at a downtown gas station one evening, Sammy was shot down by the White attendant. The man was later acquitted for killing Sammy. Pure racism!

As an adult, I realized my life was influenced by many great Black people in the Tuskegee community who had excelled in their fields, despite the racism. Among them were two family friends with whom we often interacted: P. H. Polk, Tuskegee's lifetime photographer; and Booker Felder, a fashion designer. Another family friend was Alice Coachman, my high school physical education teacher and Olympic gold medalist. Ruby Dee and Ossie Davis who were visiting relatives in Tuskegee came and spoke to us at one of our high school assemblies. Being exposed to such talented, accomplished, and undeterred people let us children know that regardless of the racism, we were expected to excel and do our part to move the race forward.

Most of my thirty-three-year professional career has been spent as a licensed clinical social worker in service to all children, especially Black children. I have worked as a family therapist and administrator for Harris County Juvenile Probation in Houston, Texas. I have been active with the National Black Child Development Initiative since its inception, receiving its highest honor, the Sarah Herbin Community Service Award, as well as its National Policy Award.

I have worked as a strong advocate for the adoption and placement of Black children and have received awards for monitoring race-related service disparities in the Harris County Juvenile Justice system. My membership in the Association of Black Social Workers, Blacks in Criminal Justice, Gamma Sigma Sigma Service Sorority, and a life membership in Alpha Kappa Alpha Sorority, Inc has strengthened my community work.

From adolescence to the present, I have fully engaged in activities and with organizations that promote equality and full inclusion. I have been a voter registrar for twenty-six years. I have maintained my credentials so that I can continue to provide citizens with the information needed to become registered voters. Black people fought hard in the South and all over the United States to get the right to vote. We are still fighting that battle to maintain and protect our right to vote. At seventy-nine years of age, I will continue that fight to maintain our voting rights and to move the race forward in any way I can, just as my parents, grandparents, and the Black Tuskegee community did before me, and as I know my children will do after me.

III

ANCESTORS AND NARRATORS

Toiling, Striving, Reaching toward the Sky

CHAPTER 12

Mattie Davis Blizzard

Editors' Note: In Mattie Davis Blizzard's narrative, she lives up to her reputation of not being afraid to say what is on her mind. She expresses her disappointment with living in Tuskegee after returning home from living in New York City for forty-seven years. She tackles the issue of her experiences living as a dark-skinned and lower-income student at school. Mattie describes her escape from Tuskegee two days after graduation to New York to work as a live-in maid. She examines some of the issues related to, possible causes of, and remedies for the current state of the city of Tuskegee. She ends by proudly relating her successful return home after managing several businesses in New York and witnessing the college success of her children and grandchildren.

During high school, I cannot remember thinking about race-related matters and civil rights that much. The thing that bothered me most in my life back then was being raised so "closed-in" by my parents and the impact skin color had on me. I am dark-skinned. In Tuskegee at that time, skin color mattered. The kids with lighter skin, or who had popular or famous professional parents, always seemed to be favored and seemed to be treated better by some of the teachers. I was an outspoken person and did not take much from anybody. Sometimes I thought I did not get the grades I deserved or was treated unfairly because of my skin color. In the school yearbook, I had wanted to be considered for the best dancer of the senior class. Instead, I was labeled the "biggest pest." As a result of being raised so closed-in by my parents and the way I felt I was mistreated in high school, I was so ready to leave Tuskegee. Two days after graduating from high school, I headed to New York, more about that later.

When I was a little girl, my paternal grandparents, Sam Davis and Cara Lee Patterson Davis, lived on Heritage Hill in Macon County. They had a farm with pigs and cows and a garden with fruits and vegetables such as watermelons, greens, and string beans. My parents took us down to the farm to get vegetables every season. When my grandfather killed pigs and cows, we drove down to the farm to get meat.

My mother's mother moved to New York when I was young. She went for better work opportunities and became a nurse. She came back and forth from New York to visit us. She made a good life for herself in New York.

Mattie Davis Blizzard's paternal grandparents, Sam and Cora Davis, were local farmers. Courtesy Mattie Davis Blizzard.

My mother worked in dietetics at the White Tuskegee High Schooll downtown that our classmates tried to integrate. She stayed there until she retired. My father, Johnny Davis, worked in maintenance at numerous businesses. He worked on campus at Tuskegee Institute, at the high school, and sometimes in Columbus, Georgia. Until I was ten, we rented a house near downtown Tuskegee. White people lived next door on both sides of our house. We played with the White children all the time. I remember my White neighbor handing me her dress over the backyard fence so I could wear it to take my fourth-grade school picture. That was how close we were. My dad and mother talked to the other White families on the street all the time. Preston Hornsby, the White county sheriff, knew my father very well. While growing up, I cannot remember my family having any race-related issues with White people. I do not remember my parents talking to us about race.

When I was around ten years old, we moved from the rented house downtown to a house that my father and uncle built from the ground up in the Greenport neighborhood. My parents never considered immigrating to the North or West because they had built their own home on their own land. They were happy here in Tuskegee. I never remembered them talking about possibly relocating, even though we had relatives coming back and forth from the North.

My grandparents and mother were never involved in the Civil Rights Movement, but my dad was always going to civil rights meetings and marches such as the Montgomery march. I was never involved because we were basically raised in lock down. We were never allowed to go places. We always had to stay home. My dad was very strict with us. My dad took me to my prom. He said, "The only thing the boy is going to do is put you in his car and take you. I can just put you in my car and take you too!"

While in high school, I worked for Ms. Vannette. I did childcare for her. That's why I dressed so well in high school. I used to wear her clothes, wash them, and then give them back to her to wear. She helped me fill out an application for a job. I told her that I had to leave Tuskegee because I was tired of Tuskegee. I did not want to be in Tuskegee anymore. She got me a sleep-in job in Long Island, New York. A sleep-in job is one in which you live in the home of the people you work for. At that time, these jobs were usually taken by Black women who worked for rich

White families in the Northeast. The family I lived with had three maids to do the housework and cooking. I was hired to do childcare.

The family had an eighteen-year-old boy and two little girls; one was about three and one was two. When I was babysitting for them, the boy would come into my room and try to have a relationship with me. I said no to him. I stayed there for six or seven weeks. I had some friends in Manhattan who had also come up North as sleep-ins. One of them, Virginia Sullins, who had traveled to New York with me, had a sister who had her own apartment on Eighty-Third Street. I moved in with Virginia's sister, two other sleep-in maids who came to stay on weekends, plus Virginia's two children. We all lived in two bedrooms. Immediately, I went out and found another job at a lipstick case manufacturing company so I could find another place to live.

I met my husband, George Blizzard, in the same building where I lived with Virginia. I used my first paycheck to get an apartment with another friend. I later moved to Seventy-Seventh Street and Douglas, across from the Museum of Natural History. My husband and 1 got married at the museum. We were young and in love. 1 was only nineteen, but we were very happy together. After we got married and had our first child, I stopped working as a receiving clerk at Saks Fifth Avenue. My second child, Timothy, came along and I went back to work there for six years until we moved back to Yonkers. At some point, I took a dietetics course at Pace University as part of a requirement to work in a daycare center.

Eventually, I started my own daycare business. I helped parents with tasks such as taking their children to school, picking them up from school, and taking them to their after-school activities. I liked having my own business because it gave me the flexibility to do what I love to do, which is clothes shopping. I love fashion and once had my own company organizing group shopping trips to various malls in and around New York City. At one point, I also had a catering business.

My husband and I loved "the New York life." There was always something to do. We also spent a lot of time with our church and our children's school activities. My husband was a well-rounded man. He worked hard and loved to do things with the family. He spent most of his career with a company that made checks and did engraving for banks like Chase Bank.

After my husband retired, he wanted to move to Virginia, but I wanted to come home to Tuskegee because it was home, and I wanted to assist with my aging parents. We came to Tuskegee and bought a beautiful big house on an acre of land. Even though my husband had retired, I continued to work in the dorms on Tuskegee University's campus. Until his death, my husband and I lived "the retirement life" and traveled a lot.

My children did not decide to stay in New York. My daughter had graduated as valedictorian of her high school, went to university for two years, and then joined the army. She now lives in Auburn, Alabama, about fifteen miles away. She has her degree and is in the Alpha Kappa Alpha Sorority, and I think she became president for a while. My granddaughters have done well and have graduated from university now. After my son graduated from high school, he went into the navy. He stayed in for twenty years and then went to school in the Philippines for five years and got his master's degree there. He now lives in Hawaii. My children went to college, have good jobs. I am proud of them. They have traveled the world, found jobs that they enjoy, and are good citizens. I think my husband and I did a good job raising them. I am happy that my daughter decided to come South. I have been able to enjoy my grandchildren and assist my daughter in raising them. It has been good to be able to participate in family activities and be a part of their lives.

I was not involved in the Civil Rights Movement. I know that racism was and is out there. To my knowledge, I cannot say that I have ever been discriminated against or treated unfairly in my jobs because of my race, other than the boy who tried to take advantage of me at my first job. I think that happened because he thought he could have his way with me because I was a Black girl. I have been lucky to have been treated fairly on the jobs that I have worked in. I am the type of person who speaks up for myself. My supervisors, coworkers, and friends knew that I was never afraid to speak up and say what was on my mind. I think that might have prevented a lot of things from becoming problems. Growing up playing with White kids in Tuskegee gave me an advantage in being comfortable with them and handling them later in life. In New York, I lived with White people with no problem. When I had my own business working mostly with White people, I gave the orders. I always could speak up for my rights.

If I had known what present-day Tuskegee was really like when we decided to move back South for retirement, I might not have moved back here. Tuskegee is nothing like the booming city that we grew up in and went to high school in. Sixty-one years after we graduated from Tuskegee Institute High School, there are hardly any stores—no clothing stores or large grocery stores. There is nowhere to go, no movie theaters like when we were young. Living in New York city for forty-seven years, I was used to just going out on the street and having hundreds of things to do. New York never sleeps. I loved that life. I loved walking the streets and all the excitement in New York. Here, most people just stay inside their homes.

We get big grants in Tuskegee, but I do not know what we do with them. We need somebody to move back here and bring their knowledge and know-how. Sometimes, I think we need to go get more White people and bring them back, so maybe we can get more recognition from state officials and businesspeople. When I left here, we had three hospitals: the city hospital, John Andrew Hospital on campus, and the Veterans Administration Hospital. What happened to all of that?

When I moved back here, I did not notice how badly things had gone. When I used to come back and forth home, I only stayed three or four days. I never stayed here for a week. Even when I bought this house, we took the home in three days. I went back to New York and closed. I knew this was going to be a big difference from living in New York, but I did not know the difference was going to be this vast. I did not know that people would not keep up their property. When I was growing up here, the neighborhoods were extremely clean and gorgeous. We had a supermarket owned by a Black family, the Bulls. The only thing we have now are dollar stores.

The kids do not have a swimming pool. We do not have a nice park or a hotel. We need to make a change, but we vote the same people into office all the time, and they do the same things all the time. Nothing! I have been here for twenty years, and we do not have a sanitation department that cleans the streets. We have a utility board that does not work. The drainage and sewage systems are poor. We pay our money for the various utilities, but we are not getting the proper services.

When I talk to my friends about the situation, they say that White people began to leave Tuskegee after all the civil rights wins. They said that Black people in Tuskegee won the right to vote and could control everything because there were more Black people than White people. Some say that White people left because our classmates had helped to integrate the schools. Over the years, I have found out that most of the Black middle-class people have left as well. It seems like there is nobody here but these young kids and old people. When the older middle-class Black people, who built Tuskegee into the booming city it was and who used to keep their yards beautiful, died out over the years, they left all those beautiful homes to their children who now live in California, Chicago, New York, or wherever they found jobs and settled down to raise their families. Many of them do not take care of the property their parents left to them because they do not live here. Some of them have become absentee landlords, and the renters do not cut the grass and keep up the houses. Nobody enforces the laws about property upkeep. It is sad to see how the city of Tuskegee has gone down over the last sixty years. I am sad because I love my hometown and I love getting together with my family and my classmates who stayed. Several of my classmates did stay and have tried their best to make the place better. It was a beautiful place for thousands of Black people in its heyday, and I think it still can make a comeback, but something has got to change.

I am not bragging, but if you come into my yard and see my house, my yard is always cut and beautiful. I take care of this acre yard by myself. I live in this twenty-room house, and I take care of it like people used to take care of their homes here in Tuskegee. Black people in Tuskegee used to be proud of their homes and their community. Those children who now own their parents' property need to do better, and the city needs to do better in providing good services that make the city a better place to live. If that happens, maybe people will start to move back to Tuskegee.

The message I want to leave with my kids and grandkids has less to do with race and civil rights and more to do with how they should live their lives to be successful human beings. I tell them that you must think for yourself; you cannot be a follower. You do not have to do what you see your friends do. Another main thing I tell my children and grandchildren is always save a penny and never let anybody see you broke. I tell them that once you get broke, nobody will help you. I worked in New York all my life, and I have never borrowed a penny in my life from anybody.

I want my children, grandchildren, and other young Black children to stand on their own two feet. Work for what they want. Go to school to learn. Get up and get a job. You don't have to go to college, but you must get a trade or skill to take care of yourself. If you live like that, you will live properly and have a good life. I did not press my kids to go to college, but they went because I told them they had to stand on their own feet and take care of themselves. My motto is help yourself. When you help yourself, you can go out and help other people.

Mattie Davis Blizzard's granddaughter, Andrea Blizzard, is currently pursuing a PhD in pediatric nursing at the University of Alabama Birmingham. Andrea represents the ancestors' hoped-for continuous upward mobility for Black people. Courtesy Andrea Blizzard and Mattie Davis Blizzard.

In the end, I would like to tell young people to live their dreams. That is what I did. I went to New York at eighteen, stayed forty-seven years, loved the New York lifestyle, had several satisfying careers, had a beautiful family, and returned to my hometown a success.

Live your dreams.

CHAPTER 13

Rosa McWilliams Henderson

Editors' Note: Rosa McWilliams Henderson discusses her ancestors' humble beginnings and the family's early strivings to move out of poverty. Her fervor for school and her desire for upward mobility were motivated by coming of age living with her parents and two siblings in a house with one room and a kitchen and having to walk four-and-a-half miles each way to and from school each day. She describes how her father's employment as a janitor at Tuskegee Institute High School helped him increase the size of their home to meet the needs of his family. Rosa's journey of ingenuity, persistence, and perseverance eventually led her to obtain her college degree on the same date as her son and daughter-in-law. One might wonder whether it was Rosa's humble beginnings, the high expectations of the Tuskegee culture, or a combination of both that led to her remarkable professional achievements and the passion for giving back to others.

After graduating from Tuskegee Institute High School in the spring of 1964, I enrolled in Alabama State College in Montgomery, Alabama, the following fall. When I arrived at the bus station, I noticed and experienced racism firsthand. There were two water fountains: one said "Colored" and the other said "Whites Only." There were two bathrooms with the same signs as the water fountains. When the Greyhound bus arrived, the White people got off the bus first, and the "Colored" people got off last. When it was time to board the bus, the White people boarded first and sat in the front, and the "Colored" people, including me, boarded last and sat in the back of the bus. This process continued during my freshman year as I rode the bus back and forth.

At Alabama State, I usually would go to the library to study and prepare for assignments around six in the evening. Sometimes we would see men suspected of being Klansmen on campus at night. It was a tense time for most Black college students in Montgomery and all over the South, but we were dedicated to the movement.

A week before the big march from Selma to Montgomery, student leaders gave us instructions on how to conduct ourselves at the march and what to wear. As I remember, all students were encouraged to join the march. On the day of the event, buses transported us to Selma, Alabama, to participate in the march to the state capitol building in downtown Montgomery. We were given water and snacks along the way. This march later became famous as the Selma to Montgomery march. Some people were beaten by state troopers, and some were bleeding. I remember a heavyset Black woman to my left who was thoroughly traumatized. It was a horrible sight to see and experience. After listening to speakers at the capitol, we walked back to campus. I think that most of us students were traumatized by that experience that day as well. After my freshman year, I did not return to Alabama State College.

My father, John McWilliams (1898–1978), was born and reared in Tunnel Springs, Alabama. As a young man, he relocated to Tuskegee. My mother, Gertha McWilliams (1913–2000), was born and reared in the Little Texas community of Macon County, Alabama, not too far from Tuskegee. When my mother met my father, she was boarding with Hester Powell, my father's sister. When my father visited his sister, he noticed my mother and began to "court" her. During that time, courting usually meant that a young man would come to the young lady's home on a Sunday evening and spend a few hours talking to her, generally under the supervision of parents or an older person.

Their relationship developed, and my parents were married on May 2, 1945. They had three children: Johnnie Lee, Rosa Mae, and Andrew. My parents did not have much money at the beginning of their marriage. We lived in a house that consisted of a bedroom and a kitchen. We had an outside toilet and a cement water well. We also had a wagon and a mule named Sam. Sam was used for transportation and helping my father with the plowing and planting.

I cannot remember my parents ever talking about leaving the South and going North. They thought they could work hard and continue making a better family life. They did. While I was still in elementary school, my father added a bedroom for me, a bedroom for the boys, and a kitchen to the existing bedroom and old kitchen. The house was on five acres of land. He liked having his own home and land, and my parents seemed satisfied.

All of us children went to Lewis Adams Elementary School. When Mr. L. M. Randolph became principal, he would visit the students' homes and talk to their parents. He wrote down the students' names and informed them of the number of the bus they would be riding and where the bus would pick them up. Unfortunately, my brothers and I did not get a bus number because the bus did not come to our community for my first two years of school. During the first and second grades, we walked four-and-a-half miles to school and four-and-a-half miles back home every day. In the third and fourth grades, the bus came to our community, but we still had to walk one mile to the bus stop in the morning and one mile from the bus stop to our house after school. I remember a coal-burning potbellied stove heated the classrooms. After fifth grade, the bus finally came to our house to pick us up in the mornings and dropped us off after school. Things were different when I went to Tuskegee Institute High School in 1960. There were no potbellied stoves for heat. The heat came from vents in the ceiling. I liked school, and I went to summer school and took two courses each summer.

My father worked at Moton Field Air Base in the 1940s. In 1951, he was hired by the Macon County Board of Education as a janitor at Tuskegee Institute High School, where my brothers and I attended. Along with being the janitor, he was also responsible for selling snacks during lunch. One day, someone in the principal's office noticed that my father had not returned to turn in the snack money from lunch. They were worried and proceeded to look for him. They found him passed out in the teachers' lounge in the junior building, holding onto the snack money bag. He had succumbed to fumes from the gas heater. They rushed him to John Andrew Hospital, where he stayed overnight. Today, many former students tell me how my father gave them milk and cookies when they did not have anything to eat and no money to pay for food. My father enjoyed his job at Tuskegee Institute High School. I think he enjoyed being around the students and being able to help some of the ones in need. I will always be thankful to the Macon County Board of Education for making it possible for him to have that job.

John McWilliams, Rosa McWilliams Henderson's father, was a farmer and custodian at Tuskegee Institute High School. Courtesy of Rosa McWilliams Henderson.

On December 1, 1955, the news came on the radio that Mrs. Rosa Parks had refused to give up her seat on the bus to a White man after a hard day of work. She was dragged off the bus by the police and taken to jail. Attorney Fred D. Gray took her case and won. The resulting Montgomery Bus Boycott helped lead to the desegregation of city buses in Montgomery. I admired Mrs. Parks for her bravery during this time. Her action was the beginning of much civil rights activity in the South.

Most Black people in Tuskegee and the South were involved in the Civil Rights Movement. My daddy would read the newspaper but never say anything about segregation. My mother could not read or write. I kept up with the news and current events of the movement. For reasons I do not know or understand, my parents and their friends and relatives never talked about segregation or the Civil Rights Movement, and they never went to any mass meetings.

Prejudice and discrimination were everywhere. I remember when Black people could not vote. I remember an upper Brantley grocery store where White people shopped and a lower Brantley grocery store where Black people shopped. I also remember going to Miller's grocery store, the clothing stores, and the drugstore, where Black and White people used the front door because there was not a back or side door. The movie theater had one side for White people to sit on and one for Black people to sit on. While I was at Alabama State College, I continued to ride the segregated Greyhound buses back and forth to Tuskegee to visit my parents. Since I decided not to go back to Alabama State for my sophomore year, I had to find an alternative to support myself.

I went to see Mr. Gaillard, the local contact for Black girls and women who wanted to go North and work as live-in maids for wealthy White families. He would connect us with an agency in Connecticut that would place us with families who needed live-in maids. I went to Hartford, Connecticut, and lived with the Smith family, who had three children. The oldest child was eight years old. I had a daily schedule for taking care of the two younger children. I prepared breakfast and lunch for them and took them for walks through the neighborhood after I finished my chores. I had a room and a bathroom in the basement, which was nice. At mealtime, I had to sit at the end of the kitchen counter, not at the table with the family. It was their choice to give me the bones whenever steak was served for dinner.

After I had been there a while, we went down to Mrs. Smith's mother's summer home on the beach for three months. Along with doing chores, I always took the two younger children down to the beach. One day, we were at the beach. A little White girl had left her group and gone into the water. I noticed they were not watching her, so I jumped up, ran into the water, grabbed the little girl, and returned her to her group. The children enjoyed playing in the sand and wading in the water.

Thursday was my day off. On Friday nights, someone from the Grand

Ole Opry would play music a few blocks away. It was only for White people, but I always got a seat and enjoyed the good country music. I remember going to Macy's department store when I was there, where the White people entered the front door and shopped upstairs. The Black people entered a door downstairs and shopped in the basement. I also remember the bus situation in 1965 was the same as in Alabama with White people sitting in the front of the bus and Black people sitting in the back. And this was Connecticut!

After my tour with the wealthy family was over, I returned to Tuskegee and enrolled in Booker T Washington Business College in Birmingham, Alabama, to refresh my clerical skills. The year was 1968–69. I was amazed that I did not have to go to the back of the bus. The "White Only" and "Colored Only" signs were down, and Black people and White people were drinking from the same water fountains . . . and using the same bathrooms. That was a huge relief for me. While going to school in Birmingham, I saw Black and White people interacting.

After my course in Birmingham, I went to see Mr. Gaillard again. He sent me to an agency in Massachusetts, where I worked with two families for three months. My job was to perform regular household chores and assist the children in their endeavors. We ate our meals on the back porch, and I sat with the family and guests at the table. They did not have television or radio but subscribed to two different newspapers. The children taught me how to play ping pong. They also used an old car tire and taught me how to swim. I learned how to paddle the boat on the water. They were Catholic. The children and I attended services on Sunday. It was a White congregation, so we sat in the back row.

After completing three months with the Warrens, I traveled to Roxbury, Connecticut. I lived with William and Rose Styron, who also were writers. The Styrons had four children. My job was to take care of the baby, Alexandra. They also had two Black ladies who took care of the house and a Black man as the groundskeeper. A White girl called Dukie took care of the three older children. She and I shared a bedroom and bathroom. One day, Alexandra asked me, "Rosa, why are you black?" I said, "That is the way God made me. You will see yellow, brown, various colors, and many nationalities. God made us all in his image."

After a month in Roxbury, Dukie and I traveled to the dock, got on the ferryboat, and traveled to Martha's Vineyard to the Styrons' summer home. The main house, the children's house, a guesthouse, and Mr. Styron's office were on the property. The Styrons welcomed me into their family. I also interacted with the family and ate at the same table. I returned home to Alabama by airplane to stay. I enjoyed my time with the Warrens and Styrons and learned much. Some years later, I received a call from one of the housekeepers wanting to know if I could come up for the summer. I said, "No. I cannot because I have a job and have bought a home."

After returning to Tuskegee for the second time, I got a job at Tuskegee Institute and attended Alabama State University in Montgomery part-time. I graduated in May 1989 with a bachelor of science degree in office administration and a minor in business management. My son, Jonathan McWilliams, graduated from Alabama State in May 1989 with a bachelor of science degree in political science and a minor in computer science. My daughter-in-law, Bregenia Ambers McWilliams, graduated from Alabama State in May 1989 with a bachelor of science degree in accounting. I had come full circle since graduating from Tuskegee Institute High and my freshman year at Alabama State College. I had experienced success in many worlds, bought a home, and had a stable professional job at a university. I had educated my son. Most importantly, I could give back to my community by serving students at the university and students in the community through my social and professional organizations.

Rosa McWilliams Henderson, graduate of Alabama State University, has dedicated her career to educational access and advocacy for Alabama's youth. Courtesy of Rosa McWilliams Henderson.

While working for the Macon County Board of Education, I was a member of the Education Support Professionals (ESP), where I served as secretary, treasurer, and on the Legislative Contact Team for twenty-two years. I was president of the organization for seven years and the editor of the ESP quarterly newsletter. I retired from the Macon County Board of Education on July 1, 2012. I am an active member of the Macon County Education Retirees Association, the Alabama Education Association, the National Education Association, the Macon County, and the National American Association of Retired Persons. I am also an active member of Shady Grove Missionary Baptist Church. My hobbies are reading, cooking, exercising, and watching television.

My life's story, having its beginning in a house composed of one bedroom and a kitchen, demonstrates the importance of equal educational opportunities for all children. My life also illustrates how important it is for parents to have employment that allows them to provide for their families. We can thank everyone, the teachers in Tuskegee who had high expectations for us; and those famous and not-so-famous people for their contributions to the Civil Rights Movement and the freedoms we now enjoy as Black people. Mrs. Rosa Parks did her part. Dr. Martin Luther King did his part. My father did his part by giving milk and cookies to hungry students who had no food for lunch at the high school where he worked as a janitor. My father must have used his limited funds to ensure the lunch money sack was not short when he gave it to the principal daily. My father never told me he gave needy kids milk and cookies for lunch. I consider his actions his contribution to the struggle. I have tried to do my part to enrich my family's legacy through the work I did and continue to do in the field of education.

CHAPTER 14

Marian Quinn Williams

Editors' Note: Marian Quinn Williams grew up on a farm near Tuskegee with parents who had limited economic resources but whose Christian and family values and pride in landownership filled their children with high educational hopes and dreams. Her ancestors had been sharecroppers, having moved to the Tuskegee area in the early 1900s for a better life. Marian's father's eventual employment at Tuskegee Institute allowed her to get a degree at a discount, participate in the Civil Rights Movement, and give back to the parallel world that had nourished her intellectual abilities. Five generations after her family's sharecropping beginnings in Tuskegee, Marian's daughter was feted for a patent she received as a professor at Tuskegee Institute's School of Veterinary Medicine. The parallel world had succeeded.

Reading the news release took my breath away. "Tuskegee University veterinary faculty member, Dr. Deidre Quinn-Gorham, is making it her mission to use her new patent to produce a multiple blade handle system for performing surgeries."[1] Although I knew she was working to receive this patent, I was still shocked to see my daughter's name in the news stating that she had received it. I immediately thought of my mother's and my father's families' humble beginnings, especially with my father's family having to move into an old house on the outskirts of Tuskegee over a hundred years ago. My father worked for the owners of that house. I thought of the picture of my formerly enslaved great-grandfather Sumpter Gibson sitting in his rocker and wondered if he could ever have imagined this moment. What contributed to this moment were an abiding faith in God, Tuskegee Institute's opportunities for employment and education, hard work, and the new civil rights laws. The latter made improvements possible for our family and millions of other Black families living in the South.

Participation in the writing of this book has been a very rewarding and enlightening experience for me. I realized how much of the history of my family is oral history. Not until the 1870 US census were all Black people explicitly listed by name, so it is often difficult for Black people to trace their history.[2] Most of that oral history that encompasses generations of families—their births, marriages, accomplishments, baptisms, and deaths—was recorded in family Bibles. Missing are the photographs! My name is Marian Quinn Williams. I was born in 1946 in Tuskegee, Alabama, as the fourth child of Charlie and Roumaine Quinn. With my three older sisters and two younger brothers, there were six children in my family.

The story of how Mom and Dad got to Macon County, Tuskegee, Alabama, is based mostly on oral history. My father told us that his family came from the small town of Ocilla, Georgia. After his father passed, the mother and children came to Alabama with other families looking for better economic opportunities. They settled in Franklin, Alabama, which at that time was a part of Tuskegee. They found an old house to live in and struggled to raise food to eat.

Survival was the daily goal; therefore, very little interest was placed on education. Jim Crow laws ensured that schools in the area remained segregated, very scarce, and underfunded for Black children. Walking long distances to and from school did allow my daddy an elementary education experience. After growing up and getting married, Daddy had to work on the farm and in the home of the White Ramsey Family.

My father seldom talked about his childhood. Later in life, I concluded that maybe his talking about his childhood and early adult life brought back such sad memories that he just did not want to relive those times. There were no photographs to tell the stories for him as it was rare for a poor Black family to own a camera or have access to a photographer at that time in the South.

My mother was born and reared in the rural outskirts of Tuskegee, near the Franklin, Alabama, area. She was the only child born to her parents, Lee Allen and Lena Gibson Allen. She met my father while walking to and from school in the rural area where they lived. My oldest sister remained their only child for about nine years.

My maternal great-grandparents lived in Franklin for many years. They owned a house and forty acres of land. My maternal grandmother's family took the name of the enslavers, the Gibsons. My mother's grandfather, Sumpter Gibson, was owned by the enslaver Gibson family. After emancipation, Great-Grandpa Sumpter and his family stayed on with the enslaver Gibson family as sharecroppers. Although slavery had been abolished, a Jim Crow socioeconomic system of scaled-down servitude was perpetuated. Sharecropping produced conditions little better than slavery, often leaving Black families with minimum food and clothing, perpetual indebtedness, and constant fear of being asked to leave the owner's property. In those days, many former enslaved people stayed on with their former owners after emancipation either out of a sense of loyalty, financial need, or fear of not being able to survive on their own. Some might have wanted to stay with the hope of one day owning their own land.

The family says that Great-Grandpa Sumpter told the story of how he came to Alabama as an enslaved person and was sold to the Gibson family. Coming from Sumter, South Carolina, he was given the name Sumpter and Gibson, the last name of the family that purchased him. Family legend has it that Great-Grandpa was treated well by his owners.

After slavery, one of the White Gibson family members continued to stay in contact with the formerly enslaved Sumpter's offspring as late as the 1970s. The White Gibson relative often paid for headstones and gave donations to the various churches attended by the progeny of Sumpter.

I do have one picture of enslaved Great-Grandpa. I look at him sitting in that rocking chair, and I wonder if he understood his situation. I look at that picture and wonder if he ever dreamed of being free, educated, and successful in life. I do believe that some of his children and offspring knew how the Jim Crow laws were depriving them of certain freedoms. Some of the children born to him and his wife never returned to Macon County once they left.

Marian Quinn Williams's enslaved great-grandfather, Sumpter Gibson, born 1863, moved his family to Tuskegee in search of a better life. Courtesy of Marian Quinn Williams.

When my parents were married, they continued to live in Tuskegee, Alabama. They did not receive formal high school educations, but they worked hard, bought some land, and became homeowners. Many of their relatives went to Detroit, Chicago, Gary, New York, and various places in Ohio. My parents seemed content with staying in Tuskegee. They thought that staying on their little spread, raising their food, and educating their children in our community schools was more rewarding. I never heard my parents express any regrets about staying in the South. They were proud of their accomplishments, especially their landownership.

I visited relatives in the North, and sometimes, they came South to visit. Some of these relatives gave the impression that they were living in Utopia. Some of them had good jobs, and their lifestyles had changed for the better. We listened to the stories. My mom and dad would often ask who was paying taxes on the land they had left in the South. Many of them had acquired cars, fine clothes, jobs, and nice apartments to live in, but very few owned homes or land in the North, and some were not paying taxes on the land they left in the South.

Some laws in the North weren't as obviously discriminatory as the Jim Crow laws of the South. However, some laws helped define where they lived, worked, and attended school. I liked the idea of visiting the historical sites with them, eating in restaurants, dressing up, and attending the big churches with relatives. On the surface, it seemed that money mattered more than skin color up there. Many of my relatives were attracted to the job opportunities and the comfortable lifestyles in the North but weren't involved in the Civil Rights Movement. Many of them tried to convince us to uproot and move to the North. We told them that we wanted to stay and participate in making changes for the better where we lived in the South.

When relatives from the North would come to visit, they were very careful about where they stopped to buy gas, food, or stay because Jim Crow laws were still in effect. Because of bad experiences living under Jim Crow laws in the South, many of my relatives came back only for funerals.

My mother became a waitress at a café located down the street from the Tuskegee Institute campus. After various jobs in Macon County, my daddy became a baker at the Tuskegee Institute cafeteria. This was a life-changing job for him. He was well paid, and he enjoyed the job. He had the skills but not the degrees; yet he was able to have a good career and retire from this job after many years of successful employment. My parents were proud, hardworking people who instilled these values in their children.

Many stories about how some of my ancestors survived Jim Crow laws are told in our family. The following incident shows how desperate White people were to keep Black and White people separated and to try to demonstrate and maintain their imagined superiority. I remember the story we were told about Uncle Clem Felton who was stopped by a White Alabama State Trooper and almost arrested. This uncle had very, very light skin and naturally straight hair. He was taking my aunt to Montgomery, Alabama, to the train station. She was going back to Chicago where she lived after migrating to the North. This was in the early 1950s. Suddenly, Uncle Clem was stopped by the White Alabama State Troopers, but he was not asked to show his license. The assumption was that he was a White man because of his appearance. He was simply asked why this Black woman was riding in the front seat with a White man. My uncle tried to think of something quick to say. He pointed to the back seat where her luggage was covered by a coat. My uncle said, "I am selling butter and eggs, and taking these with me to sell. There was no place in the back for her to sit. Therefore, she had to sit in the front with me." The troopers evidently bought the story. They warned them that if this happened again, both would be arrested. Immediately, my uncle sped to Montgomery, where our aunt caught her transport back to Chicago.

There is a family picture of another one of my mother's uncles who ran away in the early 1940s. His story demonstrates how fragile and desperate survival was for Black people in the South. My great-uncle Robert Gibson was a sharecropper, and he and another man got into a fight. A warrant for my uncle's arrest was issued. The uncle felt he would not get a fair trial. He thought of the consequences he would face as a sharecropper. He jumped aboard an opened-door freight car in Franklin, Alabama, where trains frequently passed. Once he jumped on the train and left, none of his relatives ever heard from him again. To this day, we do not have any answers as to where he went, where he may have settled, or whether he survived his escape attempt. Only his picture remains as part of our family history.

Living under Jim Crow could be awful, but many of the Black community in Tuskegee and surrounding areas made growing up and living in the Jim Crow South livable. The church played a major role in our lives. Sunday school taught us about the Bible and the importance of knowing God. My parents demanded that we attend Sunday school and church. Sunday school was held early Sunday morning for about an hour before church services began. Sunday school was taught by church adults and was divided into classes by age groups, including adult classes. Church was also a social outlet. Often there were evening services on Sundays as well. I would meet and interact with children of different ages. Dinners would be served during the long hours spent from morning to evening. Churches also acted as extensions of the local primary schools. We often had to learn speeches for various occasions, appear on programs, and learn to lead by taking on leadership responsibilities in youth organizations in the church.

Religion helped to give us hope for overcoming the Jim Crow laws in the South. I remember how the churches here in Tuskegee would hold mass meetings when the Montgomery and Tuskegee Boycotts were taking place. I would see my daddy and some of the other men in our community come home from work, change into Sunday clothes, and attend these meetings at night. When we asked what the meetings were about, they simply said that they were talking about plans for a boycott to deal with the Jim Crow laws.

Men and women in the Black community were proud to be members of the Masons and Eastern Stars. These Black fraternal organizations provided financial aid and moral support for many Black people in the community. Faced with discrimination in hotels and restaurants, these organizations would help Black people who traveled find places to sleep and eat. They also supported families in need, especially assisting the family of a member who died. These organizations helped to create hope for overcoming the daily acts of prejudice and discrimination in the outer world with their secretive meetings.[3]

Black religious, educational, social, and fraternal organizations provided respite from the ugly world of racism. Black people could worship, sing, dance, act, plan, vote, appoint, and fraternize with each other in physical and emotional spaces free of fear of racist reprisals. Black people in the South created alternative spaces that were often filled with love, joy, and kindness, which made living in the South seem bearable and ordinary in some respects.

Although most of our ancestors may not have their names written in the history books, many of them were brave and heroic historical figures in our families. Many of them were involved in the Civil Rights Movement. As a young child, I remember my mother went to the Macon County Courthouse to attend to some property tax business. She carried me and my brother who was a baby with her. The White man at the desk was very rude to my mother. My baby brother, whom my mother was holding, began to cry. The White man was yelling at her to take him out of the room. My mother was trying to fill out the papers and trying to keep my brother from crying. I thought about this when I first became a registered voter and had to visit that same area of the Macon County Courthouse.

My aunt Celia B. Chambers was a plaintiff in the *Gomillion v. Lightfoot* Supreme Court gerrymandering case. I shared information about her involvement with my American government high school students. Aunt Celia was very determined not to be drawn out of the Tuskegee city limits and lose the right to vote in city elections. I admired and respected her. She became a true mentor to me, constantly reminding me to stand up for my rights.

My family and I participated in the Tuskegee Boycott. My daddy would drive us to shop at other stores outside of downtown Tuskegee during the boycott. As children, we were told why we were participating and the positive change that would occur. Sometimes it meant doing without many things we needed and some things we wanted to help support the boycott.

After weeks and months of refusing to trade with local businesses, many positive changes happened. Many Black people were elected to city government for the first time in Tuskegee, probably since Reconstruction. My parents had to make special efforts to travel out of town to buy or trade, but it was worth it. The struggle moved forward when our Black ancestors encouraged citizens to trade with Black local businesses in Tuskegee. Black-owned Bull's supermarket became a major provider of groceries for the city and surrounding areas.

Sometimes I think of all the "what ifs." What if my ancestors had not stayed in the South or Macon County? I do think that their decision to stay was very wise. I admire the strong character that we developed because of these Jim Crow experiences. Rather than seeing migrating to the North as an end to discrimination, they stayed and used the courts to bring about changes and to rewrite the laws that enhanced the lives of millions of other Black people in the South and throughout the United States. Staying and facing the problems, they truly demonstrated Dr. Booker T. Washington's philosophy of "cast down your buckets where you are." Many people interpret this negatively, suggesting that he was promoting complacency. He did not say "cast down your bucket where you are and stay there." Those who know the legacies of Dr. Washington, Dr. George Washington Carver, and Tuskegee Institute (University) know that they were all about how to continuously improve the lives of our people through education, economic growth, and community development and outreach. That means always reaching back to pull others forward. During the late 1800s and early 1900s, most Black people in Alabama's Black Belt were emerging from the bondages of enslavement, and many could not read or write. Dr. Washington encouraged them to adopt trades that could more readily move their families out of poverty and into the working and middle classes. In doing so, Dr. Washington viewed working with one's hands as a practical low-hanging fruit way that would allow Black people to build an economic foundation and move the group forward more rapidly and more sustainably.

Growing up in Tuskegee has been a unique experience. Tuskegee was and still is indeed a small town with limited resources and facilities; however, when our family traveled to larger cities, I never got the desire to stay or reside in those large cities. I just enjoyed the exposure while I was there. I remember attending our small rural community school, New Rising Star Elementary School. Although we had limited resources, our teachers made us feel like we could do anything and be anyone we wanted to be in life. They made sure that we received a quality education. As I moved through high school, I thought about how much I wanted to be a teacher and be like my teachers. The thought stayed with me.

My parents could not afford to send me out of state to attend college. I wanted to attend college out of state, but the cost was too great. So I attended Tuskegee Institute, beginning in the fall of 1964 for half price because my father worked there. I continued to stay involved in my church and community activities while I was at the university. After graduation from Tuskegee Institute, I could have accepted a teaching position in Tennessee. I said no to that and decided to stay here in Tuskegee. After a while, I enrolled in graduate school and earned a master's degree in education. I wanted to give back to my community. I also wanted to stay involved in my church and be close to my parents, knowing that their health had begun to decline. They had worked so hard and sacrificed so much to help me reach my goal. I gladly wanted to be near them and help them to the best of my ability.

There are several things that I would like for my grandchildren to know about my life experiences growing up in the Jim Crow South. Being born and growing up in the Jim Crow South, I felt that the way we lived and the segregation of the races were the norm. We learned to accept this racial division and to make the best of our situations. Attending an all-Black rural elementary school was fully accepted. Our teachers were devoted and prepared us to compete academically no matter what schools we might attend later. I was taught to compete to be the best student. There was not even a thought or a vision of moving on to attend a White high school or a White college. I remember how we would go to downtown Tuskegee and had to go to the back window of the fast-food café to buy milkshakes, hot dogs, and hamburgers. This Dairy Queen was owned and operated by White people. We did not question why we were served at the "Coloreds Only" window. We just wanted to get there and enjoy the good tasting food. When we went to the movies, it did not matter that the same movie that we sat down to view had a wall separating us from White people.

As I got older and my exposure and experiences increased, I began to take notice of prejudice and discrimination. My values about social justice were ultimately influenced and shaped by living in the Jim Crow South. The more education I gained, the more I traveled, the more I read, and the less complacent my parents became, I began to develop my own opinions about the issue of social justice. I realized that everyone deserves equal economic, political, and social opportunities. I realized that skin color should not be the determining factor in achieving equal rights.

My grandchild and my daughter have been told about my participation in the Civil Rights Movement. This participation may be considered informal. Our parents schooled us about the Tuskegee Boycott. They also made us aware of the necessity of refusing to shop in Tuskegee to bring about changes. My family and I were all participants in this movement. I also remember telling my daughter and granddaughter about how I was an unwitting participant in integrating a fast-food restaurant in Montgomery. This happened when I was a freshman at Tuskegee Institute, which had a program called TICEP. It was commonly known as the Tuskegee Institute Community Education Program, the year-round successor of TISEP, the summer program.[4]

TICEP assigned college students to various cities in Alabama to tutor local Black K-12 students to help prepare them for school integration. One Saturday morning, as we traveled through Montgomery to our tutoring site, we became very hungry. We decided to stop at a fast-food hamburger restaurant located on Madison Ave. Black people could order or buy food from this restaurant, but they had to take it out with them. There were about five of us student workers. We were so tired and hungry that after we were given our food, we just sat and ate the food right at the table. I noticed the cashier in the restaurant was starting to stack chairs on top of the surrounding tables. Another worker started mopping all around our table. At first, we did not get it. Then the light came on, and we realized what was happening. We were not supposed to be there. We finished the food and left in a big hurry. A few days later, we found out that we had been classified as civil rights workers who had come in and integrated the restaurant.

A similar unintended participation in a Civil Rights Movement activity happened when we were assigned to live in the Pike County community as TICEP student workers. One Sunday afternoon, all of us workers decided to go to the downtown movie theater. We had been told about the segregated policies that had existed for years at this theater. We did not go with any intentions of integrating the theater. About ten of us purchased our tickets and went straight through the main door. The movie had begun, and it was dark inside, so we all sat together. We whispered to each other, "Where are the Black people?" We didn't see any. The usher later walked through and shined a flashlight on our area. Some White people got up and walked out. We thought the movie was turning them off. Finally, the movie ended, and the lights came on. We looked up, and there were all the Black moviegoers in the area reserved for Black people. They started clapping and cheering for us. We hurried out and hurried away. Word was out in the community that we had integrated the theater.

Attending Tuskegee Institute did present an opportunity for involvement in the Civil Rights Movement. The town of Tuskegee was really shaken in 1966, when Sammy Younge Jr. was killed trying to use the "Whites Only" restroom at the downtown Standard Oil gas station.

That following morning, it was announced that all classes would end and a peaceful, silent march for Sammy would take place. We all put our hurt, grief, and anger into the march. Many of us knew Sammy personally. I felt proud to take part in that march.

Later, I began to think more and more about education being the key to learning how to combat Jim Crow laws. Two of my professors, Dr. Charles Gomillion and Dr. Frank Toland, were very involved in the Tuskegee community. They used their outstanding intellect and the courts to eradicate Jim Crow laws. What if I could be a teacher like they were in the classroom? What if I could use that knowledge to teach others about their civil rights, their civic duties, and responsibilities in a democratic society? I committed my time and studies to earning a bachelor's and a master's degree in social studies education. I loved teaching civic education and American government. These efforts helped to prepare me to be an outstanding and competitive educator. Although I worked in the South, I was well equipped to teach anywhere in the United States.

Living in the Jim Crow South did affect my personal and professional relationships and how I raised my daughter. I worked and met people from various socioeconomic, racial, and cultural backgrounds. I had to work on convincing myself just to see people as humans and try not to judge them because of their race, socioeconomic, or cultural differences. I passed my philosophy on to my daughter. I taught my daughter to choose a career that she loved, get all the knowledge that she could, and always find a way to give back to her school and community.

My current activism in the Civil Rights Movement may be limited due to aging. However, I have taught my granddaughter about the current and past contributions I have tried to make. I have encouraged her to study and learn about the past and the present. She has been pictured walking over the Edmund Pettus Bridge in Selma, Alabama, talking with the late John Lewis of Atlanta, Georgia and standing beside the late Amelia B. Robinson. We try to expose her to what she has read about in history and other books. We have taken trips to Washington, DC, to visit the capital, to Georgia to visit the grave site of Martin Luther King Jr., and to Memphis, Tennessee, to see the Lorraine Hotel. All this exposure helps to educate and to pass knowledge on to our granddaughter.

Looking back over the last one hundred years, and five generations, my family has benefited from the Civil Rights Movement in major ways. My parents finally obtained the right to vote in Macon County. My granddaughter knows how to become a registered voter when she is old enough to vote. Family members can travel South now and stop to eat and stay in hotels without the fear of being refused service. College applications can be sent to any college with the expectation of being admitted based on qualifications not race. Public schools are not assigned based on race. Choosing and enjoying a neighborhood to live in can be based on affordability instead of skin color.

I can now look at a long list of career choices my family members have made that were not possible years ago. The Civil Rights Movement helped to bring about positive changes in TV programming. When I was growing up, the Black faces and programs were zero to none. Segregated facilities based on race are virtually nonexistent today. The benefits my family and I have gained from the Civil Rights Movement have been great.

I offer several pieces of advice to my daughter, granddaughter, and the Black community relative to continuing the struggle. First, we should not take any of the civil rights achievements for granted. For example, the right to vote is being attacked now. Legislatures across the country are coming up with strategies to make voting difficult and impossible for many, mostly communities of color. Many states are redrawing voting districts to favor representation based on race. Yes, we thought that after the *Gomillion v. Lightfoot* gerrymandering win, that particular ghost of drawing Black people out of districts would not come back to haunt us again, especially here in Alabama. But it has come back! Remember, our parents sacrificed and boycotted local businesses to get that Supreme Court win.

The second major advice is aimed at the most qualified applicants seeking the job. Let us not forget that the color of our skin still can be the determining factor as to who will get that job. That is why years and generations ago, Black people automatically did not apply for certain jobs. In 2022, social media, television, and newspapers are raising questions about why the NFL does not have more Black head coaches in a sport where Black players tend to dominate. Seemingly, qualified Black head coaches cannot be found.

The struggle should continue because the courts have now overturned past affirmative action rulings. So our future generations will not be able to use affirmative action to open doors to the big Ivy League colleges and universities that once included affirmative action in their registration policies. Our youth must continue to be competitive academically for higher education. We must continue the struggle and not conclude that we have arrived. For every positive step we have taken, the political system finds a loophole to cause a setback. We must be prepared for the jobs that will allow us to afford the homes and lifestyles we want. We need to establish more positive mentoring programs to support our youth.

Marian Quinn Williams's daughter, Dr. Deidre Quinn-Gorham, professor of Veterinary Medicine at Tuskegee University, was awarded a patent for a surgical instrument. Photography by Thomas Martin; courtesy of Tuskegee University, School of Veterinary Medicine.

I will forever be grateful to my daughter, Dr. Deidre Quinn-Gorham, my son-in-law, Dr. Sammy Gorham, and my granddaughter, Galen Gorham, for all the love, support and encouragement they gave to me during this project.

My descendants know the struggle is not over and that it must continue in future generations!

CHAPTER 15

Sonjia Parker Redmond

Editors' Note: Sonjia Parker Redmond describes her growing up in a rich social, intellectual, and spiritual environment in a low-income rural family in Notasulga, Alabama, approximately ten miles from Tuskegee Institute. While there was economic poverty characterized by the lack of inside plumbing, a three-room house that sometimes accommodated twelve or more people, and constant debt just to afford life's necessities, the extremes of joy and happiness and sorrow and pain coexisted in the Jim Crow environment. She expresses gratitude for the ancestors who built a stairway out of poverty for her and her rural classmates. She writes about the Jim Crow–era love story between her grandparents, their love and support of their children, and high expectations and support from her rural church and school. She credits her "toiling, striving, never ceasing, reaching toward the sky" attitude to the amazing support of her local and Tuskegee environment.

On dark Saturday nights, the young White men parked their cars in the bend of the country dirt road a few hundred yards from our rural three-room home. We could not see them, but sounds from their drunken shouts and guffawing punctuated by occasional gunfire were frightening. I cannot tell you what drove my grandfather to do what he did that night in Alabama's Black Belt. Some family members say it was his fierce protectiveness of the family and the fear that one night the shots might reach his home. Maybe it was his seething anger about how the White owner of the sawmill where he worked stacking freshly planed lumber cheated him weekly, perpetually undercounting the number of planks he was being paid pennies per piece to stack. Maybe it was the thought that no matter how hard he worked, he always had to borrow money for seed and fertilizer at cotton planting time from White men who seemed to own and control everything. Maybe it was the extra courage he received from the pint of Old Crow Whiskey in the brown paper bag that he treated himself to every weekend after giving his weekly paycheck of ten to fifteen dollars and change to my grandmother. I do not know if he discussed it with her first, but in his ire, he retrieved his shotgun from its safe resting place over the front door header, went outside to his front porch, and emptied it into the night air. In a few moments, we heard the slamming of car doors and the screeching of tires as the cars sped off in the opposite direction from our home.

I could feel the tension throughout the three-room shotgun house for days as we waited with unspoken fear for the Ku Klux Klan or some other powerful White person or group to come looking for Granddaddy Parker. For reasons we never knew, they never came to our country home about ten miles from Tuskegee Institute.

On July 14, 1946, I was born in the front room of that three-room house in the Shiloh Community of Notasulga, Macon County, Alabama, to Robenia Parker (1929), the eldest of the nine children of Jodie Parker Jr. (b. 1909) and Johnnie Mae Strong (b. 1907). My father, Charles Crittenden, and his family moved to Chicago as part of the Great Migration shortly after I was born. I saw him twice in my life.

We can trace my maternal grandfather's lineage in the United States to my great-great-grandfather Joseph Parker Sr. (b. 1841) and his unnamed parents. The 1870 census shows that he was born in Alabama and that he and his family were living in Macon County, Alabama, in the 1900 census. The 1880 census states that he was born in Georgia.

We can trace my maternal grandmother's lineage in the United States to Jordan Strong (b. 1819) and his wife, Amy Strong (b. 1821). They came to Macon County from Georgia. The September 8, 1870, US Productions of Agriculture Census for Notasulga shows a Jordan Strong of Notasulga owning fifty acres of improved land and one hundred acres of unimproved land, all with a cash value of $400. He owned five farming

Sonjia Parker Redmond's mother, Robenia Parker Bass, remained in the South to be near her parents and became a small business owner. Courtesy of Sonjia Parker Redmond.

implements, one mule, and two working oxen, all with a total value of $150. He was also the owner of thirty bushels of Indian corn. We have not been able to identify how he came to own such a large amount of property for a Black man just fifteen years after emancipation. As for Amy Strong, we learned that our family shares maternal genetic ancestry with the Bubi people in Bioko Island (Equatorial Guinea) with 99.2 percent certainty after taking the matrilineal DNA test from African Ancestry.

We do not know how our ancestors came to be in Georgia. Some enslavers brought people into ports in Savannah, Georgia. Some enslaved people came to Georgia from ports along the Florida coast and from Maryland and the Carolinas when tobacco farming had problems. Some came to Georgia from the Caribbean.[1]

When Booker T. Washington arrived in Macon County in 1881, Black Americans had only been "liberated" for sixteen years. In *Up from Slavery*, he described how most people in the area had little or no education and that living conditions were dire.[2] After emancipation, many Black Americans who stayed in the South became sharecroppers. By the early 1900s, the Parker and the Strong families were landowners. Macon County records show that in 1917 my great-grandfather Jodie Parker Sr. purchased "80 acres more or less" from J. D. Borders and his wife, Exie, another Black landowner. The Parker and Strong families were small farmers, growing most of their food and cotton as cash crops.

After my birth, I became my maternal grandparents' baby and tenth child, as my mother went to various cities in Alabama and Florida looking for work and stability, finally settling in Auburn, Alabama, a college town about twenty miles from Notasulga and Tuskegee. I visited my mother and three sisters on holidays and during summers, but I remained with my grandparents in Notasulga until graduating from Tuskegee Institute High School in 1964. Although struggling to make ends meet, my maternal grandparents, with the help of my mother, provided a fertile educational and cultural milieu for my intellectual and social development.

Even though the house I was born in only had three rooms with an outhouse, it sat on part of the Parker eighty acres. Upon his death, Great-Grandfather Jodie divided the land among his eleven children. As one of the brothers "who stayed" and paid taxes on the property, Granddaddy Jodie Parker Jr. accumulated about forty acres. That 1917 land purchase by Great-Grandfather Jodie was an extraordinary feat for a Black man in the South at that time. It made a substantial difference in the future lives of the Parker clan, especially the ones "who stayed." The land did not make the Parkers who stayed wealthy or even middle class, but it saved them from abject poverty and added an almost palpable sense of dignity. Owning those acres of land gave Grandfather Parker, an unlettered man, some semblance of independence wrapped in pride and self-respect, as it did for other Black American landowners in the South. One has not seen indignity until one has seen a White man collect his Black sharecropper family—babies and toddlers included—load them in the bed of a big cattle truck, shuttle them to work his fields before sunrise, and bring them back to a barely standing shed of a house well after sunset. As a child, I witnessed this indignity with one of our sharecropping neighbors. I noticed the looks on my grandparents' faces each time the loaded truck passed our home, and I developed the same quiet empathy and disdain for the situation that they had.

The front room of the home that my grandfather had so gallantly protected that summer night was my grandparents' bedroom. The large room served many purposes. With their bed pushed to a corner, it was also the living room where we received guests, where young men came on Sunday nights for an hour to "keep company" with the "of age" young women of the family, while my grandparents retired to the kitchen or the middle room. Yes, I had my turn there when I turned sixteen or seventeen. The front room was also where my grandma and her friends sat on the four sides of a quilting frame and quilted and gossiped. That front room was where we all gathered around the fireplace at the end of cold winter days, sharing riddles, eating parched peanuts, and listening to country or gospel music or boxing matches on the radio, as there was no television in the house until the early 1960s. The middle room, with its three double beds and a cot, sometimes slept as many as ten people. The fireplace kept us warm in winter, and its hot coals roasted sweet potatoes and dried wet clothes hung over slatted wooden chair backs. That fire also heated the irons that smoothed wrinkles from starched garments.

The third room of the house was the kitchen. The kitchen held my grandmother's pride and joy, a beautiful four-burner cast-iron Cadillac of a wood stove with double white ceramic warmers and a reservoir that heated water for baths when the fire in the burners' compartment roared. I can still smell the aroma of fresh cornbread, collard greens, stewed rabbit, and tea cakes that scented the front yard as I exited school bus number 46 bringing me home from Tuskegee Institute High School over ten miles away. Granddaddy Parker had purchased that precious stove, like the foot pedal Singer sewing machine, and the cane-bottomed rocking chairs on the front porch with a fifty-cent per month credit plan from a White traveling salesmen. Giving my grandmother a few luxuries made him proud and served as a balm to the constant hard work and poverty that marked her life.

Sonjia Parker Redmond's rural Notasulga family home where she was born and lived until graduating from high school. The farm, which sustained several generations of Parkers, was purchased in 1917 by her great-grandfather Jodie Parker Sr. Watercolor painting by James Gayles, photograph by Tasin Sabir; courtesy of Sonjia Parker Redmond.

All the traveling salesmen coming through rural Alabama at that time were White men, except for those selling insurance policies for Black millionaire A. G. Gaston's insurance company.[3] Along with the furniture they bought from White traveling salesmen, many Black people in Alabama who could afford only a few pennies a month also paid for a burial policy from A. G. Gaston.

Like most of the poor Black men in the community, my grandfather worked hard to feed and clothe his family, supplementing his meager cotton farm income with whatever other meager income they could get from local work. Sometimes the men in my rural community became migrant workers, leaving their families for months or years to go to Florida or New York to pick fruit and send money home.

Granddaddy Parker stayed in the South because of his connection to that land. Sometimes without warning, he would get the walking stick he had carved and cured from a young sapling and set off to "walk the property," sometimes with his wife, Grandma Johnnie Mae, at his side. Sometimes he walked it with one of his sons visiting from the North, and sometimes he walked alone. Even as a child, I could feel those were special times for him, but I never quite knew what to call them. I now know what it was. It was walking dignity. In good times, the land was his pride and joy. In bad times, his land was his refuge. My grandfather would never have survived a factory job up North, the sprawling and squealing traffic on city streets, or the stifling polluted big city air. The human sounds from likely adjoining apartments would have unnerved him. Like many other Black men who went North, he would have lost his grounding, footing, sanity, and dignity. I know he would not have survived it. He needed to feel the rich black dirt in his hands and under his fingernails and the peace from walking his land or sitting on his front porch in the evening breeze after a hard day's work in the fields. He could not have borne the uncertainty of renting and living in a space not his own. He might have thought that White men already controlled too much of his life.

Farming without machinery is hard work. I saw my grandfather walk behind those mules and plows from sunup to sundown, year after year. As a child, I wondered if he had walked enough miles to get to Africa. After working the farm, he would try to get as much backbreaking work as he could at the sawmill about three miles from the house. There he was often cheated or "shorted" of his pay. My grandparents planned, discussed, and made decisions together as a team. Even though he could not read, she read for him. She taught him to write his name so he would not have to sign legal documents with the X he used when she married him.

They loved their family deeply. There was no daylight between them. Through paper-thin walls, I could hear the quiet hum of their voices planning before daybreak. I always found that early morning hum reassuring. It reminded me that somebody who loved us was keeping us safe. My grandmother loved this man in faded overalls. She blushed when with calloused hands he presented her with small beautiful aqua-colored bird eggs for her breakfast. It was a humble, but luxurious gift presented with a shy grin, and she always rewarded him with a shy smile of surprise and gratitude in return. I write about this love story between a poor Black man in the South and his lovely bride during Jim Crow because it is the kind of story that has not been told enough and because it was a beautiful thing to behold—and I am sure there were thousands of other such Black love stories where the poverty or the harshness or the injustice seemed to take precedent in the telling.

Sonjia Parker Redmond's small farm owner grandparents, Jodie and Johnnie Mae Parker. Their love for each other, their family, and the land nurtured them through economic hardships and Jim Crow experiences. Courtesy of Sonjia Parker Redmond.

Even in dire circumstances, my grandparents made it work. We were often without things we needed and wanted, but we were never without food to eat. Summer and spring gardens and fruit orchards were our primary food source, with one of the Rhode Island red hens for Sunday dinners. We planted corn to feed the animals and had it ground into cornmeal for cornbread. Granddaddy Parker was always doing something to please my grandmother. The fruit orchard and her precious flower bed were gifts to her. He grew pomegranates, pears, apples, plums, figs, and peaches. The vegetable garden was filled with tomatoes, okra, mustard greens, collard greens, green and red-hot peppers, pole beans, butterbeans, and squash. There were plots of black-eyed peas, speckled peas, purple hull peas, Irish potatoes, and syrupy orange sweet potatoes. Pecan trees, black walnut trees, and peanut patches offered up snacks. Hogs and chickens provided most of the meat for our table.

During the winter, there would be salted pork from the killing of fattened hogs, Grandma Parker's canned fruits and vegetables, and the rabbits and squirrels from Granddaddy Parker's hunting. He was a fantastic marksman. There were no frozen foods because there was no refrigerator, and the block of ice that the iceman delivered in summer only lasted a couple of days. Dried black-eyed peas seasoned with a square of fatback, or what fancy restaurants now call pork belly, served with cornbread, comprised the standby dinner meal in our household over the years. Those once-dreaded peas and cornbread today make my favorite meal, and I now appreciate the lengths my grandparents went to feed and clothe us.

Granddaddy Parker and Grandma Parker were always there for their children in good times and bad. On those freezing winter mornings before we got out of bed, Granddaddy Parker made fires in the two fireplaces and the kitchen stove with the kindling and wood one of us children had had the responsibility of collecting the evening before. Grandma Parker followed by making fresh biscuits and grits, and sometimes a slice of fatback, for us every single morning, year after year. On special occasions, canned mackerel made into patties was euphemistically called salmon. There was no boxed cereal or "light bread" to ease her burden.

My grandparents always encouraged education. However, the older boys missed so much school helping on the farm they eventually dropped out and went North to work in the factories. My grandparents were proud when we won awards in school, although like many rural parents, they were sometimes embarrassed or hesitant to attend ceremonies in Tuskegee. They encouraged all their children to "own" something. All nine of their children became small business owners.

When things were bad during the Jim Crow days, my grandparents were there for the family as well. When a Black man stabbed one of my uncles in his late teens at an infamous rural crossroads "beer joint" one Saturday night, they nursed him back to health and put him on a bus to meet his brother in New York. When one of the daughters left a "no good" husband, there was always room for her and her children in that three-room house. They were there when my teenage uncle was beaten in uptown Notasulga by a White man, supposedly because the teen did not get off the sidewalk fast enough and had "sassed" him anyway. What was a poor Black man to do in that situation in a rural southern town in the mid-1950s where the Klan controlled everything? You went and got your boy, cleaned him up, and to save his life; you told him he needed to be more careful around White folk. For whatever reason, my grandparents did not send him North. Maybe they thought he was too young or that they had resolved the situation.

For southern Black and White Americans at that time, there were strictly enforced Jim Crow social norms to be maneuvered around in the presence of White folk everywhere, especially in rural towns like Notasulga. When I was growing up, if a Black person were walking on the sidewalk in Notasulga and saw a White person coming, the Black person was to move into the street and allow the White person to pass. Black people were always to address White people as "sir" or "ma'am." If a Black person were in line at the bank or grocery store, White people in my little town had the right to go to the front. After my uncle's beating incident, I learned that some of the White people in town approached my well-respected grandfather privately to say how sorry they were for what had happened. They would never have spoken out publicly against the incident for fear of being deemed what is now termed race traitors.[4] Once a White professor colleague who grew up in a rural southern town like Notasulga told me that her liberal family was as afraid of the Ku Klux Klan as we were. There were consequences for everyone, Black or

White, who dared to violate those Jim Crow norms representing superiority and subjugation.

Grandmother Parker dreamed about a better life. Although she loved my grandfather and her children and grandchildren dearly, she longed for a life without so much struggle. She had given birth to eleven children, with nine surviving. She had helped to rear numerous grandchildren, including me, from birth, when our mothers returned home, escaping bad marriages or the hard knocks of city life, and left us with Grandma Parker so they could find work and send money back home. Grandmother Parker had taught at least twelve or thirteen of us our ABCs, numbers, the Lord's Prayer, and the Twenty-Third Psalm before we went to school. She had listened to the rehearsal of hundreds of Easter Day, Mother's Day, Father's Day, and Christmas speeches for church and school programs. She had bought paper and pencils on credit at the five and dime store or was the one to disappoint when there was no money or credit for such things. She had sewn hundreds of dresses and quilts and had patched as many shirts and pants. She had cooked three meals a day for nearly half a century and washed loads of clothes several times a week. Scrubbing clothes on a washboard outside in winter months sometimes made her knuckles raw, and the smoke from the big black wash pot caused her nose to run on cold and windy Alabama days. I never knew a day in that three-room house when it was not spotless, or when the kitchen table did not have either a colorful oilcloth for weekday meals or a starched white tablecloth for Sundays. After my older aunts left home, I was the one who had to starch and iron those white tablecloths with an iron heated in the fireplace before we got electricity during my last two years of high school. I rarely remember an after church Sunday dinner without fried chicken, rice, vegetables, and a sweet potato pie or caramel cake for dessert. I often wondered how she did it. She laughed easily and could make anything, even work, seem like a festival. She often tricked us into making work fun with competitions like seeing who could pick the most cotton or shell the most peas in a set amount of time. My grandmother was responsible for the happiness and peace in that little house.

I was hers from birth, and like many children reared by grandmothers, my grandmother was my heart! She was so proud of me, and I loved her deeply and never wanted to disappoint her. She used to brag that she taught me to recite the Twenty-Third Psalm in church when I was only three. I am sure there was a lot of prompting. When I went to high school, she did not understand most of my homework, such as geometry, chemistry, and French. Still, she was fascinated by it and supported me in all my academics and extracurricular activities. I remember when she found an old pot for me to boil a lab frog in, so I could remove the flesh and label its skeletal system for biology class. She found it fascinating!

She was brilliant. She advised family and friends on how to build houses, porches, outhouses, sheds, and even a family church. She had an architect's brain. She could look at an item and determine whether it was five or six inches and whether the foundation the bricklayer was building was level by sight. Her rural elementary school of Rising Star only went to the sixth grade. Like her sisters, she wanted to continue her education after sixth grade, but she would have had to move and board with another family in an area with a Black high school. Grandma Parker's father, my great-grandfather George Strong (b. 1873), would not hear of it. He knew Black women were not always safe in many settings then. He wanted to keep his daughters near him until they were married. Besides, my grandmother's White grandfather, Billy "Boy" Miles, had told my great-grandfather Papa Strong to hold his girls close and, of all things, never allow them to work in a White man's house. Billy "Boy" knew the potential danger the "mulatto" girls might be in, as it is said that he fathered children by several Black women in the small Notasulga community in the late 1800s. A marriage certificate shows Great-Grandfather George Strong marrying my maternal great-grandmother Lula Freeman, Billy Boy's daughter, at Billy Boy's home on September 26, 1896, a few blocks from her mother's home.

Eventually, all of Great-Grandfather Papa Strong's daughters married, and most went North to Chicago. I know that Grandma Parker would have loved walking Lake Michigan on summertime evenings in Chicago with her sisters or attending classes with them, as they were a tight-knit family. She did get to fly to Chicago to attend her parents' funerals. She also traveled to Texas to visit me and to upstate New York to visit some of her children.

Sometimes people misconstrue living with economic poverty to be the same as living with constant sadness or without working-class values and aspirations. Economic insecurity does not negate love, caring, and delight in simple things. Our family found joy in preparing for and going to church on Sundays, telling scary stories around the fireplace on cold evenings, shooting marbles, and playing hopscotch, checkers, and dominos under the two towering oak trees in the front yard. These pleasures existed alongside our deep hatred for Jim Crowism and how it limited the potential of the Black community.

Along with church and school activities, there was also joy from working as a team and finishing a long, hard day of labor. There was joy in the feast of fried fish, lemonade, and churned vanilla ice cream after Granddaddy Parker ginned a bale of cotton. We all celebrated because we all had contributed to a successful family project, even if the conversation later turned to how the White cotton gin owner paid the White man whose wagon was in front of Granddaddy Parker more per pound for his cotton. It is no wonder Granddaddy Parker's seething anger and resentment toward Jim Crow racism eventually turned into weekend battles with alcohol later in his life. Sometimes it is difficult to hold love and joy and hate in the same heart.

Shiloh Missionary Baptist Church is where we spent our Sundays. A kind of preparation excitement began on Saturdays with washing, starching, and ironing everybody's clothes. Men in the family used Oxblood polish for their black or brown shoes. For the females in the house, Saturday church preparations meant getting our hair "done" with straightening combs and curling irons heated on the woodburning stove. Preparing for Sunday speeches meant practicing in front of anyone who would listen so as not to embarrass the family the next day.

Shiloh Missionary Baptist Church is where I learned to be a leader. I was the youth superintendent of Sunday school, a member of the Junior Usher Board, and Junior Missionary Society president at various times. Members of Shiloh included mostly small cotton farmers who were deacons, deaconesses, Prince Hall Masons, and Eastern Stars. Although none of the Eastern Stars women had graduated high school, they took our development seriously. They entered us into oratorical contests to compete against city kids in Tuskegee, Auburn, and Montgomery. What faith they had in us. When we came in second, third, or fourth place, you could not tell them that we had not won first place. It reminds me of what Barbara Jordan once said when her HBCU debate team at Texas Southern University tied in a debate with Harvard. She said recognizing the privilege differences, her team considered it a win.[5]

Several members of my church and extended family members were also subjects in the US Public Health Service Syphilis Study at Tuskegee and Macon County. These men were regular folk trying to care for their families and the community. The depth of racism in this country then did not allow the White study's leaders to see the humanity of these men and their families.

Mr. Charlie Pollard, a leader in my church, was the main litigant in the lawsuit filed by Attorney Fred Gray against the US government for mistreating Black men in the study. After Gray won the case, Mr. Charlie was one of the men who was invited to the White House and received a personal apology from President Bill Clinton.[6] Tuskegee Institute received federal funds to establish a bioethics center on campus and to host annual conferences for descendants and researchers.

As the church was the center of social life in the Shiloh community, the Shiloh Elementary School, a Rosenwald school, would be considered the secondary cultural center that brought joy to the community, along with encouragement and high expectations to all of us children.[7] Because of the church's association with the US Public Health Syphilis Study at Tuskegee and Macon County, it and the Rosenwald Schools are both on the National Registry of Historic Places.

Portraits of Booker T. Washington and Julius Rosenwald hung on the wall of my Rosenwald school. I did not know until later in life that they were responsible for rural Black children having elementary schools in Notasulga and throughout the South.[8] There was a potbellied coal stove in each of the three rooms of the clapboard school. There was a well for drawing drinking water and an outhouse. Even though we often received extremely worn textbooks from the brick White school in Notasulga when they got new ones, our teachers were excellent. They always reminded us that we had to do well because we would have to compete with the city kids when we transferred to Tuskegee; moreover, one day we would also have to compete with White people. They prepared mimeographed sheets of material not found in the outdated textbooks. Some say our teachers might have obtained the new material from the Tuskegee

Sonjia Parker Redmond's childhood school, Shiloh Rosenwald School, is listed on the federal registry of historic buildings. Courtesy of Sonjia Parker Redmond.

Institute library. Jarvis Givens writes in *Fugitive Pedagogy* that some Black teacher groups prepared mimeographed lessons and distributed them to Black teachers to supplement the outdated books given to Black children in the South during Jim Crow.[9] Black folk did many clandestine things to subvert the power and authority of Jim Crow. Sometimes I hear the saying that Black people do not work together. I do not know where we would be if Black people had not worked together throughout history.

Shiloh School taught me to compete. The teachers reinforced the exact high expectations of the church and those coming from Tuskegee. Two to three grades were in each classroom, and the children in the lower grades competed with the upper grades. Parents looked forward to attending school functions, including plays, maypole wrapping ceremonies on May Day, and graduation ceremonies. There would be Black poetry recitations and plays with costumes. There were songs with piano accompaniment by the first- and second-grade teacher, Mrs. Elizabeth Irving, who brought her daughter, Shirley, to the celebrations. Shirley was to become one of my good friends in high school. Mothers, grandmothers, and aunties usually came inside for the programs, while the men typically hung around outside, taking advantage of the opportunity to mingle and "have a little sip." Parents furnished the pies, cakes, cookies, and lemonade as the state of Alabama provided no funds for such activities for Black students.

How my grandparents participated in the Civil Rights Movement is interesting. Like most rural adults in my hometown, they were not leaders or members of any civil rights organization. They did not participate in marches and warned those of us yet at home not to do so. They were country folk living in a rural Black Belt Ku Klux Klan–run town. I had wanted to be one of Gray's student litigants in *Lee v Macon County*. I wanted to be in the group to integrate White schools when I was in high school. I heard about the plan to integrate the schools in Macon County and asked one of my teachers to inquire if I could join. The teacher told me that she consulted the NAACP, who said that, although I had excellent grades, I could not join the action because I lived in rural Notasulga. They could not protect my family and me from possible Klan violence. It was not safe for rural people to openly engage in civil rights activities. The student litigants in Tuskegee lived close together with all-Black neighbors who looked out for each other. I have always felt deeply indebted to my classmates Anthony Lee, Willie B. Wyatt, and Robert Judkins, and all our other schoolmates for their bravery and sacrifice in integrating Macon County schools.

My grandparents contributed to the movement quietly through our little rural Shiloh Baptist Church. They contributed beyond the sight and scrutiny of White townspeople. On the third Sunday of the month, a special collection was taken up for "Dr. King's Work." Dressed not in his weekday blue denim overalls but his Sunday suit sent to him by one of his boys up North, Granddaddy Parker would reach into his pocket with calloused hands and give each of us a nickel or dime to put into the collection plate for "Dr. King's Work." My grandparents hated Jim Crow practices and resented the perpetrators. They constantly feared that something terrible might happen to one of their children in their interactions with White people. Black parents strictly limited the possibilities for those interactions. Whenever I went into White stores with my grandmother to shop, she always led the way. I learned to always stay a step behind her and let her do the talking. They diligently strived to teach us how to cope and stay safe in one world of love and joy and in another world of imminent danger, fear, and resentment.

After leaving my small Shiloh Rosenwald Elementary School in Notasulga and attending school in Tuskegee, I lived a bifurcated existence. In high school, I was in the college preparatory homeroom, along with my middle-class classmates whose parents were professionals—teachers, lawyers, college professors, architects, business owners, doctors, and other healthcare professionals. Their parents represented the hoped-for progression of Black people. They had been fortunate to attend college or take up a trade, many there at Tuskegee Institute. They worked at the university, the Veterans Administration Hospital, the campus John Andrew Hospital, and the Tuskegee Airmen Airbase.

My classmates never knew I missed a few days at the beginning of the school year to help pick cotton on our family farm before the rains came and spoiled it. They never knew that I was using an outside toilet at home. They did not know that I was dipping the family's drinking water from a sandy spring down the road because the roots from the giant oaks in our yard had turned the well water yellow and brackish. During the spring of our senior year, my classmates talked excitedly about the colleges that had accepted them. They did not know the anguish I felt about not having applied to college. I did not even know how to get started. I kept my mouth shut, and when asked what college I would attend, I said I did not know yet.

One day the school counselor noticed that although I was one of the top students in my class, I had not received any college acceptances. She did what we hope all high school counselors have the time and inclination to do today. She called me to her office. I cannot remember the conversation as I was probably too embarrassed to say that my grandparents were too poor to send me to college, and I did not know what to do anyway. At lunchtime that day, Mrs. Jeannette Branch drove me to Tuskegee Institute. We obtained admissions and financial aid applications.

I completed the applications easily but ran into what seemed like an insurmountable situation that threatened to smother my dream of going to college. The financial aid application required my grandfather's signature, as I was required to report his meager earnings. He told my grandmother that he had worked too hard and long to sign a government form that might lead to the White man taking his land. Losing all or part of one's land had happened too often to Black men in the South. "They took his land" was something I had heard all my life. After days of crying and thinking I would die, my grandmother sneaked and signed the form without my grandfather's knowledge. I had never known her to go against his will. She did that for me. She is the reason I have my doctorate today. My grandma was my heart, and I was hers.

I entered Tuskegee Institute in the fall of 1964 and graduated in 1968. As far back as I can remember, I have always loved school. My rural yellow school bus passed through Tuskegee Institute's campus every weekday from eighth through twelfth grades. I saw the coeds walking hurriedly and purposefully across the campus. The guys looked so handsome in their ROTC uniforms, marching in formation. Sometimes if the bus windows were down, we could hear the choir or band practice. I wanted to be a part of that world of books and ideas and the hurried and purposeful walks toward the future.

Nineteen sixty-four was at the height of the Civil Rights Movement. Many of us were going to Student Nonviolent Coordinating Committee meetings on campus, even if we did not participate in all their more daring activities like sit-ins. I remember going to one session where they taught us how to dress if we were going on a march. We were advised to wear strong clothing like denim jackets, overalls, and brogan boots to protect our feet from potential violence and to keep ourselves warm in case we ended up in cold jail cells. It is interesting what the mind remembers.

My sociology faculty included Dr. C. G. Gomillion of Gray's *Gomillion v Lightfoot* gerrymandering case, a White University of Michigan exchange professor, and a White South African professor, the latter two having come to Tuskegee to make their contributions to the movement. They began training us to become social researchers as sophomores. We learned how to code and were introduced to the vast IBM counter-sorter machines. Our subjects were mostly participants in the various civil rights marches in Montgomery and Atlanta. Learning to conduct research at the marches was a safe way to be in the civil rights action and get academic credit at the same time.

Tuskegee Institute opened a new world for me. I was ready to explore independence and try new foods in the cafeteria, except for the gamey lamb I think they raised at the Veterinary Medicine School. I was prepared to listen to intriguing ideas in a philosophy class and meet new people from around the country and the world. I could not understand why some students resented compulsory vespers after Sunday dinners, as vespers is where I met and shook hands with Malcolm X and Miriam Makeba and heard and fell in love with classical guitar music. I was a complete nerd. When the dean of students, Dr. P. B. Phillips, wrote a grant for us to tutor poor Black children in rural Alabama counties to prepare them for integration, I was eager to become a part of the Civil Rights Movement by teaching those who were still living in conditions in which I had once lived. Also, it prevented me from having to seek a meaningless summer job waitressing or, worse, cleaning houses for White folk. When Dean Phillips wrote another grant establishing an exchange program between the University of Michigan, a predominantly White institution, and Tuskegee Institute, a historically Black college, I was one of the first thirteen students selected to go on exchange to Michigan in the fall of 1965. The program's goal was to enhance race relations, as we were to share our experiences growing up in the Jim Crow South.

I remember the bus ride to Michigan. I was nineteen years old and had not eaten in a restaurant with white tablecloths. Along the way, I remember having steak with A-1 sauce for the first time. I thought it was terrific, but almost everything new tasted good to me then. I had completed my first year at Tuskegee and was ready to take on the world at Michigan.

Studying at Michigan in the fall of 1965 was the first time I had gone to school with White students, and it was certainly the first time I had slept in the same room as a White person. My roommate and I had an amicable relationship, except for her continually asking me to let her feel my hair. Interestingly, I had no urge to touch hers. In classes, I was amazed at how loquacious some White students were, how they spoke without first being acknowledged by the professors, and how they challenged the professors. At first, I was a bit intimidated and thought they were very smart. Tuskegee's classroom decorum was for students to wait to be called upon by the professor and certainly not to challenge them in front of the entire class. As for the loquacious Michigan students, I soon learned that running your mouth all the time and challenging the professor does not mean you know what you are talking about.

Michigan also introduced me to another custom that would not have gone over too well at my HBCU, the panty raid. What a weird experience when I saw the White girls throwing their panties at boys waiting under their windows. All I could think was I could not afford to throw away good clothes, and more importantly, what would my religious Grandma Parker think? Grandma Parker was always with me, perched there on my shoulder like an angel, experiencing what she had longed to experience and protecting me every step of the way.

Various campus groups at Michigan invited us to discuss growing up in the Jim Crow South. The chiefly White students asked Patty Jones most of the questions as she had integrated Alabama schools. Most questions from the White students seemed naive. Most of them had had no or limited contact with Black people. The program was doing what it was meant to do, I suppose, enhancing interracial communication and understanding. Looking back, there were always people like Dean Phillips looking toward the future and creating opportunities for us to grow and give back to our people and the world.

After returning to Tuskegee from Michigan in January 1966, I found the campus teeming with civil rights activity. I kept my grandparents' warnings about not getting involved in "all that mess" to heart until the night the White service station attendant killed Sammy Younge Jr.[10] I remember students running down the dorm hallways yelling, "Sammy is dead! They killed Sammy! We are marching downtown." I guess all rational sense left us that night. Although the news reported that there was a march the next day, I remember hurriedly dressing and marching somewhere with hundreds of other students in the dark that night. I remember singing freedom songs along the way. I remember being afraid but filled with so much sadness and anger that I forgot the fear of marching at night. They had taken one of us. We all knew Sammy. Some had grown up with him. Some walked home from school with him. Some were involved with him in SNCC. I remember Sammy most for walking around campus in his SNCC attire, overalls and brogans, holding court about the movement with anyone who would listen. I cannot remember if he was on the bus or organized the trip when a group of us went to Mississippi early one Saturday morning to help register voters, but I know he did a lot of voter registration in Mississippi and Alabama.

In the ensuing days, the best that most of us could do was march, sing, and vent our anger. Some students painted a yellow stripe down the back of the Confederate soldier monument in the center of downtown Tuskegee either that night or later. Many White people did not know that their violence stirred even more resolve in the "Children of the Struggle" to fight even harder against racism and for equality.

In 1968, my senior year, when all Tuskegee students were sent home for two weeks by the university administration to quell student protests on campus, I lied to my grandmother for the first time. I told her I was not involved in "all that mess." I felt OK about lying for several reasons. I was never a leader in the movement, but it had my heart and commitment, and I knew it also had my grandmother's heart. She was afraid for all the students and me for good reasons. She was a practical woman and did not want me to get hurt or expelled from college or put my rural family in danger. I knew how far to go. I did not want to endanger the opportunity to go to college given to me by my counselor and my grandmother. She had done the unthinkable and had gone behind my grandfather's back to sign those financial aid papers so that I might become the first person in the history of the Parker family to go to college. I could not mess that up. I have much respect for those students who took the chance to lead and paid the ultimate price of suspension or expulsion and some, like Representative John Lewis, who were severely beaten. I had an amazing opportunity to meet Representative Lewis a couple of years before his death when he was a guest speaker at a fundraiser in San Francisco. We talked about my growing up in Notasulga and our shared Alabama and rural heritage. When he mentioned that he had done voter registration work in Notasulga as a young SNCC worker, I suggested that he might have registered my grandparents to vote. In those few precious moments, we were happy to see each other—so far from home. There were knowing smiles recognizing our shared pasts, how far we had come and how far we and our people had to go.

Graduating magna cum laude from Tuskegee was a memorable day for my family. My grandmother even attended a special reception for honors students at President Luther Foster's home. She told me that some faculty and administrators told her what a good student I had been. She was so proud. She had never been able to come to any of the other honors ceremonies while I was in college. I was so proud of her. She also came to see my room for the first time since bringing me as a freshman. I made a giant beautiful paper collage thank you card for her to celebrate our graduation. I can still visualize the collage and the love and gratitude it embodied.

As a result of Tuskegee's special relationship with the University of Michigan, several of us went to Michigan's School of Social Work for graduate school. I have found that White educational institutions, even those that seem welcoming to students of color, have customs that can make them feel unwelcome or less than others. Even though I had graduated magna cum laude from Tuskegee, Michigan made me a conditional admit to its Graduate School of Social Work. Being a kid at the time, I was ashamed of it. Now, having been a full professor and vice president of Student Affairs at a predominantly White institution, I am ashamed of Michigan for its actions.

I met my husband, Greg, in the fall of 1965, the semester I was on exchange at the University of Michigan. He was a business major at Michigan. We have had an amazing life together. In preparing for a career day presentation for junior high students about five years ago, we designed a game challenging the students to locate on a globe the eighty countries the Redmond family has either lived in, worked in, or vacationed in. Our highlights were living in London for three years as Greg worked with Gulf Oil Corporation and my teaching as a Fulbright Fellow in Bahrain in the Middle East, along with my youngest son, Shaka, who was in the ninth grade at the time.

Many of us who grew up in families with limited means in the Tuskegee area during Jim Crow made it to this place of upward mobility because of the culture of high expectations our ancestors had for us, even in the midst of unthinkable oppression. I am grateful for all those ancestors who paved the way for us to strive and thrive and for giving us the courage, ambition, and confidence to always reach toward the sky and resist injustice everywhere.

I am grateful that Tuskegee University was there for me and our sons, Gregory Jr. and Shaka. We have been an active alumni family helping to ensure that Tuskegee University is there for future generations of Black students. We open our home for events for Tuskegee students and their families. We have established an endowment for scholarships in my grandparents' names and donated to campus learning and housing initiatives.

To my grandfather, who protected us fiercely that dark Alabama Black Belt night; to my mother and grandmother, who were always in my corner and on my shoulders; to my sisters, aunts, and uncles who were always so proud of my accomplishments; to the Eastern Star women at Shiloh Missionary Baptist Church who entered us into oratorical contests, supervised our leadership roles in the church, and taught us to walk through life with dignity; to the teachers at Shiloh Elementary, Washington Public Junior High, and Tuskegee Institute High who taught us as if we were in university prep schools; to Sammy and John Lewis and Anthony and Willie B. and Robert and the other *Lee v. Macon County* twelve for fighting for all those who stayed; to ancestor and Presidential Medal of Freedom Recipient, Fred Gray for his brilliance and for "staying" and fighting for us all; and finally to all the unnamed ancestors who "stayed" in the Black Belt to rear their families and to fight openly and often clandestinely for justice, I carry you all with gratitude in my heart every step on this journey toward justice and equality.

CHAPTER 16

Alex Stanton

Editors' Note: Alex Stanton describes working as a teenager catching chickens in a chicken house to earn money so he could afford clothes for school. Stanton decided not to go to college and stayed in Notasulga to make a life for himself and his family. He considers himself lucky to have gotten a good-paying job with retirement benefits in the area. He was able to send all his children to college, and one even started her own business. He credits his mother with teaching him the values that led to his doing well in life and his family's upward mobility.

He beams with pride that his great-granddaughter recently graduated valedictorian from Notasulga High, the school that he and Sonjia once could not attend because of their race. He and Sonjia grew up in the same rural town, Notasulga, although they did not know each other as they went to different elementary schools and churches. They recently learned that they retrieved their families' drinking water from the same sandy spring on the side of a country road and that Alex knew Sonjia's grandfather who worked at the same sawmill as Alex's stepfather. As there was no junior high or high school for Black students in Notasulga, Alex and Sonjia joined generations of Black students whose yellow buses did not stop at the nearby Notasulga High School but traveled some ten to fifteen miles each way to the Black Washington Public Junior High School and Tuskegee Institute High School in Tuskegee. One could say that they were bused away from the all-White school instead of to it.

I always say thank God for my mother. She was a praying woman. She prayed a lot for me and my brothers and sisters. She prayed that we would grow up to be strong and straight and know right from wrong. She also prayed a lot for our safety. She had dreams of a better life for herself and her children. If she had not prayed so much for me, I do not know what would have happened to me in life. If we got in trouble, the first thing she would do was to get a chair, put it in the center of the room, and get down on her knees and pray with all of us kids watching. The second thing she would do would be to whip the person who had done something wrong with a switch that she had asked us to go outside and get. Prayer and discipline are what made me the man I am today. My sisters and brothers and I laugh about it today because once she pulled that chair out to the middle of the floor, we knew somebody was going to get it!

My stepfather and mother met and married while he was sawmilling in various areas around south-central Alabama, including Macon County, Wilcox County, and the Fort Deposit, Alabama, area. He was driving trucks for one dollar an hour for the R. P. Self Lumber Company.

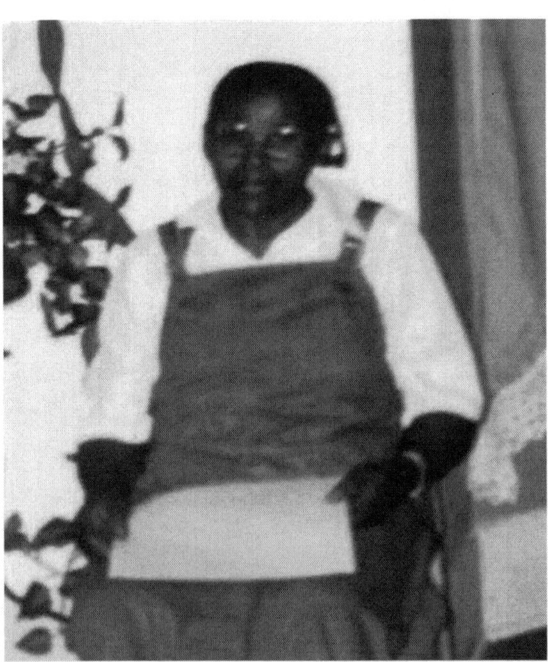

Alex Stanton's mother, Leanne Stanton, a domestic worker, saved money to build a home in Notasulga down the street from Notasulga High School. Courtesy of Alex Stanton.

Mr. Self had several sawmills in many of these places. My mother and stepfather eventually moved to Notasulga where Mr. Self also had a sawmill. Sometimes the sawmills were called planer mills because there was a huge sawlike machine that they fed the logs through to make them into smooth planks of wood in various sizes such as two by six inches or the popular two-by-four-inch planks. Some of the planks were as large as four by twelve inches and varied in length.

Mr. Self hired local White foremen to run the mill for him. The foremen hired mostly poor Black men from the area, most of whom could neither read nor write. The work was hard and backbreaking, especially during the hot Alabama summers and frigid cold winters. Most of the Black men were hired to stack the lumber after it had been planed so that it could dry flat and straight. The planks were laid with one layer going in one direction and the next layer going crosswise with space for airflow. Some of the foremen had the reputation for cheating the "colored" men, as they were called at that time. For instance, in the stacking area, the men were paid by the number of planks they stacked. Some of the foremen would reduce that number when they paid the men. The foremen kept the records, and there was nothing the poor Black men could do about it. Most were grateful for the opportunity to earn a few extra dollars to go with their farming income.

A small grocery and sundry store was located across the street from the lumber mill and had a different owner. The Black men shopped in that store for groceries for their families and sometimes for lunch for themselves. Most of the men trusted whoever the owner had hired to run the cash register and keep their records, but sometimes, they ended up paying more than they should have for whatever they bought. Maybe it was the interest payments that kept adding up because it seemed that by the end of the week many of the men owed most of their paycheck to that store. Many of them were always in debt to that store.

Along with driving the truck for Mr. Self, my stepfather sometimes worked the kiln at the lumberyard. The kiln was a kind of oven that was used for slowly drying the fresh cut lumber that had been sawed into planks from soft- or hardwood trees. The kiln drying process helped to stabilize the wood. For instance, pine trees produce softwood, and oak trees produce hardwood. They all need to be dried in the kiln and then stacked in a crisscross pattern to dry in the sun so that the planks do not warp. People did not like to buy warped wood for their building projects.

Most Black people in Notasulga were cotton farmers. I was always glad we did not have to farm. My mother was a domestic worker. She worked for the Parkers, who were White people. Mr. Parker was a mail carrier. When the kids grew up and left home, I remember that my mother went back to school. Macon County started a federal educational program for people in the Notasulga community at the old Shiloh Elementary School. My mother began to take different adult classes there to improve herself. She already had a fifth-grade education. My mother got other jobs in Auburn and finally made enough money to buy seven acres of land with a house on it. The place was located down the road a piece from Notasulga High School. Later, I built my own home a few blocks down the street from my mother's house.

I did not know much about most of my grandparents, except my maternal grandmother. I remember that my grandmother loved to fish a lot. She suffered from seizures. One day, she was fishing with my aunt on the bank of a pond. She had a seizure and fell into the water and drowned. I was twelve years old, and it broke my heart to lose her.

When I was growing up in Notasulga, things were hard for Black people. Most of the Black people in Notasulga did not have an education. Most of them worked hard every day from sunup to sundown to try to make it and still found it almost impossible to get ahead. Some, like my mother, were able to save and improve life for their families. The town was filled with Ku Klux Klansmen. They were everywhere, and they controlled everything in the town.

When I look back on how I managed with Jim Crow while I was growing up, I would say that I managed it pretty well. My major problem as a youngster was not having the opportunity to get a good job and therefore not having enough money. To get a job in Notasulga in those days, the White guy working next to you doing the same work would get more money per hour than you just because of the color of your skin. Nothing was ever fair when it came to jobs. I worked for a while for the Bentley Grass Company. For a few weeks, they would pay me well and do me right. The next week, they might short me on my paycheck. You would have to argue about that or just walk away with what they gave you. You just never had any control over what the White employers would do or would pay you after you had given them a full day's work. There were White people I would not work for because they did not want to pay you. If they did not pay you, there was nothing you could do. There was one man who would tell you that if you did not work for him, you had better leave town. Sometimes he would only want to pay you fifty cents and sometimes twenty-five cents an hour. That not only happened to youngsters but to grown men as well. Imagine you are a grown man making that kind of pay. What could you buy with that? That kind of thing was going on up until the late 1960s.

When I was a kid, everything in Notasulga was segregated. If you were walking on the sidewalk in Notasulga and a White person was coming, you had to get off the sidewalk and walk in the street. Sometimes the White men would play dominoes right in the middle of the sidewalk and Black people had to step into the street to walk around them. You usually had to say, "Yes, sir," "No, sir," "Yes, ma'am," or "No ma'am" to the White people in the town. They owned everything, and most did not want to see Black people get ahead.

White men did not mind beating up on a Black man. They used to always whip up on this one family of young Black men because they spoke up for their rights. They used to arrest them and other Black men a lot and charge them with public intoxication. There were two bars not far from downtown Notasulga on Highway 14 headed toward Auburn. They were located just outside the Macon County line in Lee County. They were located inside the Lee County line because Lee County was "wet," meaning that alcohol could be sold. Macon County was a "dry" county at the time. On the side of the first building coming from Auburn (Lee County) the beer joint sign read, "First Chance." On the second building before crossing over into Notasulga, the sign facing drivers read, "Last Chance." The Notasulga police used to sit in their cars and wait inside the Macon County line to arrest Black people coming from those beer joints, whether they were drunk or not, especially on the weekend.

There were some financial difficulties for our family. My stepfather did not have an education. I guess you could say that he had lots of mother wit. Sometimes we did good, and sometimes, we did not do so well because of the lack of jobs, low paying jobs, or always being cheated by White employers. We learned to live with it. All in all, we did fairly well and better than some Black families in Notasulga. I do not ever remember my parents thinking of leaving Notasulga and going North or West. When my stepfather married Mama, he had three children and she had three children. That made six children altogether. Like many other people in the area, we lived in a house with only three rooms in total—a front bedroom, a middle bedroom, and a kitchen. Often, we had to carry water in containers from a sandy spring down the road because there was no running water in the house. I guess my parents thought it would be too hard trying to go North with eight people in the family. So we stayed in the South and did the best that we could.

As I got older, I did not take too much stuff from people. Even I would say that I was bad. I got in trouble sometimes standing up for my rights. I was lucky though that I only stayed in jail for forty-five minutes in my life. I was accused of fighting. Later, they discovered it was a case of mistaken identity. My sister went North and thought about sending for me, but she said I was too bad. She thought I would get in too much trouble up North.

The good Lord blessed me to learn a few trades. I built my own home using the skills I had learned. My mom used to say I did not like getting my hands dirty, so I went on to other things. Sometimes I think if I had stayed with the trades, I would have gone farther in life, but I have had a good life. I got married and had five children, four girls and a boy. Unfortunately, my son died at the age of sixteen from a seizure. I think he must have inherited the seizure problem from my grandmother. I have two daughters here in Notasulga, one in Auburn, and my baby girl is in Atlanta.

In 1977, with my mother's prayers and God's blessings, I managed to get a good job in maintenance at the Neptune Water Meter Company in Tallassee, Alabama, which is about twenty miles from Notasulga. Tallassee was notorious at that time and earlier for Ku Klux Klan actions. My goal was to keep that good job and retire from there. I stayed thirty-two years and was able to provide a good living for my family. With the grace of God, I was able to do that. Another thing I did here in Notasulga was to join the Notasulga Volunteer Fire Department. You know what they say if you cannot beat them, join them. I worked there with many other White guys for forty years.

I would like my daughters and grandkids to know that I participated in the Civil Rights Movement because I always wanted to stand up for my rights. I want them to know that I wanted a better life for all of them and all Black people. I participated in protest marches in Tuskegee, and I participated in protest marches in Auburn. I never had dogs sicced on me. That happened in bigger towns like Selma and Montgomery and Birmingham. I never went to those marches in the big cities because there were too many people involved. I did have water hoses turned against me at some of the marches in Auburn and Tuskegee. I want my grandkids to know that this is what happened to their grandfather when he was fighting for them to have better lives.

Alex Stanton and his great-granddaughter, Teanna Story, who graduated valedictorian from Notasulga High, the school Alex was prevented from attending because of racial segregation fifty-four years earlier. Courtesy of Alex Stanton.

In raising my children in the South, I always told them to get a good education. I told them if you get your education, White people cannot take education away from you once you learn. Only God can take that away from you. Although I did not go to college, I was always high on education. My four daughters have good educations and good jobs. They were blessed. Two went to four-year colleges, and two went to trade schools. One daughter is over the cafeteria here at Notasulga High. Another daughter works with the Macon County School Board in Notasulga. One works at the Veterans Administration Hospital in Tuskegee. Another one has her own business, a hair salon. My great-granddaughter just graduated as valedictorian at Notasulga High. I think I did a pretty good job as a father considering the prejudice and racism that tried to hold Black people down in Notasulga. All my children went to Notasulga High School after my classmates Anthony Lee, Willie B. Wyatt, and Robert Judkins Jr. integrated it in 1963. I felt good about that. My daughter Michelle got a chance to meet Willie B. when he came up to Notasulga High one time. I introduced them and told her that Willie B. was one of the students who integrated Notasulga High School. He had a good talk with her. Michelle was so proud to meet him. Anthony came up to the school one time, and I went up to see him talk. I am grateful to Anthony, Willie B., and Robert because they are responsible for giving my children an opportunity to go to school close to home. When I was in high school, I had to ride a bus about fifteen miles to Tuskegee Institute High School each way. Since we had to catch the bus right after school ended, the kids in Notasulga had a difficult time participating in after-school activities.

People ask me how it is living in the South now. I would say that the racial situation is much better today than it was sixty years ago when we were growing up here in Notasulga. At that time, there were many Ku Klux Klansmen around. Although I think there are still a few left around here in Macon County today, there is much more respect for Black people and between the races. Chances of getting better jobs are greater. We do not have to worry that much anymore about just being cheated outright out of our pay, since there are laws now that say we are to be paid fairly. We do not have to get off the sidewalk to let White people pass. Some of the good White people never liked some of the racist things that went on. I do remember that one of the probate judges in Notasulga tried to help Black people. I also know that some of the good White people did not support some business owners who did bad things to Black people. The good White people could not always state their good intentions publicly, but in private, some of them tried to be kind and respectful to Black people.

We did not have a formal boycott of businesses in Notasulga, but as time passed, some White and most Black people did not support the local business owners who did not treat Black people right. Most of us knew a person associated with a local business who was accused of getting on the bus and beating up that cameraman when our classmates were trying to integrate Notasulga High School on their first day of school.[1] For whatever reason, they say his business did not seem to prosper after that.

Although things are much better for our people, I do worry that some of our young Black people do not know our history and how we got to this place. Some of the younger teenagers do not respect themselves or each other. It seems to me sometimes that too many of our kids here in Notasulga do not know how to appreciate the brand-new free books, air-conditioned buildings, or an integrated school close to their homes. I do not know if anyone has taught them that many Black people had to grow up like I did. We never lived on a farm, but I did work on other people's farms to make a few dollars. I do not think they know or appreciate that when many of us were teenagers, we had to do dirty work like catching chickens and crating them, so a truck could take them to be slaughtered. Our young people do not know that the White people who owned the chicken house had placed it in the middle of a Black neighborhood. They do not know that it smelled awful in the summertime. Our young people do not know that as a teenager, my friend and I met that truck from Union Springs, Alabama, once every eight weeks at ten o'clock at night because it took eight weeks for a biddie, as they called baby chicks back then, to grow to market size. They do not know that we were paid two dollars for that work. When the chicken house needed to be cleaned of all that chicken waste, the owner paid us three dollars. They do not know that, because my parents could not afford to give me an allowance, those few dollars I made catching chickens and cleaning that filth was enough for me to pay class dues, buy two pairs of Tough Rough blue jeans, and a couple of shirts for school. Sometimes, I am afraid that we give our children too much without requiring some responsibility. And sometimes I think we do not take care of each other as a people like we used to do.

We have come a mighty long way, but we must be careful to teach our young people our history. They need to know our history so they can appreciate where we are now and how far we have come and they can have a clearer vision about how much farther we must go and how they are going to help us get there as a people.

CHAPTER 17

Roosevelt Lorenzo Williams

Editors' Note: Roosevelt Lorenzo Williams led an interesting life as a child and as a young adult. His rearing was shared between his preacher paternal grandfather and his maternal grandmother who participated in an alternative economy to support him. His mother had migrated to New York and sent money back home to help support him. Although Lorenzo's paternal family owned property, had donated land to build a local school, and had helped to fund the building of a local church, there were times when they needed credit to make ends meet financially. His maternal grandmother's profession often depended on decisions made by legal authorities, and so she, too, needed credit from time to time.

Lorenzo was intelligent, ambitious, and worked his way through college on the university's five-year plan and earned his degree and military commission as a second lieutenant. His dream of becoming a second-generation Tuskegee Airman and high-ranking military officer was altered by a fateful personal decision and racism. He returned to Tuskegee to triumphantly finish unfinished business.

My grandfather donated land to Tuskegee Institute to establish a Rosenwald school named Harris Barrett, following the trend among Black people of establishing churches and schools in their rural communities in the late 1800s and the early 1900s. Harris Barrett School was named for the founder of a savings and loan association who gave

Booker T. Washington money to help establish the school. It is located across the street from the St. John AME Church, which was cofounded in the late 1800s by my great-grandfather Reverend E. D. Williams. Although St. John only has a few members now, the church still stands in the Franklin community at the corner of County Road 21 and 39 in Macon County, Alabama. This is where my story begins.

On my father's side, we can trace our ancestors back to their landing in South Carolina from Africa. My paternal great-grandfather settled in a little community south of Tuskegee, and his family and my great-grandmother's family mixed with Creek Indians in the area. Legend has it that the Franklin community was part of the Creek nation. It is said that many of the Native Americans in this area were able to avoid the long march to the West, the Trail of Tears, in the 1830s.

My paternal great-grandmother Molly Brown married Reverend E. D. Williams and they had one child, Ecolia Williams. My great-grandfather bought forty acres of land in the area and established a farm. At the same time, several of his friends were able to do the same, including Mr. Benny Hudson, Mr. Keys, Mr. Perk Alexander, Mr. Heflin, and Mr. Campbell.

My paternal grandfather, Ecolia, married Jamie Lee Baker. He was very involved in St. John Church, which was the center of the community. We would be in church from eleven in the morning until three in the afternoon every Sunday. I was baptized, grew up in, and still hold a quasi-membership there. A fellow Tuskegee Institute High student, Dr. Gwen Trawick, is still a member there, and she tries to keep it going. My great-grandfather, my grandfather, my father, my uncle Elijah Williams, my great-grandmother, and my grandmother are all buried there at St. John AME Church.

My dad, Roosevelt Williams, went to high school on Tuskegee Institute's campus where the high school was first located. It was in the old academic building, Huntington Hall. He was drafted into the army in 1944 and was stationed in France. He did basic training in Fort Benning, Georgia, and he was in a Black engineering battalion. My father said that all they did was hard labor building a railroad in France. One day, a railroad tie fell on a Black soldier's leg, and a Hispanic soldier named Lorenzo lifted the tie and saved the Black soldier's leg. My dad promised him that his first son would be named Lorenzo. That is how I got my name.

Roosevelt Lorenzo Williams and his paternal grandfather, Ecolia Williams, who took him to see serial cowboy films every Saturday morning at the segregated Macon Theatre in Tuskegee. P. H. Polk Photography; courtesy of Roosevelt Lorenzo Williams.

Upon his return to Tuskegee from France, my father and my mom, Rosa Pearl Brown, were married. I was born in John Andrew Hospital.[1] I always say that I have the mark of infinity because of the forceps mark left on my head when Dr. Mitchell used them to save my life, performing one of the first cesarean operations in John Andrew Hospital. I used to ask my mother when I was growing up what the mark was. She said, "It means you are number one!"

While I spent much time with my father's parents, my maternal grandmother raised me. My maternal grandmother and I lived off Franklin Road across the street from Ernest Howard and Edward Howard. The Howard family had about five or six kids, and they lived in a rental house there. We owned our home. We had so much fun there. We played baseball in that big open field. It is all grown up with trees now. We had a water spring in the back of the house, but we also had running water in the house.

At some point we moved from Franklin Road to Green St. I still own that property. That's where I keep pictures of my mom and my grandmother. My grandmother was my heart. When I was about four, my parents got a divorce. My mom was going to Alabama State Teachers College in Montgomery at the time. She had completed her junior year and needed money for tuition. She started scanning the newspapers looking for jobs. As a result, she became part of the Great Migration of Black people from the South to the North. She went to Spring Valley, New York, and got a job at Rockland State Hospital. They now call it the Upstate Bellevue as it is now a mental institution. As a nursing assistant at Rockland State, she qualified for onsite dormitory housing, paying a nominal amount each month. She had one bedroom, a bath, and a kitchen. She started making money and sending money back home to me and my grandmother. She never came back to stay. As a result, I was left to be raised by my maternal grandmother and my paternal grandparents.

I bounced between my maternal grandmother and paternal grandparents. I would love "going to the country" on weekends to be with my paternal grandparents. When I was in high school, I would get Mr. Keyes's school bus instead of going back Uptown where my maternal grandmother lived. In the country is where we went to church. My paternal grandfather and my maternal grandmother were the two most influential people in my life. They were my guiding lights. My dad was around, but he was in and out. He got several certificates from Tuskegee on the GI Bill.

My first school was Harris Barrett, the two-room Rosenwald cement block schoolhouse in the country that my great-grandfather had donated land for. The school had grades one through six. After graduating from Harris Barrett, students went to New Rising Star School for the seventh and eighth grades. After that, students in the community would go to Tuskegee Institute High School.

Harris Barrett had great teachers. My great-grandfather had not only provided Tuskegee University land to build the school, but he also provided them land to build what was called a teacherage, housing for the Harris Barrett teachers. That building was made of cement blocks. The skeleton of the building is still there. Tuskegee Institute provided the teachers. They had a nice place to live at the time because the house was always cool. The cement blocks provided insulation. They had a fireplace, too. I remember that the teacherage had two bedrooms, a kitchen, and an inside bathroom, which was very unusual in a rural area at the time.

I went to Harris Barrett for a week, and I liked it. My maternal grandmother on the other hand said that I was out in the country too much. She was not happy with the situation. She told my mother she wanted to bring me back to Uptown. Well, they took me out of Harris Barrett and found me a slot at St. Joseph Catholic School, which meant we had to pay tuition, and all my teachers were White. St Joseph was a fantastic school. We were expected to learn and do well. I never became an altar boy. In my seventh grade year, something happened. I'd been learning the catechism and how to say Hail Mary, Our Father, and the Apostles' Creed. I practiced very hard, and I knew all of it by heart.

Then it was time for me to be confirmed Catholic. Remember that my great-grandfather was an AME preacher. The Sunday that I was supposed to do first Communion, my great-grandfather got out of bed, came to get me, and said, "Oh no, no, no!" So, I didn't make first Communion. No, sir. That Sunday, I was at St. John AME Church, Road 27, sitting in the pew listening to my great-grandfather deliver his sermon.

The following year was the first year that St. Joseph started an eighth grade just like Tuskegee Institute High School had. Because I had not become Catholic and the demand for places at St. Joseph was high, I had to move on to Tuskegee Institute High School. Our classmates Nancy, Barbara, and Paul stayed at St. Joseph and became Catholic. When I was ordained as a deacon at Shady Grove Missionary Baptist Church, I said, "Well, let me tell you. I was baptized AME. I was trained as a Catholic, and now I'm being dedicated as a Baptist deacon. I have all the bases covered. So, when that roll is called up yonder, my name's gotta be in somebody's book."

When I got to eighth grade, my mother was still in New York. My dad had gotten an associate degree in auto mechanics at the Trades Building on Tuskegee Institute's campus. Being able to take all kinds of classes was one reason he stayed around as much as he did. My mom had gone to make money to come back to Alabama State to get her degree. However, when she got up there, she started making money and didn't come back. She would come back on vacation to see me, but she never came back to stay.

In 1962, when I was about fourteen years old, they put me on a bus right here in Tuskegee with a shoebox full of food, and I went to New York all by myself. I made three trips to New York by myself in the summers of 1962, 1963, and 1964. I met my friend Maurice Sturdivant during this time. His mother had sent him South from New York. They said it was to keep him from getting in trouble. He wasn't a bad kid. It's just that his friends were bad. It was Stuyvesant and Brooklyn, New York, you know? So they sent him South to stay with his grandmother. That's how we got to be buddies.

My first race related experience outside of Tuskegee occurred while traveling to New York on the Greyhound bus. There were "Colored Only" bathrooms and water fountains throughout stops in the South. The situation made me more aware of what my behavior should be to stay safe. Here I was out in the big racist world alone at fourteen!

When we got to New York City, going across the George Washington Bridge was an amazing experience for me. My mother lived in a little town called Nyack, New York. You could literally look out her front door down Cedar Hill Street and see the Hudson River. That was my first time seeing a river. The adventures that my mother took me on! When we went to New York City on the ferry, I saw the Statue of Liberty and the Empire State Building. I came back home with this little Empire State Building souvenir. I kept that thing for years and years. When I graduated from college, it disappeared. The comparison between Tuskegee and New York was dramatic. I found that the Caucasian people in New York might not like you, but they had to work with you! And if you had the almighty dollar, you were OK. Going to New York broadened my perspective of what freedom could look like.

I have two brothers. While I was in New York one summer, I discovered that my mom had joined this church and met this old guy who had a son named Frankie. Frankie's mother had died, so my mother hooked up with Elliot and helped to raise Frankie. The next summer I was there, mom was sitting at the table drinking a Pabst Blue Ribbon beer and she said, "I'm pregnant." Anyway, so along comes Timothy.

Other than my mom sending us money, how did my grandma and

I survive? My grandmother had about six or seven sisters, and they all had hustling capabilities. I had a cousin whose mother worked on Tuskegee Institute's campus. She got her sister a job there. She tried to get my grandma a job there too, but Grandma couldn't pass muster. So, to survive, she started working with her sister's husband who was a bootlegger. We sold corn whiskey from the house on the corner where we lived. It had a big yard, and she built another room on the back of the house for her business. It was like a bar. So, at 4:35 in the afternoon, all those people that knew how to get there would get off work from the VA and other places and come around to Happy Hour at the room on the back of our house.

Roosevelt Lorenzo Williams and his maternal grandmother, Ethel Brown Mahone, who found creative ways to provide for her grandson. P. H. Polk Photography; courtesy of Roosevelt Lorenzo Williams.

Grandma would send me up the road to get Cokes. Damn! Coke at that time cost only six cents. The customers would get their corn whiskey in a little shot glass, or they would buy a pint and add the Coke. Grandma would charge ten cents for the Coke. Happy Hour went on until about six or six thirty in the evening.

Before the day of plastic bottles and plastic gallon containers, a certain person would back his car up into our backyard. In the trunk of this old car were glass gallon jugs of corn whiskey covered with old quilts. The jugs would be wrapped up individually to keep them from breaking in transit. It was my job to help take the jugs out of the trunk and bury them in the backyard. I had to mark where I planted each jug so I or somebody else could find them. And that was my job. I would mark them with plants or stakes and keep a chart so I would know where they were buried and how many there were.

We were raided many times. We knew Preston Hornsby, the Macon County sheriff, on a personal basis. There were one or two different houses down the street that were known to sell corn whiskey. Sometimes, we had time to pour that corn whiskey down the toilet before the law arrived.

My grandmother was a really good cook, and she knew how to can foods. Everybody knew how to preserve food during that time. My great-grandfather knew Dr. George Washington Carver. Dr. Carver showed him how to make potato beds to keep the potatoes fresh through the winter. My grandfather taught me what Dr. Carver taught him, and I became part of that Tuskegee tradition. So I knew what to do during the winter when my grandmother would tell me to go pull some potatoes out of the potato bed in the garden so she could cook them. I would go and put my hand into the cone-shaped potato bed made with corn stalks, pine straw, and dirt, and pull out those huge, sweet potatoes. Having gone to the George Washington Carver Museum and seen a sweet potato about the size of a bowling ball gives me enormous respect for what the man did with plants. Can you imagine a cabbage the size of a basketball or bigger? That's what Dr. Carver was able to do. He passed that knowledge on to those gardeners and farmers around Tuskegee.

When Dr. Carver was alive, he and his students used to come around in what was called the Jessup Truck. They would come up to a meeting place. A central location in our community was our own St. John AME Church. Farmers in the community would come up to meet Dr. Carver and the Jessup Truck in their wagons. After he died in 1943, the Jessup Truck still came. I remember that those students in the Jessup Truck wore safari type hats. They would be out there from the university, but they called it "the school."

Some of my family stayed in the South, and some left. Neither my great-grandfather, grandfather, or father considered leaving the South and going North. My great-grandfather and grandfather had land, and they loved living on the land. They were proud to be landowners. Landownership also gave them financial security because they could always sell some of it for cash or use it to get loans.

My dad, Roosevelt Williams, completed a second course on campus as an LPN and moved to Birmingham. He thought he was a big-time man moving to Birmingham. Well, he stayed up there for about two years, moved back home, and ended up working at the VA. As mentioned before, my mother, Rosa Pearl Brown, went to New York for work. She would come back to visit, but there would always be this sense of her needing to get back to work. I think the work was the driver for her staying in New York. I think she enjoyed the work and life in New York as well. Her work facilitated her being able to send money and things back to me and my grandmother.

My maternal grandmother stayed in the South because she was stuck. I use the word stuck because she did not have an education. She became a property owner, so she never considered leaving her little place and what she knew. Some people in my family left the South to seek their fortune and did well, but some people stayed and did well despite the racial situation.

My grandfather retired from the VA after thirty-five years, but he had kept and farmed his land during this time. His land abutted my great-grandfather's land, which made eighty acres in the family altogether. When my great-grandfather got sick, they were able to sell off a little of the property to pay expenses. I still have seven acres of the original land that my great-grandfather owned, five acres that my grandfather left me, and I have two acres with a house on it that my grand-aunt left me. I must hang on to all that land because it was part of the original land my family owned after slavery. It is my heritage.

When the Tuskegee Boycott started, my grandparents were not afraid, but they were reluctant to get involved. The turning point in their attitudes came when they had an experience with a White butcher. There was a grocery store in town called Taylor's, and we would still go to that grocery store on Saturday mornings because he gave us credit. The shell of the building is still standing. As the movement was happening with the

Gomillion v. Lightfoot gerrymandering case with Attorney Fred Gray, my grandfather and I kept a ritual. From elementary school to high school, every Saturday morning we would drive downtown and park in front of the old Citizen's Bank and go to a movie while my grandmother did her shopping.

My grandfather and I would go to the Macon County theater and catch the morning matinee with Wild Bill Hickok at the segregated theater. He and I would watch the movie, and it was always a cliffhanger at the end. That meant we had to come back the next week and find out what happened. Afterward, we would get our popcorn and go looking for my grandmother.

We would end up at the Jitney Jungle, a grocery store on the east end of town. I remember the smell of hotdogs and onions cooking when we walked in. Oh my God! My grandma would be there. She would gather up her things and walk back up the street with us to Taylor's grocery to buy meat. One day, as usual, she stood in front of the tall meat display counter. She gave the butcher her order, and he took it to the back of the store to weigh it. The counter was so tall that she could not see what the weight was, but she thought she detected that he was placing his hand on the scale to increase the weight. The next week she went up there again and observed him dipping his hand on the scale again. After that, they never went there anymore. My grandparents had continued to shop with him during the Tuskegee Boycott because he offered credit. He also offered credit to my maternal grandma. She had told me that if I were ever hungry, just go to Mr. Taylor and get what I wanted, and he would put it on the bill. But he was cheating all of them in the process.

This is all about how my maternal grandmother and I survived. Across the bridge in Tallassee was a meat market like the one in downtown Tuskegee. My grandma would drive the fifteen to twenty miles, cross the long bridge, and make a left turn into the back of the butcher shop. It was an expensive butcher shop because you could get fresh beef, pork, or chicken. If Black people wanted to buy meat there, they had to go around to the side or back. There were lots of affluent White people shopping there. The White people owned lots of various kinds of mills in Tallassee. Tallassee was a very segregated town and was known for its Ku Klux Klan activity.

Grandma had a big old black Buick. It was so big that if you popped the trunk, you could put two bodies in there. We would have what's called two "number two" wash tubs in the trunk. She knew the guy who slaughtered the animals. For the sake of this story, let's just call him Joe. Joe had that leather or plastic apron around his neck and wrapped around his waist. It was always covered with blood, and he always looked like a mess.

We would get out of the car and stand there and watch. Joe had a 22-caliber rifle, and the workers would catch a hog, and Joe would shoot him between the eyes. He would get his workers to hang the hog upside down with hooks by his back legs. The butcher had a knife and he'd be sharpening it with a stone. He would slit the hogs' throat so the blood could drain into a hole. Afterward, my grandma would have me get a tub from the trunk and push it under the pig's head as he hung in the air. The butcher would slice the pig's stomach open, and all those entrails would come out and fall into the tub. Joe would let some of his people help me put the tub back into the trunk. I would get the other tub. By the time we left, we had two number two tubs full of entrails. Sometime between putting the tubs in the car and taking the tubs out, a covered jug of corn whiskey changed hands.

As we drove home, the smell in the car would be tremendous. We had to drive back to Tuskegee with that smell. When we would get back to 509 Green Street, Grandma would back the Buick up into the yard, and then, we would struggle to get the tubs out of the trunk into the yard and get on to the main job. My job was to dig a hole, get the water hose, run water through the intestines, and clean the feces out. I would shake them up and down until I got them as clean as I could so they could be cooked into chitlins. When the men were drinking at Grandma's Happy Hour, they often liked to have chitlins with hot sauce with their corn whiskey.

I preferred to do that job of cleaning pig intestines on a Friday or Saturday because it would take a day for me to get the smell off me. When I went back to school on Monday, I did not want to smell like intestines. I would bathe in English Leather soap. One time, I was cleaning out everything in the tub and underneath all the chitlins was a whole ham. The butcher had stuck a ham underneath the intestines for my grandma. So that's how we survived, and we did that at least once a month and sometimes twice.

That was the story of what my grandmother did to raise me. She did that all the way up to when I got to the eighth grade. She stopped after we got raided once. The police threatened that if she did not stop the bootlegging, they were going to take me and put me in a foster home. We were doing fine until somebody snitched on us. So we stopped bootlegging, and my mother increased the amount of money and other things she was sending us.

I got my first job at Reid's Phillips 66 in the summer of my seventh or eighth grade year. Mr. Reid was a lawyer, and he had a service station right outside of Tuskegee's campus. He was the first Black Phillips 66 franchisee in the state of Alabama. Mr. Reid was a Korean War veteran. He had a bad leg and had worked that disability and GI bill into obtaining the money for the service station. Oh, to open that filling station and get that building in that location was something! The building is still there. It's a car wash now.

I had to be at work at seven in the morning. That was when the attendants pumped gas, so people did not have to get out of their cars. They would drive up on their way to the VA, other work, or to school. Mr. Reid lived up on the hill about a block away from me, and I'd be there early. Mr. Reid had an enormous influence on me. He instilled or reinforced a couple of work ethic values in me. He always talked to me about working hard and setting goals. He never once bragged about being the first Black Phillips 66 franchisee. I remembered that when I was in the position of being the first Black worker at Xerox and at Allstate Insurance in Texas to hold a certain position. You can be aware of the situation but be humble at the same time. During that time, being the first Black person to do something was seen as part of the movement.

I remember when Sammy got killed. I was in that march when students from the university marched downtown that night. It saddened me to know that workers at certain business establishments were die-hard Klan members. They weren't afraid to let you know it. I think the mass exodus of the Tuskegee White population after the movement took place because they were afraid there would be retribution for things they had done to Black people there in Tuskegee. Some things happened with the sheriff's department that never made the newspaper. Police brutality was a reality in and around Tuskegee. If a White cop stopped you, you might have gotten pistol whipped if you said the wrong thing or you might have had to spend some time in jail.

In 1964 at Tuskegee University, two years of ROTC (Reserve Officers Training Corps) was mandatory for male students. The ROTC is a group of military officer training programs for students. One benefit is college tuition. One of the things that I look back upon and feel proud of is my training in the Air Force ROTC. Cadets would assemble in the Alumni Bowl on the football field by group, squadron, and flight. We would hear the commanders in their very deep military voices yelling, "Squadron! Halt" My body would just freeze. It was an amazing experience!

Some of us ROTC students had shoeshine parties every Tuesday night in the dorm. ROTC was on Wednesday mornings. Tuesday night, we would sit in the dorm and study and "spit shine" our military shoes. There was a certain pride that we took in that. There was also a certain pride because that was our first exposure to establishing that we were part of the Tuskegee Airmen legacy. My professor of aerospace studies, Colonel Herbert Carter, was a Tuskegee Airman.[2] So, when my son and I went to the Airmen Museum at Moton Field in Tuskegee this last October, I showed him Colonel Carter and told him that Colonel Carter had been my aerospace professor. My son said, "So you are a second-generation Tuskegee Airman!" I said, "Yeah, and one of my claims to fame is that Colonel Carter was there for my graduating year jump in 1969. He had been made full colonel by then."

Unlike most of my classmates, I graduated in 1969 instead of 1968 because I was on the five-year plan. I worked to help cover the cost of my tuition and room and board. I worked in Tompkins Hall, our cafeteria, from eleven o'clock in the morning to seven o'clock at night, bussing and washing dishes and cleaning up. I went to class from eight to ten in the morning. My ROTC class was at seven Wednesday mornings anyway. The five-year plan was designed for students that needed to work on campus and still go to class. I was assigned Tompkins Hall. I had a cart, and once the cart was filled with dishes, I would roll it back to the kitchen to the dish room. I had a uniform called "whites." As I would drive the cart across the floor, my classmates would catcall things like, "Hey, man, you going too slow!"

To get on the five-year plan, one had to stay on campus. My grandma was still living. At ten o'clock, I would go downstairs and change into my whites and get ready to go to work. When I got off work at seven, I would gather up food and exit from the back of the hall, go past the band cottage, past Grey Columns, past a little arbor of bushes, and end up on Church Street where I would bring food to my grandmother—every night. She was beginning to get emphysema and all kinds of heart conditions.

She still had the big car, so I would go home on Fridays and Saturdays and stay home until Monday. I had a roommate on campus, and we would use the car. I followed this routine the two semesters of my freshman year. That summer I worked for the Tuskegee Institute Summer Education Program.

My grandmother started to get sick, and she was in and out of the Tuskegee City Hospital. During Christmas of 1965, instead of going home for Christmas, I worked in Dorothy Hall, our campus guesthouse, on the switchboard because nobody else wanted the job. I was still taking her food by walking home, or if she felt like it, she would come and get me.

In my junior year, I was inducted into the Air Force ROTC in the Air Force Reserve and had ID and all that. I had pledged a fraternity and had started hanging out with my friends. My visits home became less frequent. My friends would want to do this and that. I was still trying to go home to see about my grandma, but we were having a party over here. So, when she died in March 1966, I blamed myself a lot.

I was on my own. Tina was my first girlfriend on campus. When I asked her for help, she said, "I just don't do funerals real well." That was my girlfriend, and later, she became my wife. I walked out of Sage Hall and passed out. Like my father had made a promise to a man who had helped his friend, I promised to name my first daughter after the young lady who came along, revived me, and got me to the hospital. I kept my promise and named my first daughter Andrea.

I stayed in John Andrew Hospital a few days, and they diagnosed me as having had a nervous breakdown. The loss was too much for me. There's a special bond with grandmothers and grandchildren. I have an original Polk photo of me and my grandmother and me and my grandfather, the two most important people in my life.

When the students were attempting to take over the campus to protest some campus rules and Muhammad Ali came, students were saying, "Let's burn our draft cards." I said, "Yeah, yeah," but all I burned was a piece of paper. I was not burning my draft card because, upon my graduation, I was going to be commissioned a second lieutenant in the air force.

I had a chance to fly once with Chief C. Alfred Anderson, the chief flight instructor of the Tuskegee Airmen.[3] Unfortunately, because of my poor eyesight, I didn't go to pilot's school. I went to navigation school. Navigators sit in the third seat in the cockpit. Palmer Sullins and some of my other classmates had a chance to go to pilot school and have done well. I never got a chance to travel outside the United States during my military career. My daughter works for Delta Airlines and sometimes meets some of my pilot classmates.

After navigation training, I was transferred to Sheppard Air Force Base in Texas as the branch chief. I was the first and only Black branch chief in the 3750th Training Square, and they didn't let me forget it. I had a racist White colonel. Once a skunk got in the ventilation, and I closed the building. I told everybody to go home until the Air Force Air Base could come and clean it out. The colonel heard about it, and I am told that he said. "Well, there's more than one skunk down there."

He made no pretense of not being prejudiced. He could keep me from making my rank. Having grown up in the South, I knew what to expect. George Wallace never hid the fact that he was racist. It's just that Wallace wasn't writing my efficiency reports. I had about eighty people working for me, and my secretary would tell me, "You know the colonel was down here about six o'clock this morning." So, I'd be thinking, what is he doing snooping around at six in the morning? I dealt with it to the best of my ability.

My mistake was a decision that I made. I was a physical education major in college, and I would go to the gym and play basketball. The manager of the base basketball team saw me playing and asked me to try out for the team. I did and became the only officer on the team. A tournament was planned at Lackland Air Force Base in San Antonio, and each command was to send two to four teams. When they cut the orders, they always put the ranking man at the top in terms of identifying who's going on the trip. I found out I had made the travel team. I was like, wow,

I made the travel team. So I went to my colonel and said, "Colonel, I need to be off Friday. I will take a vacation day because we're going to San Antonio. We're going to play in the base tournament Friday, Saturday, and Sunday, and I'll be back to work on Monday." The colonel said, "What! The inspector general is coming in three weeks, and you are traipsing about?" I was like, "Just one day." He said, "Well, let me think about it."

This is where I put my foot in it. The commander of 3750 Technical Training Squad was my colonel's boss. He was also one of my golfing partners. So, I went over to the commander's office, and I said, "Commander, how are you? You know we used to play golf every other Wednesday." I wasn't good, but I was the only Black man out there. He said, "Come on in. What can I do for you?" I said, "Well, I made the base travel basketball team, and we're going to go down to represent our base in San Antonio." He said, "Really? That's wonderful. That's wonderful." I can see him now. I said, "The coach has already cut the orders, and I talked to my boss, and he told me he'd think about it. I need to know because they are leaving on Friday." He picked up the phone and said to my boss, "Hey, this is the Commander. How are you doing? Hey, man, I talked to Williams, and he's been nominated to represent the base on this traveling team. He said he needs just one day off. No, this shouldn't be a problem. Right. Alright, OK, alright. Talk to you later. Hey, have a good one. Alright, bye bye." He looked at me and said, "He said OK, go ahead."

I went. When I got to work on Monday, they told me the colonel wanted to see me. He threatened me with a "fifteen," that's a transfer to a border nation. It's the air force's disciplinary tool. In these situations, you must persevere and overcome. I could have gone on and done the twenty-year career. I said no. I can't let this colonel determine my next level because, with the efficiency reports he was writing, he was telling me if I made it to the rank of major, it was going to be the best I could do. People were saying I was so good, but I needed the colonel to write that in the efficiency reports. At that point, I didn't have the stamina to persevere, so I got out of the air force.

Getting out of the air force made me strive. I learned where the rocks in the river were. I became the first Black worker at Xerox in Wichita Falls, Texas. I worked out of the Fort Worth branch and sold copy machines. My teaching skills allowed me to develop into a pretty good salesperson. I worked there until it was not financially rewarding. I left Xerox and went to work for several other companies. The outcome is that the jobs were not what I liked, but I still have the personal and professional relationships I developed over the years.

To my kids, Andrea, Michael, and Amber, I hope I have instilled in them the desire to be good at what they do. I want them to know that sometimes in jobs you must make your supervisor think it's their idea. I want them to remember to be persuasive if they are going for something. I want them to be able to show their personality. My oldest, Andrea, just achieved the Chairman's Award at Delta Airlines. She is a fifteen-year flight attendant. I was there when she got her award, and she didn't know I was going to be there.

My son, Michael, did military tours in Afghanistan, Alaska, and Germany. Since Andrea works for Delta, I visited him in Germany and stayed a week while he was waiting for his first child to be born. He lives in Mineola, Texas. He walks and raises money for veterans. Recently, I walked with him across the Edmund Pettus Bridge. Amber is the youngest. She is a great mom of three children, and she is very smart. She just sent me pictures of the grandkids, whom I need to see more often.

I am now back in Alabama. I think I moved back to Alabama because of my roots. I think of my grandmother, my grandfather, and my mom. I very easily could have gone to Alabama State in Montgomery because I was accepted there, but I couldn't leave my grandmother. Her house is long gone, but I still own that little acre of land up there. And at some point, maybe one of the grandkids might put up a trailer or a house on it. Those roots are there.

I came back because I thought I had some unfinished business. So, in 2004, I commented aloud that I wanted to go back home. Nobody was dying, and there was no emergency. I ended up getting divorced and moving back here to Tuskegee. I am now married to Marian, one of my high school classmates.

One day, I ran into Dr. Frank Leftwich who was my professor in physical education at Tuskegee and the head of the Physical Education Department. He offered me a job teaching golf on campus. Between 2008 and 2017, I taught beginning golf classes at Tuskegee University to 1,900 freshmen. Administrators used to look out the windows of the

Kellogg Administration Building where the president's office is into the valley and see the hole I talked the Buildings and Grounds Department into building for me. I loved teaching the kids and being back on campus. I had come home to the South and finished some unfinished business.

The decision to stay in the South for a lot of people was to fight for their hometown. They had to do something to make it better. Therefore, the heroes and the sheroes of that time stayed to make things better. And it did get better over time. However, sometimes making things better comes at a cost.

For Tuskegee, freedom and justice have come at a major cost—the loss of a thriving town and of jobs. The Alabama State Legislature has vetoed and strangled many advancements for the Tuskegee area. The train station is gone. The bus station is gone. A major part of the airport is gone. The campus hospital is gone. Under the cloak of law, state officials are still trying to shut down what is left of the Veterans Administration Hospital. They have already moved much of it to Montgomery. The relationship between Tuskegee University and the city has deteriorated, and that's partly our fault because of some unscrupulous people, both Black and White.

Through it all, I am hopeful that things will get better for my hometown.

IV

ANCESTORS AND NARRATORS

Frontlines of the Civil Rights Generation

CHAPTER 18

Gerald W. Billes

Editors' Note: Gerald W. Billes's father brought his family to Tuskegee from Louisiana thinking he already had a job at the Veterans Administration Hospital, only to discover that other people were competing for that same job as well. He did get the job, and his family immediately joined in the civil rights activities in Tuskegee. His father had high expectations for his children and all Black people. His family became one of the plaintiffs in the famous *Lee v. Macon Board of Education*, as Gerald's sister was one of the twelve students selected to integrate the White Tuskegee High School. While Gerald has high praise for the high expectations and academic and social environment in which he was raised, he seems to have a lesser level of enthusiasm for the planned integration of schools in Tuskegee at that time. Gerald also explores the effects skin color often had on his family.

My sister, Heloise, Chip was her nickname, was walking to a school bus stop in Tuskegee, Alabama, in the winter of 1963 when a carful of White people pulled alongside her and yelled, "Why are you going to school with them n****rs?" As a young high school teenager, she was speechless, frightened, and deeply disturbed. Chip is a light-skinned Black woman who has often been mistaken for a White person. At the time of the incident, she was one of the twelve Black students in the *Lee v. Macon County Board of Education* desegregation case who were briefly attending the all-White Tuskegee High School in downtown Tuskegee.

Our life stories are not just our own; they are also the stories of our families and the world around us that shaped us.

I was born in Alexandria, Louisiana, in 1946, just a year before my family moved to Tuskegee. Before moving to Tuskegee, my dad coached football with Eddie Robinson and taught academic courses at Grambling University. While at Grambling, Dad received a call from an army friend who asked if he wanted a job with the Veterans Administration Hospital in Tuskegee. Assuming he was already hired and that he would be making twice the money at this proposed new position, we moved to Tuskegee.

Upon arrival, Dad soon discovered that the job was a coveted position there, and he would need to compete with other qualified applicants. After an interview process, Dad was appointed the canteen director at the Tuskegee Veterans Administration Hospital.

My parents had four children, each born two years apart. My older brother was Ronald. I was the middle child, then came my sister, Heloise. My younger brother, Lynn, passed away not long after birth.

Gerald W. Billes's parents, Eugenia and I. V. Billes, moved to Tuskegee for professional opportunities and became leaders in the local Civil Rights Movement. Courtesy of Gerald W. Billes.

From the time my parents moved to Tuskegee, Dad spent his life working for the VA Hospital system. He went through a hospital directorship training program in Birmingham, Alabama, along with several other upper management Black people from the hospital. This training program and his experience at Tuskegee led to my father later being appointed VA hospital director in other cities. He finally retired from his sixth hospital as a consultant in the New Orleans VA Hospital system where he and Mom could live closer to me; my wife, Frances; and my son, Hite.

My entire childhood was spent in Tuskegee from my first year to my eighteenth birthday. My initial grammar school years were at the St. Joseph Catholic School. After discussions with my parents about my unhappiness there, they sent me to Chambliss Children's House from third grade through eighth grade. I made many friends there and still communicate with many of them today.

The years I spent in Tuskegee were some of the most enlightening and enjoyable times of my life. Tuskegee was one of the most active, educated, and vibrant Black communities in the country. My parents were insistent on each of us getting a college education and prepared for that time by buying US savings bonds that would mature about the time we were ready for college. Honestly, I didn't think we had a choice about college. All of us were going to college. That was a given as the following incident demonstrates.

I remember when my brother was attending Case University in Cleveland, Ohio. Case was an all-men's college. My brother said he had a miserable social life there. One day before the fall semester of his junior year began, my dad walked through the room where we were sitting and asked Ron when he was due back at Case. My brother emphatically said to Dad that he was not going back there. My dad stopped walking, turned to Ron, and asked, "What did you say?" Ron repeated his earlier statement. Dad said, "If you don't go back to college, you won't be here in this house." Dad took out his telephone ledger and immediately began to call other colleges. He knew the president of Fisk University, called him that night, and shipped Ron off to Fisk the following week. That was a dramatic moment for me. As my older brother, Ron set an example of what to do and what not to do at the same time. I'm certain Dad would have put Ron out of the house if he had resisted going wherever my dad set up for him. For my dad, education was imperative, especially a college education. As it turned out, Ron loved Fisk and the time he spent there.

My parents played an active role in the desegregation movement in Tuskegee, where Mom and Dad registered to vote and helped many other Black professionals register before White people shut down Black registration almost entirely. For White men and women, at that time, the only requirement was to show some form of identification to become registered. Initially, voter registration was the same for Black people. However, when White people thought too many Black people were registering and they might lose power, Black people were required to take a test to become registered to vote. Many White individuals in Tuskegee were illiterate but were not required to take a test. This racist approach to voting rights ensured that White voters in Tuskegee and Macon County remained the highest numbers of voters although the population percentages told a different story.

To further the cause of racial justice, my parents volunteered my sister, Heloise, to participate in the attempt to integrate the all-White Tuskegee High School downtown, even though it was inferior to the all-Black Tuskegee Institute High School at that time. Along with eleven other Black students from Tuskegee Institute High, Chip became a litigant in *Lee v. Macon County Board of Education*. My sister has since explained that she did not think she had a choice in the matter.

In my opinion, these students were guinea pigs in this integration experiment. My parents encouraged me to help integrate the high school as well, but I rebelled against doing it. I was in my senior year in high school, and the writing on the wall was telling me this would be a disaster for me. I could not afford to waste a year in this arena and miss going to the college of my choice. My parents agreed and turned to Heloise to represent the Billes family in the legal struggle to integrate all Alabama schools. I feared for my sister's well-being. Since the students were known by name, White people knew the addresses of each family participating in the integration movement. The KKK was prevalent in Macon County at the time, so parents and volunteers, mainly men, monitored activity around the homes of participating families.

Heloise was only a sophomore at the time and could potentially waste a year and recover from her poor learning environment. She later told me that she found herself in the middle of the worst school year of her life. My parents thought that she had a strong constitution and could integrate these less proficient high schools in Tuskegee to prove a point that White children should go to school with Black children. What a joke. The White people burned the school building in Notasulga, where my sister and other Black people were attending.

What this proved to those who were trying to make the best of this ignorance is that White people would cut off their noses not to go to school with more intelligent Black people due to their pervasive prejudice. The image of White people in that area of Alabama at that time sticks in my mind as some of the most ignorant and backward-thinking people on the planet. I did not know this was true not only in Tuskegee but in many other places in this country.

My parents kept us engaged with their full support through high school. Once we left for college, their support was primarily financial and verbal encouragement over the phone. In my parents' minds, their goal was for each of us to pursue our dreams and lead successful and independent adult lives.

Because of the segregation, there were Black people from all around the country living in Tuskegee, which drove this small middle-class community to thrive. The university attracted students, staff, and professors from many other states and foreign countries. It was an enlightening time for me and many other Black people who lived and thrived in Tuskegee.

My family lived in what might be considered today a "project" for lower-income families. In this case, the apartments were occupied by working-class individuals. I would not have ever thought we were poor due to our lifestyle where we wanted for nothing. We always had plenty to eat, took vacations, went to very good schools, and always had a roof over our heads and clothes on our backs. Since Mom was a seamstress, she made our clothes that fit very nicely.

I found Tuskegee one of the most vibrant places I could imagine growing up. We had friends and immediate family who took good care of the three of us children in every possible way. My parents were smart, directed, and goal driven and believed in education as well as perfection.

By all accounts, the VA Hospital, John A. Andrew Hospital, and

Tuskegee Institute, Tuskegee University now, hosted some of the most elite of the Black population at that time. If you were a Black doctor and wanted to work for the VA Hospital system, you were required to work in Tuskegee. If you aspired to higher education, you could attend Tuskegee University, a well-established HBCU, for college.

Tuskegee was a community of educated Black people, a lot more educated than the mostly agrarian or blue-collar White people at the time. Don't get me wrong; many in my family are contractors and auto mechanics, so I have nothing against the trades. My comment was to establish that in Tuskegee it was Black people who had a higher education level than most White people. The Tuskegee community was a kind of mecca for Black, educated, family-oriented people. As I learned after my college life, Tuskegee represented an anomaly not the rule in our country.

Dad attended Southern University in Baton Rouge where he met my mom, Eugenia Cook, and married her before going off to World War II. He was an overachiever and had two different scholarships at Southern University, one for academics and one for athletics (football in particular). He once told me that his friends called him "Red" in college. His Southern University football team were champions each year he played, so you can find his name in the Southern University Hall of Fame.

Dad brought that winning attitude to our Greenwood Little League baseball team in Tuskegee where he was coach along with my mom, his assistant coach. Our team practiced each day after school on the Tuskegee Institute High School playground. The regular practice sessions helped to form the best baseball team in the Tuskegee Little League system at that time. I had a strong arm, so I played third base, pitcher, and catcher depending on which teammates came to the game. Until he graduated from Little League, my brother played third base as well. My sister played for a short time until the other teams complained that she was a girl and was prohibited from playing in a season game. She had gotten so proficient that no other team wanted to allow her to play. We all enjoyed sports and were good at almost anything we tried to play. Our baseball team was not permitted to play the White teams because we would have shown them up by beating their socks off, LOL!

My family was a baseball and tennis family while in Tuskegee. After my baseball years with Dad and Mom as coaches, I decided to play tennis. Ron and I learned tennis from Dr. Kenney, the director of John A. Andrew Hospital, but my coach was "Slick" Holland. I started our high school tennis team by inviting Slick to be our team coach. We played on the Tuskegee Institute tennis courts. The courts were red clay like the French Open, and I watered and rolled them each week to help ensure their playing maintenance and proficiency. I remember spending all day during the summer months on those courts as I practiced and became more proficient at the game. By the end of my first summer playing tennis, the sun had darkened my skin color. That same summer, I began playing in tournaments. After high school, I played on the Tulane tennis team, although I had to make a choice for architecture or tennis. Although I continued to play tennis socially, I chose to become a professional architect due to the conflicting time the tennis team practiced and the time my architecture design studio met.

My dad had no knowledge of tennis, but both Mom and Dad supported our tennis careers. All three of us played and won tournaments in Alabama and other parts of the country under the ATA (American Tennis Association), a predominately Black organization, since the USLTA (United States Lawn Tennis Association) did not allow Black people to play tennis with them at the time.

Tennis has taken many turns over the past fifty years. At the time I played in a tennis tournament in Greensboro, North Carolina, Arthur Ashe was prominent. Arthur played an exhibition match while the tournament was underway. Ashe had broken the race barrier, and finally, tennis players were allowed to play in White run tournaments. Still, I remember White and "Colored" water fountains and facilities that reminded us that we were to be separate because we were seen as different and less than.

As a family and like most families living in Tuskegee at the time, we were isolated from the racial strife facing Black communities in most of the South. Although my nuclear family members are light-skinned Black people, we experienced discrimination like my friends and other family members when we traveled outside of Tuskegee for our sports. My mom looked White along with her entire family. My dad had brown skin with green eyes like all the children from the mix of his mom, who looked like a dark-skinned Black woman, and his dad, who looked White. Dad's mom had African and Native American ancestry, and Dad's dad was from French heritage. Whenever I visited my grandparents, I saw the rainbow of colors of skin show up at the family reunions.

Gerald W. Billes's paternal grandparents, Eva Brew Billes and Theodore "T. O." Billes *(back row, center)* with three generations of the Billes Family. Courtesy of Gerald W. Billes.

Dad had issues with the lack of initiative whenever he experienced the Black community not emphasizing education. Both my parents were relentless about our grades, which had to be perfect, and our speech had to be meticulous. My parents believed that we had to be better than any White person to be successful. Besides the credentials needed behind our names, they insisted we read about many subjects. I remember my dad purchasing a set of encyclopedias and instructing me to start at the As and go through the many volumes to Z. I made it through to the Ss, but by that time, I left home to go to college.

We were taught to be respectful to everyone. My parents never let us forget our goals or our dreams for a better future for all Black people. My dad believed that each of us had a responsibility to leave the world a better place than when we came into it. At the time, I sometimes ignored the many lessons my parents tried to teach us, and yet, I still remember and use their teachings to this day now that I am an adult. As my parents met at Southern University in Baton Rouge, they encouraged me to teach architecture at Southern, which I did for about seven years on a part-time basis. Teaching was one way of giving back as an acknowledgment to my parent's alma mater while sharing my knowledge with architecture students to become more successful.

Skin color mattered too much then in this country and still matters too much to this day. One of my first memorable experiences with racism was when I went to get my driver's license in Tuskegee. Perhaps it was not racism, but an identification of who you are based on the color of your skin. I passed the driver's test, so the White man filling out the paperwork looked at my mom and placed a W (White) beside my name, then looked at me, scratched it out, and placed an N (Negro) next to my name on the certificates. Why is this important I was thinking at the time. We left the drivers' testing area and walked to our car. I noticed for the first time in my life that White people were staring at me and my mom. She discounted those looks by saying that they do not usually see such a good-looking boy as me. Nice try, Mom, but I did not believe her even at that time. I had gotten a lot of sun that summer, and my skin was much browner than usual. My mom and I looked like a White woman walking with a "Negro" boy at the time. All I could do was smile.

On two other specific occasions, I realized that Black people were treated differently from White people in our country. Once we traveled to New Orleans from Tuskegee and stopped at a fast-food place to get a hamburger to eat along the way. The manager of the restaurant came out to our car to tell us we could not stay there to eat the sandwiches we had just ordered. My dad was upset, and my sister was so upset that she could not eat her burger. I was hungry, so I asked my sister if she did not mind me eating her burger if she did not want it.

I thought even at that time that there was no excuse for ignorance or racism, but it existed, so we had to deal with it. My sister was sensitive to such things, but I thought to myself that these people must change over time. If I got upset with every stupid act anyone made, I would be upset all the time.

Another incident that left an impression on me occurred when we were traveling to California. This was a three-day drive across the country, so we had to stay overnight. My grandfather went with our immediate family. My dad did a lot of the driving, so when he was tired and wanted to stay the night, he asked my mom and his dad, who both looked White, to get a hotel room to stay the night. To me, this was an indication that the color of your skin mattered in this country. All I could think was how good it would be when these prejudicial and discriminatory practices changed.

A young Gerald W. Billes (*far right*) with mother, siblings, and his paternal grandfather, Theodore "T. O." Billes, on a family trip to California. Courtesy of Gerald W. Billes.

My father, I. V. Billes, began his management career in Tuskegee. After seventeen years, Dad planned our family's exit from Tuskegee after my high school graduation by packing the car with necessities, dropping me off in New Orleans on Tulane University's campus where I lived in the dormitory, and continuing their drive to Butler, Pennsylvania, where he served his first term in an all-White hospital as its assistant director.

In 1964, I was the first Black student to attend the Tulane University School of Architecture and the first Black graduate from the School of Architecture. Two-thirds of my freshman class did not graduate due to the rigor of the coursework. This was my first encounter with both talented and intelligent White people. From my experience in Tuskegee, I was under the impression that Black people were the more intelligent and talented humans of our species and that most White people were ignorant, uneducated racists. Although things are still difficult racially in our country based on the current national and state political climate, my Tulane experience taught me that those percentages might have been a little off.

I knew I was integrating Tulane University in 1964 and needed to be the best in my class. I ranked number one in my finishing class in architecture. I applied and attended MIT's Graduate School of Architecture in Urban Design and completed these courses at the top of my class. I was the product of Tuskegee Institute High School and that meant something to me.

I am one of the few architects with licenses in architecture, interior design, planning, and construction. I credit Tuskegee for giving me the excellent early beginnings of my education, which have contributed to any success I have achieved professionally.

One important thing I remember my dad telling me was that I had to be better, more educated, and maintain more licenses than my White counterparts; otherwise, I would never be respected. Respect was his mantra and mine now. Everyone will not like you, but they will respect you for your knowledge. To hear this from my dad meant a lot since he was my mentor.

Tuskegee was a place of friendship, a place where a Black person was respected for his talents and not taken for granted. Many Black people of high standards lived and thrived in Tuskegee. The Tuskegee Airmen were another group of upwardly mobile Black people who had fought in World War II with honor. I asked my parents about this elite group of pilots. My dad knew one of them, but I did not get to know the history of the airmen except through my friend and classmate Colonel Palmer Sullins, who is considered to be a second-generation Tuskegee Airman. I would like to fly a plane and feel honored to have had such a distinguished group of men and women representing Tuskegee so capably.

Skin color means too much in our society. My view of White and Black people was somewhat distorted due to my upbringing in Tuskegee. When I began my college life at Tulane University in New Orleans, I had expected a lot of the same experiences I had in Tuskegee. My world was turned upside down there. I soon learned that there are smart Black people and there are smart White people. There are ignorant White people and ignorant Black people.

My life now is such a product of my experiences in Tuskegee, building on what I now know is atypical. When someone asks me about where I grew up, they ask because they don't pick up an accent or sign of a location where my English was learned or spoken. Almost everyone knows about Tuskegee University and the Tuskegee Airmen. Few people know about the VA Hospital or the other hospitals that trained many Black doctors, nurses, and administrators. I appreciate my time in Tuskegee. The lessons I learned about education and family life should be shared with the world.

Each of us has a relevant story to tell about our childhood and the many experiences we each had growing up. Hopefully, these stories will be appreciated and act as catalysts to keep the United States moving toward a more democratic society. This task must be taken on by people of all races, creeds, and colors.

Then, there will never again be the need for a carful of White people to yell, "Why are you going to school with them n****rs?" *to anyone.*

CHAPTER 19

ANTHONY T. LEE

Editors' Note: The headstone for Detroit Lee, Anthony T. Lee's father, reads "Trailblazer" for his incessant work fighting Jim Crow in the South during the 1940s, '50s, and '60s. Unable to acquire his own yearned-for law degree due to time and economic circumstances, Detroit Lee used every opportunity to file lawsuits against discriminatory activity in Tuskegee. He wanted his sons and daughter to have an equally excellent education, not a separate education, thus lending his son, narrator Anthony to be the lead plaintiff in *Lee v. Macon County Board of Education*.

Anthony gives us an inside view of a family whose existence seemed to be built for resisting and protesting injustice against Black people in the South. Anthony writes about family time, the effects of his and his father's resistance on his mother, family time around the breakfast table, and the family's decision to lead one of the most consequential legal protests for human rights and dignity in the South.

Imagine a sixteen-year-old, having the courage to say, "Send me. I will go to defend freedom and justice." That was Anthony.

SOMETIMES I CANNOT BELIEVE THE life I have lived. At seventy-nine, I feel I have lived several lives fully. With God's guidance, I am blessed to have enjoyed them all. While I still have much life to live and plans to bring to fruition, I have been asked on numerous occasions by family, friends, and those I have tried to help along the way how I want to be remembered. With humility, I would like for people to remember that there was a job to be done, and by happenstance, I got the opportunity to do it. I stepped up to the plate and did the job to the best of my ability. It was a job that I loved doing and was happy to do.

As a teenager in 1963, I, Anthony T. Lee, was one of the main plaintiffs in the case that eventually desegregated all schools in Alabama. The case was *Anthony T. Lee and Henry A. Lee, by Detroit Lee and Hattie M. Lee, their parents, and next friends, et al., Plaintiffs, United States of America, Plaintiffs and Amicus Curiae v. Macon County Board of Education et al., Defendants.*[1]

My mother, Hattie M. Lee, came from the Greensboro area in Hale County, Alabama. She was the youngest of nine children. As she was the baby and her mother had died in childbirth, her brothers and sisters were very protective of her. They would not allow her to do domestic work outside of the home. Nearly all my mother's sisters and brothers stayed in the South, probably to be near each other. My mother's major aspiration in life was to have a family and take care of her children and husband. She loved taking care of us, her home, and other children in the neighborhood as well. She was a beautiful part of the equation that kept us loved, fed, clean, safe, and emotionally healthy. She made it possible for the other side of the equation, my father, Detroit Lee, to go out into the world, stare systemic racist practices in the face, and use the legal system to tear them down.

My father's parents and siblings were all born in Texas. Most stayed in Texas, but some migrated North, specifically to Chicago. From an early age, my father loved to read, and he was a good student. As a teen, he read Booker T. Washington's *Up from Slavery*. He read where Washington said that if you made it to Tuskegee, you would be given an education.[2] My father wanted an education more than anything, so in his teens, he hopped a train from his home in Texas and made his way to Tuskegee. When he arrived in Tuskegee, he worked for a while with the Civilian Conservation Corps, one of the programs President Franklin Delano Roosevelt used to put people back to work and improve the country during the Depression. My parents were married around 1940. My father was twenty-one and my mother was about four years younger.

My father went into the US Army and qualified for various veterans' benefits. My parents eventually had five children. I was born in the hospital at the Tuskegee Airmen Air Base. Being in the military and trying to go to school at the same time was a bit much for my dad. With five children to feed and not much time for study, he began to put more focus on trying to provide the best possible education for his children. My older brother was one of the first Black children in Macon County to go to the previously all-White St. Joseph Catholic School. After he started there, all of us went to St. Joseph. When I was in the sixth grade, my sister Mary was graduating from St. Joseph and going on to Tuskegee Institute High School. At that point, my father enrolled my younger brother and me in Children's House, Tuskegee University's laboratory school at the time, which was an elementary and junior high school mostly for the children of Tuskegee University's faculty and staff.

Along with education, my dad loved the law. His dream was to be a lawyer. In those days, there were people called reading lawyers. One could work in a law office for a long time and read and study and become a lawyer. He did that for a while but never was able to reach his goal of becoming a lawyer. One of his greatest thrills in life was traveling to New Orleans to see Thurgood Marshall in action. He was impressed with Mr. Marshall's skills and the fact that he had all those big books. My father talked about that experience forever.

My father was always reading and studying the law. He was one of the first Black veterans in Macon County to be able to use the GI Bill to buy a home. Fighting injustice was the name of the "struggle" for him. He read and read and petitioned and petitioned injustices until he won. He also helped many Black people secure their Social Security benefits. Many of them did not know how to fill out the mountains of paperwork and follow up with the various queries from government officials. Because of his being well-read and being able to understand legal issues easily, he was a great help to many people in the community.

My dad worked for the Veterans Administration Hospital in Tuskegee for twelve years but was eventually fired. He was accused of violating the Hatch Act by running for probate judge of Macon County, a seat that had never been held by a Black person.[3] While he narrowly lost the race, he paved the way for other Black people to win in the future, as the office has not been held by a White person since his narrow loss. The Hatch Act, passed in 1939, restricts certain partisan political activities of federal employees. Sometimes my father's political activism had consequences for the family. The VA job was a very good job with very good benefits. My father knew what he was doing when he ran for probate judge. After being fired, he was undeterred in his social justice work, and he subsequently took other jobs such as owning and driving taxi cabs to take care of his family.

Despite being deep in the struggle and having threats to our lives, my parents never considered leaving the South. Once my father made it to Tuskegee, he committed himself to improving the situation for Black people in any way that he could. He believed in improving conditions for family and Black people where he was. My mother's close-knit family was in the area, and she would never have considered leaving them. She held our family together at home while my father was making his mark in the world. Although he was not able to get his law degree and at times it was difficult economically for the family, my parents were where they wanted to be and doing what they wanted to do. They fought injustice in the South wherever and whenever they could.

My father received much community support for his various civil rights actions, and he supported others in their fight against injustice. We recently found letters that he wrote to the NAACP in the early 1940s requesting assistance in establishing a chapter in Tuskegee. Many people still remember his work with the NAACP. He was also an active member of the Tuskegee Civic Association (TCA). He was a deacon at Mount Olive Baptist church and was a Freemason. He always kept his eye out for social justice inequities and continuously brought them to the attention of political officials or initiated lawsuits until the day he died. As a matter of fact, when he died, he had an active case against the VA Hospital for injustice. His tombstone at Fort Mitchell reads, "Trailblazer." And that is what he was!

While growing up in Tuskegee, I did not experience the direct personal day-to-day injustices and slights that others living in smaller towns in Alabama might have experienced. I was one of the younger children in the family, and my parents and older siblings were very protective of the youngest two of us. Rarely did we go out alone into situations that might have been dangerous. I remember one of my older brothers having a negative experience at the local segregated Dairy Queen, but my father quickly took care of that situation.

Tuskegee Institute, Alabama
P. O. Box 517,
August 25, 1944.

Miss Ella J. Baker
Director of Branches, NAACP,
69 5th Ave., New York, 3 N. Y.

Dear Madam:

Having had a very successful meeting of interested people in a local chapter of the N.A.A.C.P, I am requesting the necessary blanks and organization material.

The enthusiasm is very high. We have set our next meeting for next Thursday, August 31, 1944. At which time we hope to set up our local organization as suggested by your organization booklet. Therefore, please send this material by return Air Mail.

Very truly yours,

Detroit Lee
Local Organizer.

A letter from Detroit Lee, Anthony Lee's civil rights activist father, to Ella Baker, then national director of NAACP branches, seeking permission to start an NAACP chapter in Tuskegee, dated August 25, 1944. Courtesy of the Anthony Lee Family.

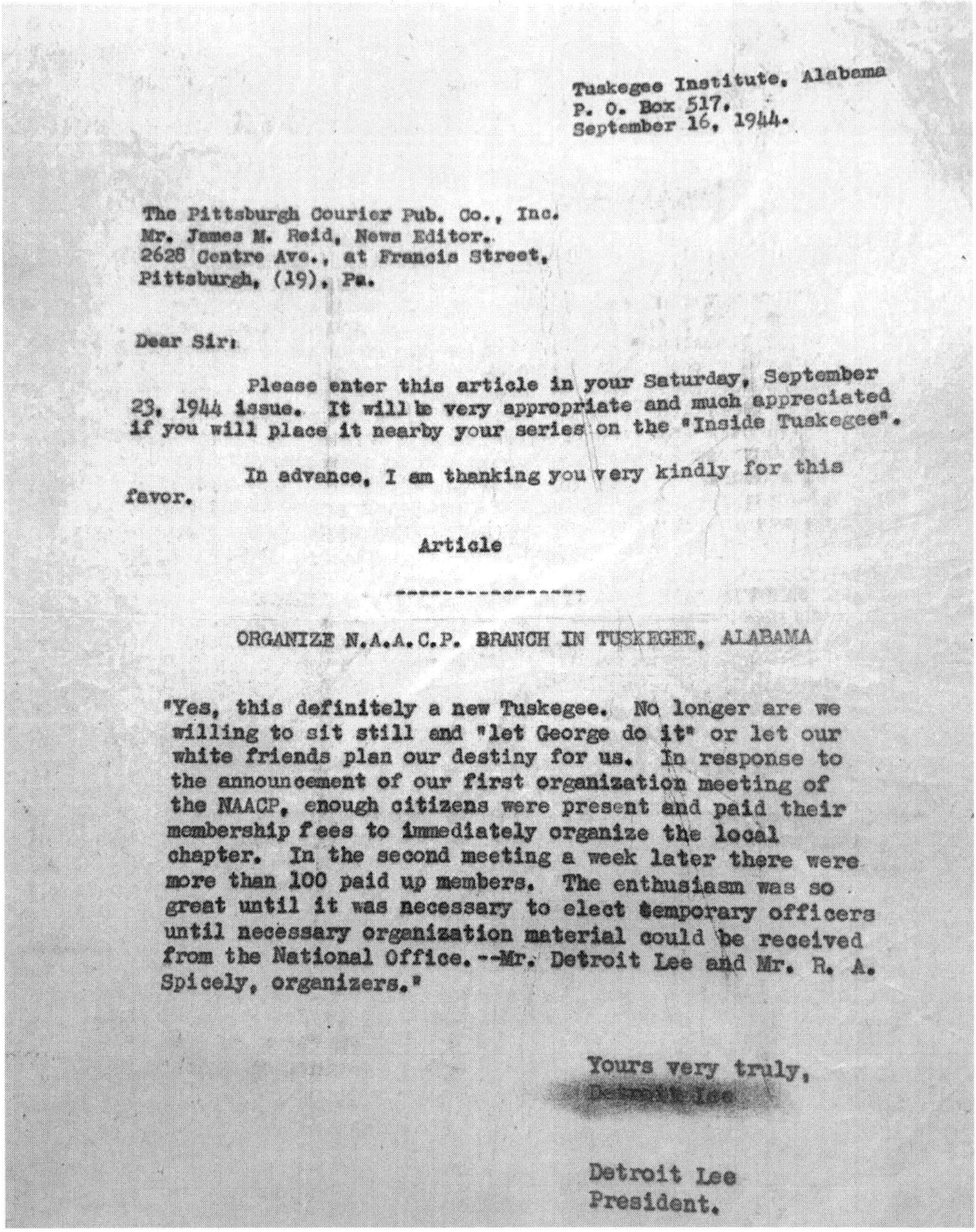

Tuskegee Institute, Alabama
P. O. Box 517,
September 16, 1944.

The Pittsburgh Courier Pub. Co., Inc.
Mr. James M. Reid, News Editor.
2628 Centre Ave., at Francis Street,
Pittsburgh, (19), Pa.

Dear Sir:

Please enter this article in your Saturday, September 23, 1944 issue. It will be very appropriate and much appreciated if you will place it nearby your series on the "Inside Tuskegee".

In advance, I am thanking you very kindly for this favor.

Article

ORGANIZE N.A.A.C.P. BRANCH IN TUSKEGEE, ALABAMA

"Yes, this definitely a new Tuskegee. No longer are we willing to sit still and "let George do it" or let our white friends plan our destiny for us. In response to the announcement of our first organization meeting of the NAACP, enough citizens were present and paid their membership fees to immediately organize the local chapter. In the second meeting a week later there were more than 100 paid up members. The enthusiasm was so great until it was necessary to elect temporary officers until necessary organization material could be received from the National Office.--Mr. Detroit Lee and Mr. R. A. Spicely, organizers."

Yours very truly,

Detroit Lee
President.

A letter from Detroit Lee to the *Pittsburgh Courier* announcing the formation of the local Tuskegee NAACP Chapter, dated September 16, 1944. Courtesy of the Anthony Lee Family.

Growing up, I went to a Black church and a Black school and had jobs in Black businesses as a teenager. Although we were aware of the systemic racism of separate educational, eating, and recreational facilities, we were kept from most of the everyday indignities. The Black community in Tuskegee created its own community with its own churches, social clubs, and employment opportunities. Even at the Black VA, there was a movie theater and sports facilities. Black teenagers were given after-school jobs in some of the Black businesses that thrived in Tuskegee.

Many of us were introduced to the fight for racial justice early on. My friend Willie B. Wyatt and I started early trying to break down some of the systemic racial barriers. We were in our middle teens when we tried to integrate some of the White churches in Tuskegee. Of course, they closed the doors in our faces. We were accompanied by our fathers for protection during these early escapades into protesting prejudice and discrimination in Alabama.

My family set the stage for my ideas about social justice and civil rights. My mother cooked every day, and every day, everyone sat at the kitchen table and ate breakfast. We were required to read the newspaper daily. At breakfast, after one said his or her Bible verse, they had to discuss a current event that they had read about in the newspaper! Every day! I remember being seven or eight and raising my hand in the air after my Bible verse and saying loudly, "I like Ike!" sometime during Eisenhower's 1953 campaign for president! I always really enjoyed that time with my family. At that breakfast table, I also learned about my parents' values of social justice. It was bred into all of us to help our family, the Black community, and others in society. Being committed to God's role in our lives, fighting for social justice, and getting along with others were my family's basic values.

My father wanted to start his school desegregation lawsuits against Macon County and the state of Alabama with my older brother as a plaintiff and Mr. Gray as the attorney earlier than it happened. He went to Mr. Gray continuously over a period of years. Unfortunately, the timing was not right because he was already handling the *Gomillion v. Lightfoot* case, the major gerrymandering voting rights case in Tuskegee. He knew there would be a conflict, and he really did not have the time to handle two major civil rights cases at the same time. My parents were also plaintiffs in the *Gomillion v. Lightfoot case*.[4]

Daddy was a pusher when it came to civil rights. He did not take no for an answer. He thought of asking another lawyer to take the school desegregation case because he was impatient. When he wanted something done, he wanted it done then. Gray made a deal with my father that after he finished with *Gomillion v. Lightfoot*, he would take his case. After he won the *Gomillion v. Lightfoot* case in the US Supreme Court, that's exactly what happened. He took my father's case.

In 1963, Mr. Gray filed the following case: *Anthony T. Lee and Henry A. Lee, by Detroit Lee and Hattie M. Lee, their parents, and next friends, et al., Plaintiffs, United States of America, Plaintiff and Amicus Curiae v. Macon County Board of Education et al., Defendants.* I was ready! When it happened, I was ready! I wanted to be a part of this social action! I would have been very disappointed had I not been chosen. In the past when the NAACP planned these kinds of legal actions, the leaders would want to put what they considered their best foot forward by selecting the strongest representatives. In this case, the leaders wanted to select the students who were academically the strongest. There were discussions about who would be the best candidates to ensure success of the action. There was a bit of a vetting process by either the NAACP and/or the TCA. In the end, students were selected because their parents were committed to the Civil Rights Movement and were willing and capable of providing the needed support to their children. As far as I know, no one was drafted; they were all volunteers. Most of the parents were people that my father knew from his work in the movement.

There was a safety element involved in the selection process as well. All twelve of those selected lived in secure Black communities in Tuskegee. At the time, my family had moved from our exposed house on the Notasulga Highway, where anyone could have driven by and done anything and easily escaped to Auburn or Montgomery, Alabama, on the freeway. We had moved to a house in the heart of one of Tuskegee's Black communities, where the road provided one-way in and out access. All the neighbors kept watch for unidentified cars that approached our home, providing us with a significant degree of security. Other plaintiffs lived in Black subdivisions, and their neighbors looked out for them as well.

Lee et al. v. Macon County Board of Education had made it possible for the twelve of us Black students to begin school at the all-White Tuskegee

High School in September 1963. When we arrived at Tuskegee High School for the first day of school, we were turned away and told that we could not go in because then Governor George C. Wallace had closed the school. He had the power to do this because, at the time, he was the ex officio head of all the Boards of Education in the state. Gray had to go back to court to enjoin him from interfering. In the meantime, all the White students went to a newly created private school called Tuskegee Academy. Wallace openly helped to solicit money for the administration of this private school. For those White students who did not go to the academy or could not afford to go, state buses were provided for them to be transported to nearby White high schools in Notasulga or Shorter, Alabama.

As a result of Wallace's actions, we were divided into two groups and bused to the all-White high schools in Notasulga and Shorter. I was not afraid because every day all I had to do was look behind the bus. Daddy and Marsha Sullins's dad drove behind the bus nearly every single day that we went to Notasulga High. They made sure we were safe. In addition, the federal marshals were always surrounding us to provide protection. When my group arrived at Notasulga High School, all the White high school students had left the school. As we were all in grades nine through twelve, the Notasulga Elementary School remained open.

I guess the major frightful incident occurred on the first day of school. Although there were White federal agents on the bus with us, somehow a White reporter sneaked onto the bus at the beginning of our trip. I guess some of the White policemen or someone else had been watching us closely and saw him get on the bus. When we approached Notasulga School, we could see many White police and sheriff department cars from surrounding towns and counties, including the notorious Sheriff Jim Clark from Selma. They had come as a visible show of resistance. Some of the policemen and local people boarded the bus while we were still on the bus, beat the cameraman, and smashed his camera. Apparently, he saw them coming and was able to hide the film in his shoe. I have often tried to get access to the film, but I have had no success. I have heard that the *New York Times* tried to find the film, but they could not get access to it either. The cameraman is now deceased.

When we got to the school and tried to disembark, the mayor of

Notasulga, Jim Rea, told us that we could not go to the school because if one more student went to the school, it would create a fire hazard. We returned home until Gray could get an injunction to enjoin the mayor from further activity denying us access to schooling at Notasulga High.

There were two to three Black students in each of grades nine through twelve at Notasulga High. There were three of us in the twelfth grade: Robert Judkins Jr., Willie B. Wyatt, and me. The teachers were very good to us. We were a good support system for each other. We met regularly with the other students and parents in the desegregation group to discuss what was going on and how to deal with the various situations. Some of the students in our group occasionally went to school social activities at Tuskegee Institute High, the all-Black high school.

The school year went reasonably well. What is it that all twelfth graders look forward to? Graduation day, right? The other two students and I put so much energy into planning our graduation ceremony. We wanted pomp and circumstance and all the celebration, only to get to school that day and it was closed because someone had burned down the school auditorium. The principal unceremoniously gave us our diplomas. Fifty years later, Notasulga High School invited us all back to participate in the graduation ceremony, and they gave us new diplomas!

In the end, Wallace's interference in the desegregation of Tuskegee High School had far ranging consequences. The injunction that Gray filed against him in 1964 and eventually won not only enjoined him from interfering in desegregation attempts in Macon County but it also enjoined Wallace from interfering in future school desegregation cases throughout the state of Alabama. Gray had been prevented from getting his law degree in Alabama. He had said at that time that he was going out of state to get his law degree and would come back to Alabama and desegregate everything in the state. With the ruling on the injunction that he filed against the governor of Alabama, he darn well did what he had promised years earlier because the injunction affected all the school systems in the state, except those that were already under some federal action.[5] Effectively, all Alabama schools were ordered to integrate.

After "graduating" from Notasulga High, Willie B. and I applied to the all-White Auburn University and became the first Black undergraduate students to be accepted and to go there. Harold A. Franklin, a Black graduate student, had already been accepted into the university.[6] I applied to Auburn University to show other people that it could be done. Autherine Lucy had already integrated the University of Alabama in 1956. In addition, Auburn University was right down the highway from home.

Since Willie B., my fellow Notasulga classmate, enrolled in Auburn with me, the experience was much better than if I had been there by myself. During our first quarter at Auburn, we could not get student housing because the university said they had no more space. A fellow Tuskegean who formerly owned the Carter store in Tuskegee had a relative in Auburn who rented us a place. We moved into student housing in the second quarter. They gave us the dorm supervisor's apartment, which meant that we were still somewhat separated from the rest of the students. That is how that first year at Auburn was, but we sort of adjusted. We went to football games and other activities, of course. At that time, we still had some Alabama State Trooper protection. We were never by ourselves as they were always around. No one ever tried to physically harm us, but it was an uncomfortable atmosphere sometimes. But, hey, we were there! We were Auburn University college students, and we were doing the things that college students do, although we had very few interactions with other students. I became the first Black student to go to Auburn for four years and graduate. Samuel Pettijohn Jr., a Tuskegee University student who transferred to Auburn in his junior year to complete a physics degree, graduated one quarter before I did and became the first Black undergraduate to graduate from Auburn.

After Auburn University, I applied and was accepted to Rutgers University Law School. All almost went well. Although I am happy that I was able to do what I wanted to do in terms of helping to desegregate schools and a major university in the state of Alabama and would never change any of it, there was probably a major personal and professional consequence for me later in life. The only thing I ever wanted to become in my life was a lawyer. My whole body and mind were committed to that goal. All my experiences in life had guided me toward this goal. It was 1968–69, and the Vietnam War was raging. I wanted to go to law school and not into military service.

Many of my White fellow students were getting deferments by teaching. When I got to New Jersey, I taught third grade for a whole year while I was in law school. In applying for a deferment, the Alabama State Draft Board refused to transfer my draft status to New Jersey. I always suspected that my civil rights activities in Alabama played a part in their action. I was drafted.

When I was in the military, a person was not allowed to be a legal clerk unless they had a law degree. Nevertheless, at every turn, from the first day I got to Vietnam, I told them I wanted to be in the legal department. As I was arriving, the legal clerk was leaving, so I got the position. I saw very little fighting action in Vietnam. Some things the Lord must take care of, rather than oneself.

Going into the military really disrupted my life and thinking. When I got back to the United States, things were very different. I was a different person. I attempted to go back to law school at Rutgers, but it did not work. I came back home to Alabama and initially did some legal work, such as title searches for Gray's office. My father had gotten a job with the Alabama Pardons and Parole Department and encouraged me to take the test. I did well on the test and became the first Black parole officer in the state of Alabama. During that time, I also became the director of a halfway house in Montgomery that housed parolees. I did this job for twelve years. I went into that job initially to have a job, and I thought I could help somebody along the way. The difficult part was that the job changed from one with a social work orientation to an enforcement orientation, which required me to wear a gun. When you wear a weapon as part of your job, one does not know what might happen. That was not for me. With a weapon, I was expected to protect myself and other people. That was not for me.

Sometimes in life, people put pressure on you to do certain things. One always tries to rise to the level that they are trying to push you to and encourage you to be at. Sometimes it gets to be a little bit too much.

I tried to tell my family for a long time that that job was not for me and that I wanted a different direction. It seemed that no one was listening, so I just left town. I decided to "run away from home" at the age of thirty-eight! I went to San Diego, California! I went as far as I could go—all the way to the Pacific Ocean! A little bit farther, I would have been in Mexico! I did not tell anyone I was going. I did not want to go North because of the weather. I had lived in that cold in New Jersey, and I did not like the cold.

Although I had a brother in Los Angeles, I was not going to California to stay with him. I did not want to live with him or contact him until I got settled. I did not even call him initially because the first thing he would have done would have been to call my mom. Remember, I literally ran away from home. No one knew where I was. I had no plans, but I just needed that time to be with myself and make my own way in a different environment. My family was quite upset when I left. I know my mother was really, really, really hurt. I know that. They did not know where I was. They put a search party out for me. They didn't know that my leaving without telling anyone was what I had to do at that time in my life.

After arriving in San Diego, I applied for and was accepted into a union-oriented job. I had always been a supporter of unions. Luckily, I did not have to fill out any application or have references or experience. The first thing I did with my first paycheck was to pay my union dues because I wanted to do it right. I did not want the lack of a union card to stand in the way of my advancement. I knew that without a union card, it could be difficult to keep a position, especially for a Black person in those days.

I worked with the San Diego Convention Center helping to manage and set up all the big shows and events that came to the center. The job was high paying, and the company had hired very few Black people. Black people had to fight to get and keep those union jobs because White people wanted to keep them for themselves. The union was not always fair to everyone. I climbed the ranks in that job and in the union. I did very well. I enjoyed the job so much that, most often, it did not feel like work. I have always liked to assemble things, and the job involved some of that. I loved working with different people to get a job accomplished. I became a union steward and had the opportunity to help others advance and deal with legal issues in the union and on the job. I was happy there for twenty-five years.

There was racism in California as well, but it was not nearly as harsh as the racism I had experienced in Alabama. White people are always going to try to maintain their dominance, no matter what, and that is just what they tried to do. Although I had more education than most of them, there were times when the racism came through, and they still tried to "put me in my place." I was not always accepted with open arms. If you are trying to reach your goals, you must stick with your goals. You must make your own way.

The prejudice and racism were a challenge, but I accepted and enjoyed the challenge. I have no doubt that my experiences growing up in the South helped me tremendously. In communicating, I knew how to approach White people. I knew how to get my way and still achieve the goals I wanted to achieve. It took a lot of work because they were not always welcoming. I had to force my way in and that's exactly what I did. I enjoyed the challenge anyway, and I reached my goals.

To illustrate how racism plays a part no matter where one is in the United States, I recall a situation that was political also. I wanted to be a union representative. That is an elected position. My job as union steward required me to go to different job sites and meet different people, rather than staying in one area. Time came for the election of the union representative position I was running for. I had worked in various places, more people knew me, and they were going to vote for me. At the very last minute, the union delayed the election so that a White person who had their endorsement would have time to earn the reputation among the rank and file as I had. Even though the other guy had a head injury and was even hospitalized, they still pushed him over me. This was despite the fact that I was much more qualified and much more ready to work. But that's how things go sometimes. I still stayed there, worked there for twenty-five years, and retired at sixty years of age. I made the kind of money that I wanted to make, and it gave me a great retirement.

After getting established, I eventually contacted my family. When I got together with my brother in the Los Angeles area and he was about to retire from the post office, I was able to get him a job working with me at the Convention Center. I know it was difficult for my close-knit family not to know where I was, but I had to do this for myself. If I had contacted them earlier, I would not have had the opportunity to show myself what I could do on my own. "Running away to San Diego" helped me find myself and how I wanted to live—at that point in my life. Again, I am convinced that events had to go in the order that they did for me to accomplish what I accomplished in San Diego. Going there on my own, knowing no one, and getting a great job that I loved and advanced in were things that I was able to do on my own, independently of anyone else. That course of events fulfilled a need in me. I just needed to get away and make my own way. I needed to do this for myself. If they had found me before I got myself together, they would have put more pressure on me to come back home. I would not have had the experiences that I had in life.

Auburn University celebrates the fiftieth anniversary of integration firsts. *Left to right:* Harold Franklin, first African American to attend Auburn; Willie B. Wyatt Jr., one of the first freshman to enroll at Auburn; Samuel Pettijohn Jr., first African American to graduate from Auburn; and Anthony Lee, first African American who enrolled as a freshman to graduate. Courtesy of Auburn University.

I believe a lot of things in life are spirit led. I believe that a person's life does not just materialize out of the clear blue. God puts us in places that he wants us to be so we can do what he wants us to do and what we want to do in life. I have no doubts that all that happened in this situation was in the plan. I am going to say "God's" plans because I just wanted to escape home. There were some difficult parts, but things worked out. I never wanted to go and stay in California for the rest of my life. I was always thinking I would just go there, get a good job, and return home.

I always wanted to come back home, and I did. And I am continuing my work to improve the community here.

As I stated earlier, my life has been a journey of trying to right some of the wrongs in society. God put me in a situation with my parents who prepared me for the journey. My mother held down the fort at home, loving us, caring for us, consoling us, and taking care of our mental health. Although she was often a bit more hesitant and afraid for the safety of her children, she also felt deeply about civil rights issues and supported my father in his passionate and determined efforts to attack injustice and make a better life for Black people in Macon County and Alabama. She went through a lot having to be the strong support in the house for everyone. She was the one who most often took the threatening phone calls against my father and me and the family. She was very protective. I never disagreed with her because she knew what she was doing. Once we did have a disagreement when the *New York Times* wanted to publish some pictures that a photographer had taken of us at Notasulga High. I wanted them published, and she said no. I realize now that she was right. It would have made us more of a target.

And without Detroit Lee for a father, I probably would not have been able to make the contributions I have made to society in my young life. Ironically, the strong upbringing that I received from these two people also gave me the strength to reclaim my life at age thirty-eight, travel far from home, and live a life of work, fun, and service to others. I continue that work now. I am currently on a few community boards including the NAACP, and I serve as president of my high school Reunion Club. I was recently invited to join a lawsuit as a plaintiff to remove a statue of a Confederate soldier from downtown Tuskegee City Square. Efforts to remove the statue have been going on for over fifty years by various people in the community. The statue has been cared for over the years by the United Daughters of the Confederacy. Attempts to have the statue removed at various times have resulted in its being painted with a yellow stripe down the back by students after the murder of Sammy Younge or painted all over at other times. After each incident, the Daughters or someone would have it cleaned. More recently, former Tuskegee Mayor Johnny Ford sawed one of the legs off the statue hoping it would fall. It did not. The park could not be used for four or five months because they were afraid the statue would fall on someone. The Confederate soldier's leg was replaced by some group, the statue was washed, and it looks brand new. I have been removed as a plaintiff in that case, as the county commissioners are in negotiations.

As I think about the political and socioeconomic situation of Black people in this country now, I think it is extremely important for us to achieve economic stability for our families. I have started a project that hopefully will turn into a movement for the Black community. In our youth, the mantra Black parents would constantly repeat to their children was, "Go to college, get a good education, and get a good job." That is still good, but most jobs are not as secure as they used to be because of social change and rapidly changing technological opportunities. For instance, the major employers here in the South are pretty much what I call automobile plantations, where they build automobile parts, pay minimum wage, and work people very hard. When these workers get home, they have no energy to participate in community enhancement activities for their children, themselves, or the community. Most of the companies are very impersonal and hire through employment agencies. People often work part-time, or they work about six months full-time, and they want to change jobs because they are burned out, get no benefits, and there is no union to negotiate for them.

My idea is to introduce Black people, young and old, to various income producing programs online where they can make a very good living and have time to live and improve their lives and their communities. One also must change the mindset because people are so tied to the forty-hour work week or having several low-paying jobs.

In Tuskegee, we are not going to get any kind of big employers to come here. We do not need them if we can use the computer so that people can make a good living. It is time for us to eliminate poverty in Macon County. I would like to start with Tuskegee and then go throughout the Black Belt and farther with the use of technology. We must stop doing things the old way. The use of technology will free our people to be involved with their families and community building. Black people can become their own employers with many tax advantages. Like they say, small businesses are the backbone of the country. This is a project that I am working on for now and for the future of our community.

Students and their parents involved in the court-ordered desegregation of Macon County Schools in 1963 through *Lee v. The Macon County Board of Education* case brought by attorney Fred D. Gray. Courtesy of the Tuskegee University Archives, Tuskegee University.

CHAPTER 20

Palmer Sullins Jr.

Editors' Note: Palmer Sullins Jr. was born into a family of leaders in the fight for justice in the South. His mother, Della Sullins, has a street in Tuskegee named in her honor. She was one of the most noted women in the Civil Rights Movement in the South.[1] She was on the original board of the Tuskegee Civic Association. Like other parents in this section, Palmer's parents willingly allowed their daughter, Marsha, to be one of the twelve plaintiffs in the *Lee v. Macon County* case that integrated all schools in Alabama.

Palmer credits his mother with being the person who always guided him and encouraged him in his academic and professional journey. His family provided him with the strength of conviction to follow different paths such as learning to fly airplanes as a young boy and teaching swimming to adults at the age of ten. Now a full colonel, he continues the work of his civil rights leading ancestors as he leads an initiative for the construction of a memorial to the Tuskegee Airmen at the Tuskegee National Historic Airmen Site. The Sullins family took advantage of all the opportunities offered by the parallel world in Tuskegee and spent their lives not only trying to ensure that those opportunities were open to others but that all Black people in Tuskegee, Macon County, and throughout the South would be able to participate equally in society.

Sixty-six years ago, on October 6, 1959, when I was just thirteen years old, my civil rights activist mother, Della Sullins, began her speech to the Tuskegee Civic Association with the following:

> When change is in evidence, it is logical to assume that there has been an awakening. Change, as we speak of it now, means "the passing from one condition to another." With change must come an awakening, a realization, and a reaction. One should not become too upset by resistance to change. Primarily, this is a natural reaction.
>
> Peacefully the South has slept, satisfied with its "way of life," but suddenly it awakes at midnight, a frightened, confused, upset South which has suddenly discovered that the veranda on which the veranda-sitters once sat is rotted and the mint from which the julep was once sipped is wilted. The realization is that there can no longer be a "Southern way of life"; there must and will be an American way of life.[2]

My parents, Della Mae Davison and Palmer Sullins Sr., met in the 1940s in Tuskegee, Alabama, while working at the Veterans Administration Hospital, commonly known as the VA. Palmer Sr. was born in Macon County, while Della was born in Indian Hill, South Carolina, and grew up in Charlotte, North Carolina. At the time, Dad worked in the Recreation Department, and Mom was a nurse residing in the Veterans Administration Hospital Complex Nurses' Home; this was a housing facility for single female nurses who came from various states, often at young ages, to work at the hospital. My parents married in 1942. As a team, they would mount a powerful community assault on Jim Crow practices in Tuskegee with subsequent consequences for all of Alabama and the South.

Segregation was alive and well in the South in the early 1940s. Tuskegee in Macon County offered a unique environment for Black people in the South. Tuskegee Institute was a major employer and social and political influencer in Alabama, attracting people nationally and internationally to the area. My parents were highly committed to involving themselves in ways that would benefit the Tuskegee community and Black people. Raising their children and preparing them to give back to the community was included in the equation. There were three of us, Alan Davison, Marsha Marie, and me, Palmer Jr.

Mom moved to Tuskegee after completing a diploma in nursing at Lincoln School of Nursing in North Carolina. She was only nineteen when she graduated college, but she was well prepared to tackle the road

Palmer Sullins Jr.'s parents, Della Davison Sullins and Palmer Sullins Sr., mounted a focused assault on Jim Crow practices in Macon County. Courtesy of Palmer Sullins Jr.

ahead. She took the Civil Service Exam in 1938. Her high scores resulted in her move to Macon County. My mom told me, "It was much different from Charlotte when I moved to Tuskegee. Tuskegee was more rural, so I spent a lot of time attending activities on Tuskegee Institute's campus and at the VA." My mother became the first person in the state of Alabama to be awarded a BA in nursing in 1949. The Tuskegee University School of Nursing had the first nursing baccalaureate program in Alabama, even among White universities. She remained with the VA for thirty-three years. She culminated her professional nursing career with ten additional years teaching psychiatric nursing at Tuskegee Institute and Troy State University.

Dad did not complete high school but was an avid reader and mostly self-taught. He kept himself very much up to date on what was happening in the world around him. The Jim Crow South was his home and leaving was never a thought.

Some of my dad's five siblings did move away from the South, while others remained. We have learned that my father's grandfather was a Confederate soldier from Tennessee who remained in the Roba, Alabama, area of Macon County after the Civil War. He and my great-grandmother were the parents of my dad's father, Christian Sullins.

I was never around Dad's siblings who moved away, and I have limited knowledge of their reasons for leaving or whether they thought moving from the Jim Crow South provided any benefits. I assume that success and fulfillment factored into their not returning home to Macon County. My Dad's younger sister, Julia Sullins Hamilton, who stayed, became an entrepreneur. She opened and operated Master Dry Cleaners at the Franklin Road entrance to the Tuskegee Institute campus. Her business was successful for many years until she became ill in the early 1960s. Although Community Cleaners, another Black-owned business, was next door, her biggest competition was Greg's Cleaners, a White-owned company located in downtown Tuskegee. Greg's Cleaners attracted all the White clientele in Tuskegee, as well as all the Black people who lived on the east side where Greg's was located.

Three of my mother's seven siblings relocated to Tuskegee because of the opportunities experienced by their elder sister, my mom. I do not recall any regret by my parents for staying in the South. Dad and Mom tried their best to make it "home" and a better place for other Black people, their children, and themselves to live.

Those relatives who followed Mom to Tuskegee got diplomas and worked in printing, homemaking, and nursing. During those times, opportunities for education and employment in Tuskegee were very good for them compared to their experiences elsewhere in the South.

Tuskegee News quoted my mother saying, "My daddy was very education-minded and told me he hoped I made it with my head and not my hands. He said I could do anything I wanted, from digging ditches to washing dishes for someone else's kids or getting an education." My Mom said, "I hated washing dishes and knew I had to go to school to learn." Jim Crow was alive and well in North Carolina also. Mom described discrimination while growing up in Charlotte, but her strong family helped her deal with those situations. She went on to say, "I remember a seafood place downtown. I always wanted to eat there after seeing lobsters in the window. I wasn't allowed to eat there then. When everybody was able to eat there years later, I went. The food wasn't any better than anywhere else."

My parents were members of Butler Chapel AME Zion Church in Tuskegee. Butler Chapel was where Booker T. Washington taught his first classes before establishing Tuskegee Normal. My first pastor was Reverend William E. Carson. Reverend Kenneth L. Bufford followed Reverend Carson. I mention them because they were pastors during my childhood when the civil rights of Black people were grossly violated and protests from Black communities were rising. Dr. Martin Luther King Jr. visited mass meetings held at various churches in Macon County, including Butler Chapel.

My parents were well entrenched in the fight to gain civil rights and clear obstacles prevalent in Macon County's school system. As a result, a massive boycott of the predominantly White Tuskegee business community was called for along with other civil rights actions. Several university community members and faculty established the Tuskegee Civic Association (TCA). At this moment, Mom and Dad launched a total commitment to working with other dedicated Macon Countians to achieve equal rights for everyone. My mother was membership chair in the early years of the TCA. Dr. C. G. Gomillion of the famous *Gomillion v. Lightfoot* Supreme Court gerrymandering case was president.

I was born in 1946 in John Andrew Hospital on the Tuskegee Institute Campus. I entered kindergarten at Chambliss Children's House, the university's laboratory school on campus. The school was kindergarten through eighth grade. It was an excellent elementary school for an aviation-minded kid like me, as Tuskegee Institute had a Reserve Officers Training Corps (ROTC) program where many of the Tuskegee Airmen received assignments for on-campus teaching and Moton Field air base

THE TCA EXECUTIVE COMMITTEE 1960

George C. Busby
Vice-President

Rev. S. T. Martin
Vice-President

C. G. Gomillion
President

Rev. K. L. Buford
Vice-President
Chr. Community Welfare Committee

Frank J. Toland
Vice-President
Chairman, Program Committee

William P. Mitchell
Executive Secretary
Chairman, Voter Franchise Committee

Lyman B. Jeffries
Treasurer

TUSKEGEE CIVIC ASSOCIATION

ORIGIN AND OBJECTIVES

More than thirty-nine years ago a group of men in Greenwood began holding meetings to discuss matters of civic interest to the group. These "Men's Meetings" were held at irregular intervals, under the leadership of Dr. G. Lake Imes, and later, Reverend Charles W. Kelly. In 1938, the group organized as the Tuskegee Men's Club, adopted a constitution, and began meeting regularly. In 1941, the constitution was revised to admit women to membership and change the name of the organization to the Tuskegee Civic Association.

The general objective of the Association is to promote through group action the civic well-being of the community. Specifically, the objectives may be stated as follows: The study and interpretation of local and national trends and problems; the collection and dissemination of useful civic and political data; and intelligent and courageous civic action.

Frank Bentley
Assistant Treasurer

Mrs. B. C. Johnson
Member-at-Large

Mrs. Della D. Sullins
Chairman, Membership Committee

Miss Mattie Johnson
Recording Secretary

Mrs. Charlotte Lewis
Historian

Mrs. Laura McCray
Chairman, Youth Education Committee

Lynwood T. Dorsey
Member-at-Large

Dr. Stanley H. Smith
Chairman, Public Education Committee

Otis Pinkard
Chairman, Legal Redress Committee

D. L. Beasley
Member-at-Large

James A. Johnson
Chairman, Economic Education Committee

Palmer Sullins Jr.'s activist mother (*row 4, left*), Della Davison Sullins, membership chair of the Tuskegee Civic Association, was also the first nurse to graduate with a bachelor of nursing degree in the state of Alabama. (TCA), 1960; courtesy of the Tuskegee University Archives, Tuskegee University.

duties after World War II. As a result of the airmen working on campus, their children were eligible to attend Children's House. I became friends with Danny James Jr. and Lee Archer Jr., who were both airmen's children. Danny was the son of Tuskegee Airman General Daniel "Chappie" James, the first Black four-star general. Lee was the son of Tuskegee Airman "ace pilot" Lee Archer Sr. Lawrence Roberts, the father of TV personality Robin Roberts, was another Tuskegee Airmen assigned to Tuskegee Institute. Robin was also born in John Andrew Hospital while her father was assigned to Tuskegee. Other important aviation figures on campus included Chief Charles A. Anderson, whose sons Alfred and Charles also went to Chambliss Children's House. Chief Anderson turned out to be my life-long mentor.

Chief Anderson was the chief instructor pilot for Tuskegee Airmen's primary training in Tuskegee. Chief Anderson is known as the Father of Black Aviation and is remembered for his historic flight when he took First Lady Eleanor Roosevelt on a flight over Tuskegee. Tuskegee Institute President Dr. Frederick D. Patterson, founder of the United Negro College Fund, brought him to Tuskegee in the early 1940s to administer the pilot training for the school. In 2014, the US Postal Service released a stamp in his honor. He remained in Tuskegee after the war and continued to teach flying at Moton Field until his death on April 13, 1996, at eighty-six years of age.[3] We addressed each other as "best friends," as shown in the photo he signed for me a few days before his death. I am so glad he stayed in Alabama.

My high school days were a continuation of focusing on things that interested me. As a result, I often found myself in the minority regarding career and athletic interests. I knew no other classmate who was interested in flying or competitive swimming. The only one at Tuskegee Institute High School who showed interest in swimming was an underclassman named Tom Joyner, the renowned "Fly Jock" radio host and brother of our classmate Albert Joyner.

Tom and I were the only persons to receive the sports letter "T" in swimming from Tuskegee Institute High School. We were featured in the class of '64 yearbook. During my junior and senior years in high school, I also lettered in football, specializing as a punter. I knew that punting would be an important asset in my college years.

I decided to attend Tuskegee Institute for several reasons. Tuskegee had offered me many unique opportunities early in my life, often by exciting and accomplished people now noted in the history books. I was blessed to have had them touch my life. Living close to the campus and my parents' continued involvement in community and civil rights issues made Tuskegee Institute the only college for me. Several colleges recruited me for my swimming athletics achievements, but none could equal the experiences afforded while growing up in Tuskegee. Jim Crow was still alive and well, but Tuskegee and the Black community guided me to the building blocks to achieve despite the evil traditions of racial prejudice and discrimination that surrounded us.

I attended Tuskegee on a swimming scholarship, earning many championship honors. I lettered in swimming for four years and two years in football. My punting ability developed in high school paid off as I hoped it would. In 1964, Reserve Officers Training Corps (ROTC) was mandatory for all male students during the first two years at Tuskegee. Initially, I participated in the air force, but I switched to the army during my last two years of college with army aviation as my focus.

The university contracted Chief Anderson's School of Aviation for ROTC aviation training for the army and air force. Cadets going into military aviation took these classes. My relationship with Chief Anderson had afforded me hours to obtain a private pilot's rating before qualifying for the ROTC program. What an extraordinary show it was when Tuskegee Institute ROTC celebrated Armed Forces Day annually. When I was a child, the faculty erected military displays for the army and air force in the quadrangle in front of Logan Hall, Hollis Burke Frissell Library, and the then Science Building on the Tuskegee Institute campus. The event was awesome for me because, miraculously, Chief Anderson was always there with his airplane. I was always in awe when I saw the Cessna 120 on campus because there was no runway nearby. I could not understand how it got there and was too shy to ask Chief Anderson about it.

At the age of nine, during the Annual Armed Forces Day event, I overheard Chief Anderson explaining his concern to onlookers viewing his plane that his sons did not show much interest in flying the way he hoped they would. Then, I walked up behind him, pulled on his shirt tail, and asked, "May I be your son?" He turned to me with a huge smile and answered, "You mean you want to fly?" I said yes, and we adopted each other at that moment as "father and son." He explained that on each Armed Forces Day, he would wake up at daybreak, take off from Moton Field, land on Franklin Road a couple of miles from campus and taxi to the quadrangle. The mystery was solved. I received forty hours of training with him, which went toward my commercial rating. Again, my mother was in the background, coaching and encouraging me to keep charging and achieving. She knew that Jim Crow still lurked in the shadows.

Upon graduation from Tuskegee in 1968, I was commissioned as a second lieutenant in the US Army in 1968 at Ft. Bragg, North Carolina. Tuskegee Institute athletic director Dr. Edward L. Jackson asked me if I were interested in assuming the head swimming coaching position. He was retiring, and my former swimming coach, Dr. Frank Leftwich, would replace him as athletic director. My military career was beginning to unfold, and my commitment to active service was coming due. I had another whisper in my ear from my mother to add the coaching chapter to my life. I sent a request to the army to grant one one-year delay of reporting for active duty, and to my surprise, it was granted.

I assumed the head swimming coach position and taught as an academic instructor in the Department of Physical Education until the summer of 1969. What a great experience. The transition from student to coach and faculty was made easy thanks to those who had been classmates and were now my students. We adjusted to the situation together. My duties also entailed assisting football special teams with punting. Talents developed in my early years in Tuskegee were once again manifesting themselves and pushing me forward.

While my parents supported my development and life pursuits, they did the same for my brother and sister. Their decision to allow my sister and the family to become plaintiffs in the famous *Lee v. Macon County Board of Education* case put the family at the forefront of one of the most significant civil rights cases in Alabama history. My sister, Marsha Sullins, was one of the student litigants who integrated Macon County schools.

My brother, Alan, and I, as well as Marsha, my little sister, were submitted for acceptance in the integration effort at then all-White Tuskegee High School. Only Marsha was selected. That was fine with my parents. Our family, united, embraced the potential challenges ahead with eyes wide open. I remember my mom and dad gathering us together and explaining the dynamics of what was about to take place. They described the uncertainty about the reactions from the local White citizens. We, as children of parents dedicated to the cause, were mentally prepared for the events on the horizon. We specially made sure that Marsha knew and felt that her family was fully behind her with support. My dad and mom accompanied her to the school on the first day, and my dad often followed her bus to the new school.

Palmer Sullins Jr.'s sister, Marsha Sullins Slocum, reviewing legal papers from the Macon County school desegregation case with her mother, Della Davison Sullins. Courtesy of Palmer Sullins Jr. and *Tuskegee News*.

I have been blessed to achieve the rank of colonel in the army and receive numerous honors because of the support, mentoring, and opportunities I received growing up in Tuskegee. In 2014, I received the Federal Aviation Administration's highest award, the Master Pilot Award. It recognizes individuals who have exhibited professionalism, skills, and aviation expertise while piloting aircraft and have conducted fifty or more consecutive years of safe flight operations. On May 18, 2018, I was honored by my hometown of Tuskegee by being awarded the Chief Charles A. Anderson Lifetime Achievement award. I am also grateful to have received numerous military awards, including the Bronze Star. I became Louisiana's first Black major command (MACOM) commander in the National Guard.

Trained to fly at age nine by famed Tuskegee Airmen chief flight instructor, Charles A. Anderson, Palmer Sullins Jr. became a colonel in the US Army. He is honored on the cover of *The International Comanche Society*. Courtesy of Palmer Sullins Jr.

My community service has included being chairman of the board of the Friends of the Tuskegee Airmen National Historic Site, president of the Black Pilots of America, and president of the Tuskegee University Athletic Hall of Fame. I am a life member of Kappa Alpha Psi, a community service fraternity. I owe it all to the support of my family and mentors who nurtured my talents as a youngster in Tuskegee during the Civil Rights Movement.

My personal and professional pursuits have been fulfilled and began early in life. Logan Hall on the campus of Tuskegee Institute contained a swimming pool, which allowed me to develop into a competitive swimmer as a youngster. I had the opportunity to begin teaching others to swim when I was only ten years old. Many of my students were adults. I called it then, and I call it now, giving back.

I am dedicating my life now to preserving the Tuskegee Airmen legacy. As the chairman of Friends of the Tuskegee Airmen National Historic Site, Inc., I work to ensure that youth and those who visit the museum can continue to walk the hallowed grounds where the airmen trained. People need to know some of the historic accomplishments Black people made in Alabama under Jim Crow. Their achievements resulted from the commitments of "those who stayed" and worked tirelessly to achieve, regardless of the trials and tribulations presented by racism.

I owe so much to "those who stayed" and lit the pathways for me to follow. I have ventured into diverse directions, including education, athletics, the military, and nonprofit community service. Childhood mentors, my parents, and a broader Black community supported me. They understood the struggles and committed themselves to inspiring changes during Jim Crow, especially through the youth. My successes in life are directly linked to being taught to take advantage of opportunities and to look beyond the horizons while moving in positive directions wherever I am.

Like most people, I have had to deal with various life challenges. However, the solutions usually appeared because of what was drilled into my head by "those who stayed." Their influences and philosophies remain fresh in my mind today. Times have changed since Lewis Adams and Booker T. Washington impacted the Tuskegee community, but adjustments still must be made. My Jim Crow generation, in many cases, was prepared to move forward due to our immediate environment. Unfortunately, Jim Crow's aftermath continues to take its toll on our people, and all who value freedom and justice must continue to do their part to prepare the next generation of activists for equality.

CHAPTER 21

Willie B. Wyatt Jr.

Editors' Note: Willie B. Wyatt Jr. and his family were also stalwarts of the Civil Rights Movement in Tuskegee. They joined the Tuskegee Civic Association, the NAACP, and the Tuskegee community of everyday people fighting for freedom and justice during the 1950s and 1960s. Willie B., as he is affectionately known by his classmates, accepted his family's decision to join the Tuskegee Twelve as plaintiffs in *Lee v. Macon County Board of Education* to integrate Alabama schools.

Resistance to injustice in those days often resulted in indignities such as name-calling, bomb threats, and beatings. This group of students would suffer many, but the first was the White superintendent's requirement that the twelve Black students take IQ tests before they entered a school that their parents paid taxes to support.

At the age of seventeen, Willie B. was already a seasoned civil rights warrior as he and his classmate, Anthony Lee, had practiced integrating White churches in Tuskegee with their parents at an even younger age. Again, the parallel world encouraged, supported, and helped protect Willie B. and his family in their resistance to injustice.

My granddaughter, Sonya Clark, became the fourth generation of Wyatts to graduate from Tuskegee University. Education of the Wyatts all began with my father, Willie B. Wyatt Sr., who went to Tuskegee Institute in 1948 under the GI Bill. He graduated in 1951 and moved the family to Austin, Texas. In 1957, Tuskegee Institute offered him the opportunity to teach electrical construction, and he moved the family back to Tuskegee.

The decision to migrate to Tuskegee from Austin was not taken without discussion and anguish from the extended family that was settled in Texas. My grandmother, aunt, great-aunt, and great-uncles had heard of the Montgomery Bus Boycott and the upheaval Dr. King's work was causing. They were all fearful that Dad was taking the family into harm's way and that the Ku Klux Klan would be riding all over Alabama. Despite their objections, we did move to Tuskegee.

I enrolled in the Washington Public School the day after Labor Day in 1957. My early days at Washington Public were a throwback for me, as I was not accustomed to having Black teachers. I attended Holy Cross Catholic School in Austin with all White nuns through the fifth grade. I enrolled in Washington Public as a sixth grader.

The next shock came when I learned that classes would not have a full complement of students until early October, as some of my classmates who lived in rural areas had to pick cotton and harvest crops in September. Some of their parents and grandparents were sharecroppers. Nevertheless, I eventually settled in.

Within the first months of returning to Tuskegee, my parents joined the Tuskegee Civic Association (TCA). Several community activists had formed the TCA to fight for voting rights and against gerrymandering in Tuskegee. The meetings were held on Tuesday nights. My and Harold White's parents would ride together to the meetings. Harold and I have been classmates and friends since we were five years old, before my family moved back to Texas after my father graduated from Tuskegee Institute.

I looked forward to these Tuesday meetings, as my sisters and I would get to stay at Harold's house with his older sisters. I got to watch more than just the Columbus, Georgia TV stations we received with the rabbit ears TV antenna at our home. Harold had an outside TV antenna that received stations from Montgomery, Alabama, as well! While our parents were at the TCA meetings dealing with the critical issues of racial injustice that affected our lives and our futures, we were doing what kids do, enjoying each other and television.

My parents were members of Mt. Olive Baptist Church. They supported the Civil Rights Movement with financial contributions through the church. They refused to shop in Tuskegee and traveled to surrounding towns and counties to shop. My parents' actions supported the TCA mandate not to shop locally in the city of Tuskegee.

As the TCA was organizing boycotts in Tuskegee, it also planned social actions with other civil rights groups such as the NAACP and local and national civil rights lawyers. Fred Grey, a local civil rights lawyer, had filed and won the Tuskegee voting rights gerrymandering case, *Gomillion v. Lightfoot*.[1] The school desegregation case was next on his agenda.

Through a series of meetings with TCA leadership and Attorney Gray, a group of students and parents filed a school desegregation lawsuit against Macon County public schools. TCA leadership and Gray set the expectations for participants in the case to integrate the school system in Macon County. The expectations were that parents should be in jobs that would not be affected if their children participated in the lawsuit. Their children should be well-mannered and emotionally stable. The students chosen to participate should also have good grades.

My parents told me I would be one of the students named in a lawsuit to integrate Macon County public schools. The decision did not bother me at all. I looked forward to it and was not afraid. I knew a few White students who went to the White high school in Tuskegee by name. In addition, I remembered the story of Orval Faubus, governor of Arkansas, blocking the entrance of the Little Rock Nine to the all-White Central High School. I was comforted that President Dwight D. Eisenhower had sent federal troops to protect the students. I knew the same would be done for us by our then-president, John F. Kennedy, if necessary.

I, along with other students, was tested (IQ) to ensure we could keep up with the White students. Upon reflection, I believe that the superintendent wanted to ensure that the Black students from around Tuskegee Institute (University) did not have higher IQs than White students in the county school system.

After a series of federal court hearings in Opelika, Alabama, federal Judge Frank M. Johnson Jr. handed down the order to integrate the Macon County public schools. Judge Johnson often handed down court decisions that enhanced civil rights in Alabama.[2]

Our first attempt to attend class was the first week of September 1963. Students and parents were briefed by the US Department of

Justice on what to expect on the first day. We were told to report to the Macon County Superintendent's Office to travel by bus to the White Tuskegee High School. Upon our arrival at the school, Captain Pryor of the Alabama State Troopers boarded the bus and read us a proclamation from Governor George Wallace. It stated that the law prohibited us from entering this White school. Pryor instructed the driver to return us to the Macon County Superintendent's Office, where our parents were waiting. The US Department of Justice attorneys instructed us to return home, emphasizing that we should not try to reenroll in Tuskegee Institute High, the Black high school, as our lawyers were going back to court.

Attorney Gray got a court date within a week with Judge Johnson. The hearing results were that Wallace was issued an injunction preventing the Alabama State Troopers from interfering with the integration of the White Tuskegee High School. Ignoring the order and continuing the interference, Wallace called out the Alabama National Guard to prevent us from entering Tuskegee High. Some days later, we were bused back to the school after Attorney General Robert Kennedy had federalized the Alabama National Guard, taking them out of Alabama state control.

We entered Tuskegee High School for the first time under the protection of the federalized Alabama National Guard. We were directed to the library to get class schedules as we entered the school. As we were beginning to get class assignments, White students' parents began arriving to withdraw their children from the school. My first days of class were uneventful. The teachers tried to put on a good face, and class sizes were very small. My largest class had three people in it. There were twenty-six teachers for thirteen students. I was one of the three seniors involved in the desegregation of Macon County public schools.

On November 22, 1963, President John F. Kennedy was assassinated. Although the Black students were saddened to learn of the assassination, the White teachers seemed to enjoy the moment. The teachers told us to go to the teacher's lounge to watch the news.

During the Christmas holidays, the state Board of Education determined that keeping Tuskegee High School open was not feasible because it was not economical to operate with only thirteen students. After returning to federal court in early January, the now twelve Black students were divided into two groups. Six went to each of the two remaining

White high schools in Macon County: Shorter High School in Shorter, Alabama, and Notasulga High School in Notasulga, Alabama.

Classmates Anthony Lee, Robert Judkins Jr., and I went to Notasulga High School. On the way to Notasulga, the Alabama State Troopers and US Marshals followed the bus. On my first day going to Notasulga High, the mayor of Notasulga, Mr. Rea, met the bus. He denied us admission to the school, citing that admitting six more students would present a fire hazard.

I saw my first violence during this desegregation attempt on that day in Notasulga. As we left Tuskegee and headed to Notasulga, a White freelance photographer boarded the bus out of the sight of the state troopers. Once the mayor left the bus, state troopers came through the backdoor and began to punch and prod the photographer until he was able to run off the bus. Local townspeople then accosted him. Someone had noticed the photographer getting on the bus in Tuskegee and reported him to the authorities in Notasulga.

Later in the week, we again had to obtain federal orders to attend Notasulga High School. About a month after we arrived at the school, it was set on fire at night, and the Notasulga fire marshal deemed the high school unsafe. Our lawyers went back to court again, and Judge Johnson ordered the local Macon County Board of Education to provide accommodations for us to attend classes at Notasulga High School. Temporary classrooms were set up in the gym using portable chalkboards. A typical school day involved three study halls and three courses. The instructors led classes for two or three students. All the White students had left the school, so the student body was a total of six Black students. During our time in 1964 at Notasulga High School, a detail of US Marshals and FBI Agents followed our bus daily and staked out in front of the school to protect us.

As we continued the school year, our parents were constantly talking with each other. We also had meetings at students' homes where we could tell all the parents how we felt about things and what was being said in the schools. All the students had Neighborhood Watch groups on their streets. These neighbors had agreed to watch at all times of the day and night for unfamiliar cars or persons who might have intentions of engaging in threatening or violent behavior. I lived on a dead-end street with two other students in the group, Patty and Wilma Jones. Next door to our house lived Dr. Wasserstrom, a White University of Michigan professor who had come to Tuskegee Institute to be the dean of Arts, Letters, and Social Sciences. There was an agreement among Mr. Jones, my father, and Dean Wasserstrom that they would not put up with any harassment by people from outside the neighborhood. Our fathers were prepared to use lethal force to protect our families and us and then call the local law enforcement to come and get the remains if necessary.

Willie B. Wyatt Jr.'s parents, Willie B. Wyatt Sr., a civil rights activist and staunch defender of his family from segregationist threats, and Thelma Green Wyatt. Courtesy of Willie B. Wyatt Jr.

Notasulga did not offer trigonometry as a math class, but Tuskegee Institute (University) offered us seniors a class for three hours a week to meet the requirements for our high school diploma. The Tuskegee community came together to support us.

Graduation from Notasulga High School in 1964 for the three seniors was very simple. The principal, citing KKK threats, presented the three seniors with our diplomas on May 24, 1964, and declared that day the last day of school. There was no ceremony, no audience, no parents, or friends. It was not until May 2012 that the senior graduating class of Notasulga High School allowed the other surviving senior and me from 1964 to participate in their graduation ceremony, which was fifty years overdue. We were both grateful.

Willie B. Wyatt Jr. and Anthony Lee were invited back fifty years later to formally participate in graduation at Notasulga High School since their ceremony was cancelled in 1964. Courtesy of Willie B. Wyatt Jr.

I missed my classmates at Tuskegee Institute High School. I always felt forgotten because they never talked about it. I have since learned that they appreciated the sacrifices that we made. I also recently learned that our 1964 yearbook staff tore Anthony's, Robert's, and my picture from a Tuskegee Twelve photograph and clandestinely mounted them individually among their senior pictures. They have welcomed us to all the events of the TIHS Class of 1964 Reunion Club. Anthony and I have both served as president of the club. The class has come out to support us as adults and be a part of the recognition we get from local and state leaders.

I watched James Hood and Vivian Malone integrate the University of Alabama in the fall of 1963. Since I had listened to Auburn football on the radio, and since Auburn was a state school not far from Tuskegee, I thought I could go to college there. In doing so, I could save my family some money. Going to Auburn was my idea. My parents were opposed, but I did everything possible to gain admission. There was no consulting with the TCA, the NAACP, or any other group. I had gone through Notasulga with Anthony Lee, and we had talked about not stopping with the integration of the Macon County school system.

I enrolled in Auburn University as one of the first two Black freshmen to integrate that school in the fall of 1964. The first obstacle at Auburn was housing. Our admissions letters stated we were accepted, but no housing was available. In the first quarter, we lived in a rooming house in the Black community about a twenty-minute walk to campus.

In the second quarter of our freshman year, we moved into the dormitories on campus. I lived in a dormitory with another Black student, Anthony Lee, as my roommate. Harold Franklin, the first Black graduate student at Auburn, lived next door in the dorm. We had no social life, and the southern White people scorned us.

My Auburn experience was not a good one. There were constant catcalls and staring but never making eye contact. Some professors assigned seats that put me in the back of the room or at angles that made it hard for me to see the blackboard. Some classes had study sessions, but no one would let me know when and where they were. I overheard conversations about the study sessions after the fact.

In time, I made friends with some upperclassmen from out of state. I liked playing table tennis in the recreation area of the dorm. If I played with one of my friends and the ball hit the floor, some bystanders would purposely step on it. Reporting this to the counselor only got a shrug of the shoulders.

At the end of my year at Auburn, I had had enough. My parents began worrying about my safety since I had some late classes. I had also worked and saved some money, so my parents did not have to pay tuition at Tuskegee for my older sister and me. I transferred to Tuskegee Institute.

I never planned to leave the South; however, as I attended Tuskegee Institute (University) and became a commissioned officer through the Reserve Officers' Training Program (ROTC), I realized that the world was much bigger than Tuskegee. My first awakening came in 1966 when I had a summer job with the US Forest Service in Minturn, Colorado.

It was my first time being far away from home and living and working among strangers. I worked with students from other universities, including Arizona, Minnesota, Colorado, and Louisiana. These guys were White and showed no prejudice. We lived together, cooked, washed clothes, and socialized together. Their actions were totally different from my past experiences with White people.

It seems that my family has a legacy of making difficult decisions that improve conditions for their families and Black people in general. My maternal grandfather, Jessie Green Sr., sacrificed and was absent from his family for long periods as a Pullman porter on the railroad in the 1940s.[3] Making that sacrifice helped his family live a working-class existence.

My grandfather had relocated to Denver, Colorado, from Austin, Texas, in the early 1940s. Subsequently, he worked for the railroad for a run between Denver, Colorado, and Portland, Oregon. I did not see or talk to him often, but I remember my mother speaking about him making good money on a good job and helping other Black people along the way.

My maternal uncle, John D. Green, was one of a small group of Black students to integrate the University of Texas at Austin in 1955. Although I was very young, I remember the buzz around Grandma's house about Uncle John. And my father had the courage to offer up his only son to possible physical and psychological harm to fight for equal educational opportunity for all Black people in Alabama, the South, and the nation. Being exposed to these accomplished and fearless relatives willing to take chances to improve the lives of their families and the Black community probably shaped my activities later in life in Alabama.

I graduated from Tuskegee Institute in 1968 with a degree in industrial technology. After graduation, I took a duty tour in Vietnam as a commissioned officer and was commissioned as a second lieutenant in the US Army Signal Corp in May 1969. I completed the signal officer basic course at Fort Gordon, Georgia, in November 1969 and had orders for Fort Sill, Oklahoma, to be the signal officer for a 155 MM field artillery battalion. I was promoted to first lieutenant in August 1970 and received orders for Vietnam. I arrived in Vietnam on August 8, 1970, and my initial assignment was to be the officer in command of three signal sites in the Mekong Delta. Platoons of US Army persons trained in communications operated these sites. My communications platoon provided radio communications during live fire exercises to field troops and headquarters. In February 1971, I transferred to brigade signal headquarters in Saigon. My duties were to design and ensure the installation of circuits to support the troops on the ground. My additional responsibility was to give the morning briefing to the brigade commander on overnight communication outages. I returned to the United States in July 1971 and ended active duty.

Willie B. Wyatt Jr. receiving the Bronze Star in Saigon in 1971. Courtesy of Willie B. Wyatt Jr.

Returning to the United States, I had no thoughts about staying in Alabama. I had worked with and spoken with employers in the North. I could not see staying in Tuskegee for employment and raising a family. I wanted more for my family since I had seen a big new world. My BS in industrial technology–electronics and my veteran status would give me better opportunities in the North.

My first civilian job was as a commercial marketing representative for Mobil Oil Corporation in Buffalo, New York, from 1971 to 1973. My desire to move closer to family led me to my second job as placement director at DeVry Institute and later as dean of students at DeVry in Atlanta, Georgia, from 1974 to 1980. The graduate placement director at DeVry was mainly responsible for identifying employers in the Southeast who needed persons with electronic backgrounds.

I later joined Southern Bell/AT&T as a PBX supervisor in Atlanta. My twenty-two-year career at AT&T allowed me to move to several jobs in the company, retiring as project manager. As a manager in international operations, I worked in and traveled to numerous European countries. I was the first Black person to work in that position at AT&T. I retired in 2002.

I talk to my grandchildren about my upbringing in the South as I visit them. It is hard for them to believe that Black people struggled so hard for fundamental equality. I have lived through situations they have never had to face, that is, living without the same legal rights as other human beings.

I want my grandchildren to know these things about their grandfather. I was one of the plaintiffs who brought the case to integrate the Macon County public schools in September 1963. The eventual ruling in this case led to the integration of all public schools in the state of Alabama.[4] I was among the first two Black students to integrate Auburn University as undergraduates in September 1964. I met Dr. King at the end of the Selma to Montgomery march in 1965.

For my children and grandchildren, especially Sonya, who has decided to embark upon a corporate career, I talk to them about avoiding the pitfalls in corporate America. I speak to them about the importance of forming bonds with coworkers and supervisors. Most importantly for Black people, I counsel them to maximize their financial opportunities in the corporate setting to secure their financial futures. I tell them not to reinvent the wheel but to seek out experienced people as mentors.

Willie B. Wyatt Jr., with his granddaughter Sonya Clark,
a fourth-generation Tuskegee University graduate.
Courtesy of Willie B. Wyatt Jr.

I have spent my postcollege and postmilitary life in corporate America, where I continued to experience discrimination in job title, promotion, job location assignments, and salary. My upbringing in the South taught me to work around obstacles. As I have spoken to groups of students on high school career days, I have shared my life experiences with them.

Living in the Jim Crow South gave me a value system to be ever mindful of how far we as a people in this country have come. I was born at a time in history that has allowed me to live through major transitions in social justice. My family has been brave, bold, and adventurous enough to break barriers and fight for justice. I have witnessed voter suppression and voter registration. I have witnessed police brutality, as well as seeing

Black people challenge the legal system to obtain justice. I have lived through my family's fight for the right to vote and not having their children relegated to segregated settings. I have also witnessed the election of the first Black president of the United States. We have come a very long way, but the fight continues.

I can never remember my parents discussing leaving the South to go North or even back to Texas. Knowing my parents, I can only surmise that there were several reasons for their decision to stay in Tuskegee. They had uprooted their family once in a major relocation from Austin to Tuskegee, and they probably did not want to repeat it. Secondly, despite Jim Crow being ever present, my father and mother had made a good middle-class life for our family. My parents had secure jobs, and their children had friends and good schools to attend. My parents had developed deep friendships and social and political roots throughout the community. I also think my parents had committed to the civil rights struggle in the South. The fight for equality in the South was a major part of their lives, and I know they did not want to give that up. They were very invested in improving the situation for all Black people in the South and the United States.

I shared an experience with my family that sums up where Black people have been, where we are, and where we hope to go. The family experience occurred in the summer of 1964, the same year the bodies of Michael Schwerner, Andrew Goodman, and James Chaney were found in an earthen dam in Mississippi. The nation was in turmoil, but major change was coming. That same year, President Lyndon Johnson signed the Civil Rights Accommodations Act. It forbade discrimination on the bases of race, religion, or national origin at all public accommodations.[5] I was traveling from Austin to Tuskegee with my father and two of my sisters. Around lunchtime, we stopped in Jackson, Mississippi, and had a sit-down lunch at a restaurant in the Holiday Inn.

Sitting there in that restaurant was a powerfully prideful moment for my father. During all the years of my family going back and forth to "home" in Texas to visit family, we had to pack our fried chicken and stop at a park along the highway to eat. Sitting there in that restaurant with my family, I could see my father's relief and pride at that moment. He had suffered indignities as a Black man in the South. He had made what must have been a difficult decision to put his only son on the front lines and in harm's way to fight for what my grandchildren take for granted as fundamental human rights.

Sitting there, we all knew he was thinking about the past, the present, and the future for Black people in this country. We could see him exhale a bit and smile slightly with a faint nod toward future victories. The moment was unforgettable for Dad and for his children, who had witnessed him lead his family on the walk toward justice.

Group photo of the Tuskegee Institute High School Class of 1964 in 2014. Photography by Thomas Martin; courtesy of Thomas Martin.

Epilogue

This study uses narratives written by a group of 1964 graduates of a segregated high school in Tuskegee, Alabama, to explore an understudied aspect of American history—why people stayed in the South before, during, and after the Great Migration. Their narratives tell intergenerational stories of resistance, social mobility, and perseverance. They also support findings in the literature that most Black people stayed in the South because of landownership, the desire to be close to family, and later for the opportunity to participate in the Civil Rights Movement. However, for the families in this study, there is an additional set of unconventional reasons for staying. These additional reasons for staying included access to gainful employment, education, the ability to own homes and businesses, and to fight injustice in the South outside of the traditional boundaries of the Civil Rights Movement. These reasons add another dimension to the still-emerging scholarly literature focused on why Black people stayed in the South.[1] This set of reasons is also deeply connected to the exceptional Black community in which the group of septuagenarians came of age, that is, the parallel world that developed around Tuskegee Institute. In the final analysis, the narratives point to questions of what happens when conditions for a parallel world deteriorate and lead to an examination of the implications for Black exceptionalism and Black upward mobility in today's society.

The history of Tuskegee and the dynamic Black community that it helped to develop serve as a model for understanding how culturally rich and economically dynamic Black communities formed in the South despite the everyday antagonisms and violences of Jim Crow. The narratives in this study provide a singular perspective on the role Tuskegee Institute played as the foundational cultural, social, and economic engine for the community. Beyond just Tuskegee, the narratives illustrate the role historically Black colleges and universities (HBCUs) across the South played as anchors for Black business districts, migratory destinations for Black professionals, and in establishing social values and practices. One of the most valuable ways that dynamic Black communities anchored by HBCUs provided resources for Black people to stay in the South, despite racial segregation, was through the creation of parallel institutions.[2] Across the nation, Black people established their own newspapers, churches, social organizations, professional organizations, and schools as they were excluded from mainstream White organizations and institutions. In Tuskegee, Booker T. Washington, his supporters, and his successors created gainful employment opportunities for Black professionals and the Black working class alike at the Veterans Administration Hospital, the John A. Andrew Hospital, and Moton Field, home of the Tuskegee Airmen. These opportunities attracted Black talent and made middle-class status possible for thousands of Black citizens in Macon County.

As a result, ancestors were able to create a parallel world of social opportunities for their children, including the Boy and Girl Scouts, team sports, tutoring, music lessons, and exposure to the arts, travel, and, possibly most importantly, to extraordinarily accomplished people. These experiences instilled key values of upward mobility in the Black children coming of age in the community. The parallel world also provided the organizational foundation for two landmark civil rights cases, one heard before the Supreme Court.[3] Consequently, these institutions and organizations helped develop Black leadership, challenged ideas about Black inferiority, provided social and economic resources to the larger Black community, and led to an upwardly mobile populace.

As a community, Tuskegee exemplified this system of Black community building. Alongside the famed architect of this community, Booker T. Washington, were Black scholars and leaders including George Washington Carver, Bess Bolden Walcott, Charles Gomillion, and P. B. Phillips. In addition, everyday people like the ancestors of the contributors of this project also embodied the values and the upwardly mobile intentions of Tuskegee's dynamic Black community.[4] For example, classmate Ray Adams's formerly enslaved great-grandfather Lewis Adams was the raison d'être for the existence of Tuskegee Institute. Carolyn Foster Bivins's great-grandparents heard about "the school" and drove their young children to Tuskegee in a wagon to help build a better space for a better life. They moved into a house down the street from Tuskegee's Butler Chapel Church where they helped to build many of the new campus buildings. Several classmates' ancestors, including Roosevelt Lorenzo Williams and Annie Jean Baker Reed, donated land to the new Tuskegee Normal School for local primary and Rosenwald schools and teachers' homes in rural areas surrounding Tuskegee. Nancy Hooten Garrison's Tuskegee graduate relatives settled in rural areas in Alabama and founded educational institutes in rural Black communities to make education available to all Black people throughout the South.

Additionally, when discussing contributions to the Civil Rights Movement or the Black freedom struggle in general, there is a tendency for writers to focus on noted leaders of the movement. This study reveals the overwhelming involvement of the mostly unheralded ancestors and children in Tuskegee that made a difference in the movement. Many of the contributors to the parallel world, young and old, joined together and formed a powerful resistance to Jim Crow practices of the day. They became litigants in legal cases aimed at improving equal rights for Black people in the Tuskegee area. Marian Quinn Williams's aunt was one of thousands of Tuskegee residents who were redistricted out of the city limits in the 1950s and became a litigant in *Gomillion v. Lightfoot*. Anthony Lee Jr.'s, Willie B. Wyatt Jr.'s, Palmer Sullins Jr.'s, and Gerald W. Billis's parents put their most prized possessions, their children, on the front lines to integrate the White Tuskegee High School. Their actions resulted in the landmark *Lee v. Macon County Board of Education* case that desegregated schools in Alabama. Harold White's father and Anthony Lee's father became leaders in the Tuskegee Civic Association and the community, even though they did not have college degrees, as did most others in leadership positions in the TCA.

Almost all the narrators' parents resisted the logics of White supremacy in less spectacular but just as essential ways and made contributions to uplifting their people. Barbara White Atkinson-Liggins's father warned a White man not to call him "uncle," and her mother politely collected her girls and left a store, never to shop there again, when she was treated unequally. Rosa McWilliams Henderson's father, a janitor at the high school, gave milk and cookies to hungry students without the money to pay for them. Milton Donald's grandmother and other parents "volunteered" them as teenagers to take grocery orders for elderly neighbors when their families shopped in surrounding towns during the Tuskegee Boycott. Sonjia Parker Redmond's grandfather, an unlettered man in the then racially oppressive town of Notasulga, Alabama, gave each of his grandchildren an untraceable nickel or dime to put in the monthly rural church collection plate for "Dr. King's work."

However, as was the case in many places in the country, desegregation proved to be a double-edged sword for Tuskegee. As an example of parallelism, Tuskegee flourished as a separate community when Black professionals had few economic opportunities elsewhere. The parallel world had created a social community of educated and middle-class Black people. However, desegregation meant educated Black people did not have to travel to Tuskegee to find opportunities. As Carolyn Moss Woodard's father and grandfather predicted, the majority White towns of Montgomery and Auburn "squeezed" out the Black businesses in Tuskegee, and institutions that had provided professional, skilled, and unskilled jobs for thousands of Black people in Tuskegee were downsized or closed. Moton Field and the Veterans Administration Hospital were significantly downsized by those outside of the Black Tuskegee business and political community. John Andrews Hospital and the Greyhound bus station were closed. These situations "did not bode well" for the economic well-being of the community. These changes complicate imagining Tuskegee as a model for creating dynamic Black communities in the contemporary moment.

Furthermore, as new possibilities opened across the nation and beyond, they drew Black residents away from the community. Gerald W. Billes's father dropped him off to matriculate at Tulane University on his way to a major job opportunity in the North after working in administration at the VA for over fifteen years. Several members of the high school graduating class went North for college. Ray Adams talked about major corporations in the North recruiting Black people during the late 1960s and early 1970s. Narrators who completed ROTC received their commissions and went North and West. As White residents continued to leave the city because of civil rights losses and older members of both the Black and White middle class started to pass away, the population and tax base of the city of Tuskegee decreased even further. In this way, the history of Tuskegee since the end of the Civil Rights Movement follows the same path and pitfalls experienced by Black-led cities from Newark, New Jersey, to Haynesville, Alabama.[5]

Nonetheless, many members of the civil rights generation were able to take advantage of the success their parents and grandparents found by staying in the South, by moving away to avail themselves of professional opportunities worldwide. Leaving the South in the wake of the Civil Rights Movement in the late 1960s, their migratory experiences ran against broader migratory shifts during the period when more and more Black people opted to remain in the South and moved to southern cities like Atlanta and Houston. Instead, many of the narrators moved to northern cities and even across the Atlantic to fully use the intellectual and professional preparation their families had worked hard for them to acquire.

However, the lure of Tuskegee also drew some members of this generation back home after they had explored the world and the opportunities it offered. Mattie Blizzard came home to help with her ailing parents. Lorenzo returned to take care of unfinished business. While these returnees joined the stream of Black people moving back to the South, their decisions to return to Tuskegee as opposed to larger cities such as Atlanta, Houston, or even Montgomery provide valuable insights into the ways familial and social concerns drove Black homeplace migration during the New Great Migration—a set of migratory experiences that remain largely outside of historians' understanding of Black migration.[6]

Yet, the promise of Tuskegee still lies open. HBCUs remain key social institutions for the nation's Black community. With record increases in enrollments at HBCUs across the nation, the end of affirmative action in higher education, and renewed interest in the revitalization of Black business districts, the historical importance of examining the history of places like Tuskegee increases. Furthermore, these histories suggest compelling new directions for future research from quantitative studies of HBCUs as engines of economic uplift to the ongoing educational, economic, and psychological importance of HBCUs in a nation still struggling with anti-Black racism. Thus, as each new generation of scholars and students is drawn to Tuskegee, they bring with them the hope and promise that define the history of this extraordinary place.[7] In fact, Tuskegee still offers an alluring model for the future of Black freedom through economic empowerment. As the narratives in this study reveal, reclaiming aspects of Washington's economic model and balancing them with the Black political empowerment that emerged alongside the 1964 graduating class of Tuskegee Institute High School could serve as the foundation for the next phase of the Black freedom struggle.

The narratives in this volume illuminate an influential moment in the history of Tuskegee and the nation more broadly. Sitting at the cusp of two of the most important demographic movements in American history, the Great Migration and the New Great Migration, the migratory decisions of the ancestors and the narrators highlight the changing ways Black people used mobility to pursue their ideas of freedom and opportunity. Furthermore, the narratives illustrate the singularity of a time and place where Black people built an economically diverse and resource-rich community in the Jim Crow South. Through the creation of a parallel world, the community experienced significant upward mobility among those who migrated to the area or stayed in the Tuskegee area. Moreover, the narrators provide a window into one of American history's most important social movements, the Modern Black Freedom Movement. As key actors and witnesses to the Civil Rights Movement and stakeholders of its promises, their choices delineate how migration, opportunities for upward mobility, and freedom have been, and remain, deeply connected.

Notes

Foreword

1. Fred D. Gray, *Bus Ride to Justice: Changing the System by the System: The Life and Works of Fred Gray, Preacher, Attorney, Politician* (Montgomery: Black Belt Press, 1995), 117–18, 122–24. Fred D. Gray represented the plaintiffs in a series of landmark civil rights cases, including *Lee v. Macon County Board of Education*, which ultimately desegregated all public school systems in Alabama not under court order already, and *Gomillion v. Lightfoot*, which helped pave the way for the Voting Rights Act of 1965.

2. Gray, *Bus Ride to Justice*, 10.

3. Gray, *Bus Ride to Justice*, 13.

Introduction

1. Stephen A. Berrey, *The Jim Crow Routine: Everyday Performances of Race, Civil Rights, and Segregation in Mississippi* (Chapel Hill: University of North Carolina Press, 2015), 2–3. Jim Crow describes both the local and state laws as well as the social and cultural practices that enforced racial segregation in the American South between the end of Reconstruction and the legislative successes of the Civil Rights Movement in the 1960s.

2. Nancy L. Leech and Anthony J. Onwuegbuzie, "Recursivity," in Lisa M. Given, *The SAGE Encyclopedia of Qualitative Research Methods* (Thousand Oaks, CA: SAGE Publications, 2008), 745.

3. Michelle Butina, "A Narrative Approach to Qualitative Inquiry," *American Society for Clinical Laboratory Science* 28, no. 3 (July 1, 2015): 190–96.

4. For more on the ways power dynamics shape the collection of oral histories, see S. Armitage, *Speaking History: Oral Histories of the American Past, 1865–Present* (New York: Springer, 2016); A. Sheftel and S. Zembrzycki, *Oral History Off the Record: Toward an Ethnography of Practice* (New York: Springer, 2013); Donald A. Ritchie, *Doing Oral History* (New York: Oxford University Press, 2014); Paul Thompson, *The Voice of the Past: Oral History* (New York: Oxford University Press, 2017).

5. For more on composer William L. Dawson, see Gwynne Kuhner Brown, *William L. Dawson* (Champaign: University of Illinois Press, 2024); Mark Hugh Malone, *William Levi Dawson: American Music Educator* (Oxford: University Press of Mississippi, 2023); Eileen Southern, *The Music of Black Americans: A History* (New York: Norton, 1983), 427. Dr. William Levi Dawson (September 26, 1899–May 2, 1990) was an American composer, choir director, professor, and musicologist. He served as choir director at Tuskegee Institute from 1931 until 1956. His many compositions include, "There Is a Balm in Gilead" (1939), "Steal Away" (1942), "Every Time I Feel the Spirit" (1946), "Swing Low" (1946), and "Ain'a That Good News" (1967).

6. Robert N. Brown and John Cromartie, "Black Homeplace Migration to the Yazoo-Mississippi Delta: Ambiguous Journeys, Uncertain Outcomes," *Southeastern Geographer* 46, no. 2 (2006): 189–214; Pete Daniel, *Dispossession: Discrimination against Black Farmers in the Age of Civil Rights* (Chapel Hill: University of North Carolina Press, 2013); William W. Falk, *Rooted in Place: Family and Belonging in a Southern Black Community* (New Brunswick, NJ: Rutgers University Press, 2004);Valerie Grim, "Black Farm Families in the Yazoo-Mississippi Delta: A Study of the Brooks Farm Community, 1920–1970," PhD diss., Iowa State University, 1990; Carol B. Stack, *Call to Home: Blacks Reclaim the Rural South* (New York: Basic Books, 1996).

7. Ronald J. Grele, "Values and Methods in the Classroom Transformation of Oral History," *Oral History Review* 25, no. 1/2 (1998): 57–69; Steve Cohen, "Shifting Questions: New Paradigms for Oral History in a Digital World," *Oral History Review* 40, no. 1 (2013): 154–67. Some have said that the narratives in this project are too hagiographic. As many scholars have described, first-person written and oral history narratives are often served up with a bit of nostalgia.

8. Tuskegee University, "History and Mission | Tuskegee University," accessed September 11, 2022. Tuskegee attained the status of a university in 1985, so throughout most of the introduction, it is referred to as Tuskegee Institute.

9. Charles S. Johnson, *Shadow of the Plantation*, (Chicago: University of Chicago, 1934), 8–10; William Warren Rogers, Robert David Ward, Leah Rawls Atkins, and Wayne Flynt, *Alabama: The History of a Deep South State, Bicentennial Edition* (Tuscaloosa: University of Alabama Press, 2018), 90; Christopher D. Haveman, *Rivers of Sand: Creek Indian Emigration, Relocation, and Ethnic Cleansing in the American South* (Lincoln: University of Nebraska Press, 2016), xi, 3, 235; "Tuskegee," Encyclopedia of Alabama, accessed September 11, 2022. The Muscogee Nation originally inhabited the land that would become Tuskegee, Alabama, before their removal with the passage of the Indian Removal Act of 1830 and the signing of the Treaty of Cusseta on March 23, 1832. Tus-

kegee was founded in 1833—one year after Macon County, Alabama, was established. Tuskegee became the county seat of Macon County the same year it was founded. Named for Nathaniel Macon, a white politician from North Carolina, the county attracted large numbers of White settlers after the remaining Native Americans were removed from the area in 1836 following the Second Creek War. As White settlers poured into the county, so did the enslaved African people who would clear the land and make it profitable. The fertile Black Belt soil of the county meant that cotton cultivation did well there, and by the 1850s, it was an agricultural center and "the heart of a powerful plantation area." Johnson, *Shadow of the Plantation*, 10.

10. Robert J. Norrell, *Reaping the Whirlwind: The Civil Rights Movement in Tuskegee* (Chapel Hill: University of North Carolina Press, 1998), 13–14.

11. Tuskegee University, "History and Mission | Tuskegee University."

12. Norrell, *Reaping the Whirlwind*, 15.

13. Crystal R. Sanders, "'We Very Much Prefer to Have a Colored Man in Charge': Booker T. Washington and Tuskegee's All-Black Faculty," *Alabama Review* 74, no. 2 (2021): 125–26.

14. Darlene Clark Hine, "Black Professionals and Race Consciousness: Origins of the Civil Rights Movement, 1890–1950," *Journal of American History* 89, no. 4 (2003): 1279–94. Our discussion of Tuskegee as a parallel world is deeply informed by Darlene Clark Hine's concept of parallelism.

15. Sanders, "'We Very Much Prefer,'" 100–102. For critiques of Washington's emphasis on industrial education by historians, see James D. Anderson, *The Education of Blacks in the South, 1860–1935* (Chapel Hill: University of North Carolina Press, 1988); Glenda Elizabeth Gilmore, *Gender and Jim Crow: Women and the Politics of White Supremacy in North Carolina, 1896–1920* (Chapel Hill: University of North Carolina Press, 2013); Donald Spivey, *Schooling for the New Slavery: Black Industrial Education, 1868–1915* (Westport, CT: Greenwood Press, 1978), 66. Raymond W. Smock, *Booker T. Washington in Perspective: Essays of Louis R. Harlan* (Oxford: University Press of Mississippi, 2011). Recently, scholars have worked to complicate Washington's embrace of industrial education. See M. Christopher Brown, "The Politics of Industrial Education: Booker T. Washington and Tuskegee State Normal School, 1880–1915," *Negro Educational Review* 50, no. 3 (July 1 1999): 123; Karen J. Ferguson, "Caught in 'No Man's Land': The Negro Cooperative Demonstration Service and the Ideology of Booker T. Washington, 1900–1918," *Agricultural History* 72, no. 1 (1998): 33–54; Jarvis C. McInnis, *Afterlives of the Plantation: Plotting Agrarian Futures in the Global Black South* (New York: Columbia University Press, 2025); Pamela Newkirk, "Tuskegee's Talented Tenth: Reconciling a Legacy," *Journal of Asian and African Studies* 51, no. 3 (2016): 328–45; Robert J. Norrell, *Up from*

History: The Life of Booker T. Washington, repr. ed. (Cambridge, MA: Belknap Press, 2011).

16. Norrell, *Reaping the Whirlwind*, 44; Sanders, "'We Very Much Prefer,'" 104, 121, 111.

17. Ellen Weiss, *Robert R. Taylor and Tuskegee: A Black Architect Designs for Booker T. Washington* (Montgomery: NewSouth Books, 2012), xv; Emmett Jay Scott and Lyman Beecher Stowe, *Booker T. Washington: Builder of a Civilization* (Garden City, NY: Doubleday, Page, 1916); For more on Black world making, see Jayna Brown, *Black Utopias: Speculative Life and the Music of Other Worlds* (Durham, NC: Duke University Press, 2021); Adom Getachew, *Worldmaking after Empire: The Rise and Fall of Self-Determination* (Princeton, NJ: Princeton University Press, 2020); Alyosha Goldstein, "Introduction: Abolitionist World-making," *American Quarterly* 75, no. 2 (2023): 359–64, Robin D. G. Kelley, "From the River to the Sea to Every Mountain Top: Solidarity as Worldmaking," *Journal of Palestine Studies* 48, no. 4 (August 1, 2019): 69–91; Judith Madera, "Early Black Worldmaking: Body, Compass, and Text," *American Literary History* 33, no. 3 (September 1, 2021): 481–97.

18. Sanders, "'We Very Much Prefer,'" 100.

19. Weiss, *Robert R. Taylor and Tuskegee*, xv.

20. George Washington Carver earned his bachelor of science degree at Iowa State College of Agricultural and Mechanic Arts, now known as Iowa State University, in 1894. He then earned his master of science in bacterial botany and agriculture in 1896. Linda O. McMurry, *George Washington Carver: Scientist and Symbol* (New York: Oxford University Press, 1981), 42, 12; "George Washington Carver," Encyclopedia of Alabama, accessed September 11, 2022; Sanders, "'We Very Much Prefer,'" 117; Christina Vella, *George Washington Carver: A Life* (Baton Rouge: Louisiana State Press, 2015), 313.

21. Kimberly C. Ransom. "There Are Children Here: Examining Black Childhood in Rosenwald Schools of Pickens County Alabama (1940–1969)," PhD diss., University of Michigan, 2021, 2. For more on the Rosenwald Schools Program, see Anderson, *Education of Blacks in the South*; Stephanie Deutsch, *You Need a Schoolhouse: Booker T. Washington, Julius Rosenwald, and the Building of Schools for the Segregated South* (Evanston, IL: Northwestern University Press, 2011); Vanessa Siddle Walker, *Their Highest Potential: A Black School Community in the Segregated South* (Chapel Hill: University of North Carolina Press, 1996); Mary S. Hoffschwelle, *The Rosenwald Schools of the American South*, (Gainesville: University Press of Florida, 2006).

22. For more information, see Dana Chandler and Edith Powell, *To Raise Up the Man Farthest Down: Tuskegee University's Advancements in Human Health, 1881–1987* (Tuscaloosa: University of Alabama Press, 2018).

23. "Black Hospital Movement in Alabama," Encyclopedia of Alabama, accessed September 11, 2022; "John Andrew Kenney, M.D., 1874–1950," *Journal of the National Medical Association* 48, no. 1 (January 1956): 75.

24. The John A. Andrew Memorial Hospital was named in honor of John Albion Andrew, who was governor of Massachusetts during the Civil War and related by marriage to the trustee who funded the construction of the new building for the hospital. Chandler and Powell, *To Raise Up, 16.*

25. In 1947, the hospital played a critical role in Tuskegee Institute becoming the first historically Black college or university and the first school in Alabama where students could earn a degree in nursing. Chandler and Powell, *To Raise Up*, 59.

26. Booker T. Washington, "From the *AJN* Archives: Training Colored Nurses at Tuskegee," *American Journal of Nursing* 114, no. 2 (2014): 22–23. While Tuskegee became the first historically Black college or university and the first school in Alabama where students could earn a degree in nursing in 1947, Tuskegee Institute was training Black nurses before the establishment of the degree in the decades immediately following the establishment of the school.

27. Norrell, *Reaping the Whirlwind*, 27; Jennifer D. Keene, "The Long Journey Home: Black World War I Veterans and Veterans' Policies," in *Veterans' Policies, Veterans' Politics*, ed. Stephen R. Ortiz (Gainesville: University Press of Florida, 2012), 161–64.

28. Founded in 1895, the National Medical Association (NMA) is the largest and oldest national organization representing Black physicians and their patients in the United States. "About Us—National Medical Association," accessed March 16, 2024.

29. Norrell, *Reaping the Whirlwind*, 28.

30. Although the study is commonly referred to as the Tuskegee Syphilis Study, the authors chose to refer to it as the Syphilis Study following the example of the National Center for Bioethics in Research and Health Care. Tuskegee University, "Syphilis Study Legacy Committee | Tuskegee University," accessed September 19, 2022.

31. Fred D. Gray, *The Tuskegee Syphilis Study: The Real Story and Beyond* (Montgomery: NewSouth Books, 1998), 24; Ada McVean, "40 Years of Human Experimentation in America: The Tuskegee Study," McGill Office for Science and Society, January 25, 2019.

32. For more details on the legal battle, see Gray, *Tuskegee Syphilis Study*; "Tuskegee Syphilis Study," Encyclopedia of Alabama, accessed September 11, 2022; McVean, "40 Years of Human Experimentation." In the aftermath of the study, the participants and their families were awarded $10 million and med-

ical treatment for life. Attorney Fred Gray, who wrote the foreword for this book, was the lawyer who brought the court case and won compensation and an apology for the victims from then-President Bill Clinton. The study also played an influential role in the passage of the National Research Act of 1974, which now requires researchers to obtain informed consent for all research on humans and established Intuitional Review Boards (IRBs) within academia and hospitals. Nonetheless, the study is frequently cited as one cause of Black mistrust in the medical establishment.

33. "G. L. Washington, Ex-Official at Howard U., Dies," *Washington Post*, accessed March 16, 2024.

34. J. Todd Moye, *Freedom Flyers: The Tuskegee Airmen of World War II* (New York: Oxford University Press, 2012), 31. The airfield, Moton Field, which is now home to the Tuskegee Airmen National Historic Site, was funded by Julius Rosenwald and named in honor of Tuskegee's second president, Robert Russa Moton.

35. Moye, *Freedom Flyers*, 34.

36. Norrell, *Reaping the Whirlwind*, 25.

37. Leslie Brown, *Upbuilding Black Durham: Gender, Class, and Black Community Development in the Jim Crow South* (Chapel Hill: University of North Carolina Press, 2009), 249; Maurice J. Hobson, *The Legend of the Black Mecca: Politics and Class in the Making of Modern Atlanta* (Chapel Hill: University of North Carolina Press, 2017), 16.

38. Jessie Parkhurst Guzman, *Crusade for Civic Democracy: The Story of the Tuskegee Civic Association, 1941–1970*, (New York: Vantage Press, 1984); "Tuskegee Civic Association Flyer," Encyclopedia of Alabama, accessed March 16, 2024. TCA was founded on April 13, 1941, at a meeting held at Greenwood Missionary Baptist Church. It sought "to promote through group action the civil well-being" of Tuskegee's Black community.

39. Norrell, *Reaping the Whirlwind*, 41. Hasan Kwame Jeffries, "Black Freedom Movement," in *Keywords for African American Studies*, ed. Erica R. Edwards, Roderick A. Ferguson, and Jeffrey O. G. Ogbar, vol. 8 (New York: New York University Press, 2018), 22. The Modern Black Freedom Movement extends the traditional timeline of the Civil Rights Movement back to World War II and forward into the Black Power Movement. It also expands the movement's traditional parameters to include struggles for both human and civil rights.

40. Gray, *Bus Ride to Justice*, 4–5. In *Gomillion v. Lightfoot*, the Supreme Court ruled that the redrawing of Tuskegee's boundaries by city officials to ensure the election of white candidates in the city's political races was unconstitutional.

41. "Tuskegee Boycott," Encyclopedia of Alabama.

42. Norrell, *Reaping the Whirlwind*, 96, 99.

43. Gray, *Bus Ride to Justice*, 116, 3–5.

44. Gray, *Bus Ride to Justice*, 118–21.

45. Gray, *Bus Ride to Justice*, 217–18.

46. Norrell, *Reaping the Whirlwind*, 138.

47. Gray, *Bus Ride to Justice*, 217–18.

48. James Forman, *Sammy Younge, Jr.: The First Black College Student to Die in the Black Liberation Movement* (New York: Grove Press, 1968), 192, 23–24.

49. Forman, *Sammy Younge*, 35, 56, 67, 72; Norrell, *Reaping the Whirlwind*, 180.

50. Norrell, *Reaping the Whirlwind*, 175–77.

51. Norrell, *Reaping the Whirlwind*, 181.

52. Norrell, *Reaping the Whirlwind*, 331.

53. Norrell, *Reaping the Whirlwind*, 211.

54. Krista Johnson, "An Uncomfortable History: Montgomery Academy Leader Recognizes School's Contribution to Racial Division," *Montgomery Advertiser*, accessed February 23, 2024.

55. Norrell, *Reaping the Whirlwind*, 216.

56. Norrell, *Reaping the Whirlwind*, 204–5.

57. Hasan Kwame Jeffries, *Bloody Lowndes: Civil Rights and Black Power in Alabama's Black Belt* (Fredericksburg: New York University Press, 2010), 245.

58. For more on why African Americans stayed in the South during the Great Migration, see Luther Adams, *Way Up North in Louisville: African American Migration in the Urban South, 1930–1970* (Chapel Hill: University of North Carolina Press, 2010); Karida Brown, *Gone Home: Race and Roots through Appalachia* (Chapel Hill: University of North Carolina Press, 2018); William W. Falk, *Rooted in Place: Family and Belonging in a Southern Black Community* (New Brunswick, NJ: Rutgers University Press, 2004); Laurie B. Green, *Battling the Plantation Mentality: Memphis and the Black Freedom Struggle* (Chapel Hill: University of North Carolina Press, 2009); Maurice J. Hobson, *The Legend of the Black Mecca: Politics and Class in the Making of Modern Atlanta* (Chapel Hill: University of North Carolina Press, 2017); Bernadette Pruitt, *The Other Great Migration: The Movement of Rural Blacks to Houston, 1900–1941* (College Station: Texas A&M University Press, 2013).

59. Stewart E. Tolnay, "Educational Selection in the Migration of Southern Blacks, 1880–1990," *Social Forces* 77, no. 2 (1998): 487–514.

60. Ransom, "There Are Children Here," 1–2.

61. For more information on the history of Black high schools in the South, see Anderson, *Education of Blacks in the South*; Horace Mann Bond, *Ne-*

gro Education in Alabama: A Study in Cotton and Steel (Tuscaloosa: University of Alabama Press, 1994); Jon N. Hale, *A New Kind of Youth: Historically Black High Schools and Southern Student Activism, 1920–1975* (Chapel Hill: University of North Carolina Press, 2022).

62. Sanders, "'We Very Much Prefer,'" 99–100. For more on Black Americans receiving graduate level education in the North, then returning to the American South, see Crystal R. Sanders, *A Forgotten Migration: Black Southerners, Segregation Scholarships, and the Debt Owed to Public HBCUs* (Chapel Hill: University of North Carolina Press, 2024).

63. For more on the role economic factors played in the Great Migration, see Davarian L. Baldwin, *Chicago's New Negroes Modernity, the Great Migration, and Black Urban Life* (Chapel Hill: University of North Carolina Press, 2007); Ira Berlin, *The Making of African America: The Four Great Migrations* (New York: Penguin, 2010); Leah Platt Boustan, *Competition in the Promised Land: Black Migrants in Northern Cities and Labor Markets* (Princeton, NJ: Princeton University Press, 2020); James N. Gregory, *The Southern Diaspora: How the Great Migrations of Black and White Southerners Transformed America* (Chapel Hill: University of North Carolina Press, 2005); James R. Grossman, *Land of Hope: Chicago, Black Southerners, and the Great Migration* (Chicago: University of Chicago Press, 1991); Alferdteen Harrison, *Black Exodus: The Great Migration from the American South* (Oxford: University Press of Mississippi, 1992); Nicholas Lemann, *The Promised Land: The Great Black Migration and How It Changed America*, (New York: Vintage Books, 1992); Joe William Trotter, *The Great Migration in Historical Perspective: New Dimensions of Race, Class, and Gender* (Bloomington: Indiana University Press, 1991); Joe William Trotter, *Black Milwaukee: The Making of an Industrial Proletariat, 1915–45* (Urbana: University of Illinois Press, 2007).

64. "Lifting the Veil of Ignorance Statue in Tuskegee," Encyclopedia of Alabama, accessed February 23, 2024.

65. Forman, *Sammy Younge, Jr*, 147. For more on TISEP, see Jeffries, *Bloody Lowndes*; Brian Jones, *The Tuskegee Student Uprising: A History* (New York: New York University Press, 2024); Percival Bertrand Phillips, "Looking Back Nearly 60 Years: The Tuskegee Institute Community Action Corps (TICAC)," *Spectrum* 8, no. 2 (Spring 2021): 131–39; "Tuskegee Receives National Park Service Grant to Preserve Civil Rights History," Tuskegee University, accessed June 15, 2022. The Tuskegee Institute Summer Education Program (TISEP) and the Tuskegee Institute Community Education Program (TICEP) were student outreach programs, mainly focused on tutoring students across the Black Belt counties of Alabama. Dr. Percival Bertrand Phillips, who was dean of students at Tuskegee, founded the program in the fall of 1963. Initially, students from

Tuskegee served as tutors in the program. As the program grew to offer additional services, and even establish a newspaper, the program received grant funding, and the students from Tuskegee were joined by college students from dozens of other institutions of higher education from across the nation, including many White students from St. Olaf College. Frequently, TISEP and TICEP are used interchangeably as some students only worked in the summer program, while some worked year-round. For more on TISEP and TICEP, see Tierra Cole, "TICEP," 3 T's Movement (blog), accessed March 17, 2025.

66. St. Olaf College, "St. Olaf to Award Honorary Degree to Educator, Civil Rights Advocate."

67. For more on everyday forms of resistance in the Jim Crow South, see Robin D. G. Kelley, "'We Are Not What We Seem': Rethinking Black Working-Class Opposition in the Jim Crow South," *Journal of American History* 80, no. 1 (1993): 75–112; Berrey, *Jim Crow Routine*.

68. Norrell, *Reaping the Whirlwind*, 175–77.

Chapter 1

1. For more on Lewis Adams, see Norrell, *Reaping the Whirlwind*; "History and Mission | Tuskegee University," accessed September 10, 2022. Encyclopedia of Alabama. "Tuskegee Institute National Historic Site," accessed September 10, 2022.

2. Booker T. Washington, *Up from Slavery: An Autobiography*, (New York: Doubleday, Page, 1907), 112.

Chapter 2

1. The Order of the Eastern Star was the women's auxiliary organization attached with Freemasonry. Prince Hall Masons began during the Revolutionary War in response to the all-White Masons in the United States refusing membership to Black men. "Prince Hall Masons," National Museum of African American History and Culture.

2. *The Official Railway Guide: North American Freight Service Edition* (New York: National Railway Publication Company, 1896). The Chehaw station was located on the Tuskegee Railroad, which connected Tuskegee, Alabama, to Montgomery, Alabama.

Chapter 3

1. Eileen Southern, *The Music of Black Americans: A History* (New York: Norton, 1983), 427.

2. Jennifer H. Lansbury, *A Spectacular Leap: Black Women Athletes in Twen-*

tieth Century America, (Fayetteville: University of Arkansas Press, 2014). Alice Coachman Davis (November 9, 1923–July 14, 2014) was a teacher at Tuskegee Institute High School. She specialized in high jump and became the first Black woman to win an Olympic gold medal in the London games in 1948.

3. House Joint Resolution No. 322: Celebrating the Life of Dr. James H. M. Henderson, Virginia Cong. (2010); Chandler and Powell, *To Raise Up the Man*, 102. Dr. James H. M. Henderson (August 10, 1917–December 3, 2009) was a world-renowned physiologist who worked with Dr. George Washington Carver and performed extensive research while working at Tuskegee Institute. Dr. Henderson was also a very active and important part of the Civil Rights Movement.

4. "Pearly Gates," IMDb, accessed July 22, 2022. Viola Billups, a member of the Tuskegee Institute High School class of 1964, started performing immediately after high school and has been a sensation in England and other parts of Europe for decades. Viola continues to perform and to host a radio show in London.

5. Faith Karimi, "It's Now Illegal in Georgia to Give Food and Water to Voters in Line," CNN, March 26, 2021.

6. Maya King, "Gov. Brian Kemp Wins Re-Election in Georgia, Topping Stacey Abrams," *New York Times*, November 9, 2022. Brian Porter Kemp has served as the eighty-third governor of Georgia since January 2019. A Republican, he was the twenty-seventh secretary of state of Georgia from 2010 to 2018 and a member of the Georgia state senate from 2003 until 2007.

7. King, "Gov. Brian Kemp." Stacey Yvonne Abrams (born December 9, 1973) is a politician, lawyer, voting rights activist, and author who served in the Georgia House of Representatives from 2007 to 2017, serving as minority leader from 2011 to 2017. Abrams founded Fair Fight Action, an organization to address voter suppression, in 2018. A voting rights activist, her efforts have been widely credited with boosting voter turnout in Georgia.

Chapter 4

1. Gray, *Bus Ride to Justice*, 116–22.

2. Weiss, *Robert R. Taylor and Tuskegee*, xv.

3. Donald P. Stone and Julian Bond, *Fallen Prince: William James Edwards, Black Education, and the Quest for Afro-American Nationality*, (Snow Hill, AL: Snow Hill Press, 1990).

4. Andrea D. Lewis and Nicole A. Taylor, *Unsung Legacies of Educators and Events in Black Education* (New York: Springer, 2019), 156.

5. Gray, *Bus Ride to Justice*, 217–18.

6. Jeffries, *Bloody Lowndes*, 81.

Chapter 5

1. E. Franklin Frazier, *Black Bourgeoisie*, (New York: Simon and Schuster, 1997), 5.

2. D. Jordan. "Bennie Douglas Mayberry: An Unsung Hero," *Journal of Natural Resources Life Science Education* 24, no 1 (1995); B. D. Mayberry, ed., *B. D. Mayberry*, NewSouth Books, accessed September 25, 2022.

3. For more information on *The Urantia Book*, see David Bradley, *An Introduction to the Urantia Revelation* (White Egret Publications, 2008); Sarah Lewis, "The Peculiar Sleep: Receiving the Urantia Book," in *The Invention of Sacred Tradition*, ed. James R. Lewis and Olav Hammer, 199–212 (Cambridge: Cambridge University Press, 2007); Sarah Lewis, "The Urantia Book," in *UFO Religions*, ed. C. Partridge, 129–98 (London: Routledge, 2003); Larry Mullins, *A History of the Urantia Papers* (Boulder, CO: Penumbra Press, 2000).

4. Douglas Mayberry, "Recent Revelations Revealed—So You Know!," *RevelatoryTruths* (blog), accessed September 25, 2022.

Chapter 6

1. Scott and Stowe, *Booker T. Washington*, 136, 274.

2. For more on the Rosenwald schools program, see James D. Anderson, *The Education of Blacks in the South, 1860–1935* (Chapel Hill: University of North Carolina Press, 1988); Stephanie Deutsch, *You Need a Schoolhouse: Booker T. Washington, Julius Rosenwald, and the Building of Schools for the Segregated South*, (Evanston, IL: Northwestern University Press, 2011); Walker, *Their Highest Potential*; Mary S. Hoffschwelle, *The Rosenwald Schools of the American South* (Gainesville: University Press of Florida, 2006); Ransom, "There Are Children Here."

Chapter 7

1. Norrell, *Reaping the Whirlwind*, 41.

Chapter 8

1. Stewart Emory Tolnay and E. M. Beck, *A Festival of Violence: An Analysis of Southern Lynchings, 1882–1930* (Champaign: University of Illinois Press, 1995), 270.

2. For more on *The Negro Motorist Green Book*, or *The Green Book*, see Mia Bay, *Traveling Black: A Story of Race and Resistance* (Cambridge, MA: Harvard University Press, 2021); James W. Loewen, *Sundown Towns: A Hidden Dimension of American Racism* (New York: New Press, 2018); Cotten Seiler, *Republic of Drivers: A Cultural History of Automobility in America* (Chicago: University of Chicago Press, 2009); Gretchen Sorin, *Driving While Black: African American*

Travel and the Road to Civil Rights (New York: Liveright Publishing, 2020); Candacy A. Taylor, *Overground Railroad: The Green Book and the Roots of Black Travel in America* (New York: Abrams, 2020). *The Negro Motorist Green Book*, or *The Green Book* for short, was an annual travel guide that provided Black travelers with information about lodging, restaurants, and gas stations that served Black people. The guide was published by Victor Hugo Green between 1936 and 1966.

3. Stewart Burns, *Daybreak of Freedom: The Montgomery Bus Boycott* (Chapel Hill: University of North Carolina Press, 2012), 41.

4. For more information on Black Masonic organizations and their community-building efforts, see Peter P. Hinks and Stephen David Kantrowitz, *All Men Free and Brethren: Essays on the History of African American Freemasonry* (Ithaca, NY: Cornell University Press, 2013); Paul Ortiz, *Emancipation Betrayed: The Hidden History of Black Organizing and White Violence in Florida from Reconstruction to the Bloody Election of 1920* (Oakland: University of California Press, 2005). Black Freemasonry dates back to the colonial era, and Black Masonic organizations played an influential role in challenging the logics of White supremacy in the Jim Crow South.

Chapter 9

1. For more on the history and identity of Gullah people, see Melissa L. Cooper, *Making Gullah: A History of Sapelo Islanders, Race, and the American Imagination* (Chapel Hill: University of North Carolina Press Books, 2017).

2. For more on Alfred "Chief" Anderson, see Blanche Wiesen Cook, *Eleanor Roosevelt* (New York: Penguin, 1992); Daniel Haulman, *The Tuskegee Airmen Chronology: A Detailed Timeline of the Red Tails and Other Black Pilots of World War II* (Athens: University of Georgia Press, 2018); David Stout, "Charles Anderson Dies at 89; Trainer of Tuskegee Airmen," *New York Times*, April 17, 1996.

Chapter 10

1. For more on class tensions in the Black community in Tuskegee, see Frazier, *Black Bourgeoisie*, 63–66.

2. Stephanie Toone, "Ahead of Impeachment Vote, John Lewis Makes Plea for 'Moral Obligation' to Impeach Trump," *Atlanta Journal-Constitution*, n.d., sec. Nation & World News.

3. Fatima Goss Graves, "Opinion: The Most Powerful Moment of Ketanji Brown Jackson's Testimony," CNN, March 24, 2022.

4. "Samkee America, Inc. Announcement Puts Macon County on Path for Even More Economic Success—Macon County Economic Development Authority (MCEDA)," accessed July 16, 2024.

Chapter 11

1. For more on George Washington Carver and his extension work with Black farmers, see Allen Jones, "Improving Rural Life for Blacks: The Tuskegee Negro Farmers' Conference, 1892–1915," *Agricultural History* 65, no. 2 (1991): 105–14; B. D. Mayberry, *The Role of Tuskegee University in the Growth and Development of the Negro Cooperative Extension System, 1881–1990* (Tuskegee, AL: Tuskegee University Cooperative Extension Program, 1989); Christina Vella, *George Washington Carver: A Life* (Baton Rouge: Louisiana State University Press, 2015); Chandler and Powell, *To Raise Up the Man Farthest Down*; Felix James, "The Tuskegee Institute Movable School, 1906–1923," *Agricultural History* 45 (July 1971): 201–9. McMurry, *George Washington Carver*; Thomas Campbell, *The Movable School Goes to the Negro Farmer*, (Tuskegee, AL: Tuskegee Institute Press, 1936).

2. Forman, *Sammy Younge*, 27.

3. Forman, *Sammy Younge*, 119–20.

Chapter 14

1. "Tuskegee University Veterinarian Acquires New Patent for a Medical Device," Tuskegee University, last modified December 20, 2021, accessed July 14, 2022.

2. Rhonda Evans, "Research Guides: African American Genealogy: The 1870 Census," accessed July 4, 2024.

3. For more on Black Masonic organizations, see Hinks and Kantrowitz, *All Men Free and Brethren*; Ortiz, *Emancipation Betrayed.*

4. "Tuskegee University Partnership Receives National Park Service Grant to Preserve Civil Rights History," Tuskegee University, accessed July 4, 2024.

Chapter 15

1. "Atlantic Slave Trade to Savannah," *New Georgia Encyclopedia*, accessed October 4, 2022.

2. Washington, *Up from Slavery*, 121, 141.

3. "A. G. Gaston," *Encyclopedia of Alabama*, accessed October 4, 2022.

4. Mab Segrest, *Memoir of a Race Traitor: Fighting Racism in the American South* (New York: New Press, 2019), ix.

5. Barbara Jordan and Shelby Hearon, *Barbara Jordan, a Self-Portrait* (New York: Doubleday, 1979), 93.

6. "About the USPHS Syphilis Study," Tuskegee University, accessed October 4, 2022.

7. Ransom, "There Are Children here," 5–6.

8. Jarvis R. Givens, *Fugitive Pedagogy: Carter G. Woodson and the Art of Black Teaching* (Cambridge, MA: Harvard University Press, 2021), 208.

9. Givens, *Fugitive Pedagogy*. I recently heard Jarvis Givens make a presentation on his book *Fugitive Pedagogy*. He talked about how Carter G. Woodson and the Colored Teachers Association used to prepare packets of material for Black teachers because the teaching of Black history was outlawed in many states.

10. Forman, *Sammy Younge*, 192.

Chapter 16

1. Norrell, *Reaping the Whirlwind*, 161.

Chapter 17

1. Gray, *Tuskegee Syphilis Study*, 35.

2. Jeremy Gray, "Tuskegee Airman Retired Lt. Col. Herbert Carter Died Today, Reports State," AL.com, November 9, 2012.

3. David Stout, "Charles Anderson Dies at 89; Trainer of Tuskegee Airmen." *New York Times*, April 17, 1996.

Chapter 19

1. *Lee v. Macon County Board of Education*, 267 F. Supp. 458 (Dist. Court 1967).

2. Washington, *Up from Slavery*, 166–68.

3. US Office of Special Counsel, "Hatch Act Overview."

4. Gray, *Bus Ride to Justice*, 209.

5. For more on *Lee v. Macon County Board of Education*, see Joseph Bagley, *The Politics of White Rights: Race, Justice, and Integrating Alabama's Schools* (Athens: University of Georgia Press, 2018); Forman, *Sammy Younge*; Gray, *Bus Ride to Justice*; Leon Jones, *From Brown to Boston: Desegregation in Education, 1954–1974* (Metuchen, NJ: Scarecrow Press, 1979); Norrell, *Reaping the Whirlwind.*

6. Neal Reid, "Legacy of Harold A. Franklin, Auburn University's First African American Student, Preserved at Special Dedication Ceremony," Auburn University, Office of Communications and Marketing, accessed July 4, 2024.

Chapter 20

1. For more on Della Sullins, see Davis W. Houck and David E. Dixon, *Women and the Civil Rights Movement, 1954–1965* (Oxford: University Press of Mississippi, 2009); Gray, *Bus Ride to Justice*; Brian K. Landsberg, *Revolution by Law: The Federal Government and the Desegregation of Alabama Schools* (Lawrence: University Press of Kansas, 2022); "New Scholarship Program Honors

Tuskegee's First Nursing Graduate," *Journal of Blacks in Higher Education*, October 13, 2019.

2. Houck and Dixon, *Women and the Civil Rights Movement*, 113.

3. David Stout, "Charles Anderson Dies at 89; Trainer of Tuskegee Airmen," *New York Times*, April 17, 1996.

Chapter 21

1. Gray, *Bus Ride to Justice*, 121–24.

2. "Johnson, Frank M.," Encyclopedia of Alabama, accessed July 4, 2024.

3. For more on Pullman porters, see Robert L. Allen, *Brotherhood of Sleeping Car Porters: C. L. Dellums and the Fight for Fair Treatment and Civil Rights* (New York: Routledge, 2015); Beth Tompkins Bates, *Pullman Porters and the Rise of Protest Politics in Black America, 1925–1945* (Chapel Hill: University of North Carolina Press, 2003); Cornelius L. Bynum, *A. Philip Randolph and the Struggle for Civil Rights* (Champaign: University of Illinois Press, 2010); Melinda Chateauvert, *Marching Together: Women of the Brotherhood of Sleeping Car Porters* (Champaign: University of Illinois Press, 1997); Blair L. M. Kelley, *Black Folk: The Roots of the Black Working Class* (New York: Liveright Publishing, 2023); Andrew E. Kersten and Clarence Lang, *Reframing Randolph: Labor, Black Freedom, and the Legacies of A. Philip Randolph* (New York: New York University Press, 2015); Larry Tye, *Rising from the Rails: Pullman Porters and the Making of the Black Middle Class* (New York: Henry Holt, 2005). Pullman porters worked as attendants on sleeping cars on railroads. They were historically Black men, and working as a Pullman porter was considered a middle-class job in most Black communities.

4. Gray, *Bus Ride to Justice*, 217–18.

5. "Civil Rights Act (1964)," National Archives, October 5, 2021.

Epilogue

1. For more on the scholarly literature related to why African Americans stay in the American South, Adams, *Way Up North*; Brown, *Gone Home*; Falk, *Rooted in Place*; Green, *Battling the Plantation Mentality*; Hobson, *Legend of the Black Mecca*; Pruitt, *Other Great Migration*.

2. Hine, "Black Professionals and Race Consciousness," 1279.

3. Hine, "Black Professionals and Race Consciousness," 1279.

4. Caroline Gebhard, "A Legacy of Women's Leadership at Tuskegee Institute," in *Alabama Women: Their Lives and Times*, ed. Susan Youngblood Ashmore and Lisa Lindquist Dorr (Athens: University of Georgia Press, 2017), 222.

5. Jeffries, *Bloody Lowndes*, 238.

6. For more on the history of the New Great Migration, see Beatrice J. Adams, "Why the New Great Migration Matters," African American Intellectual History Society, January 8, 2024.

7. "HBCUs See a Historic Jump in Enrollments," NPR, August 13, 2022, sec. Education; "The End of Affirmative Action," *New York Times*, accessed July 17, 2023; Stephan Bisaha and Shalina Chatlani, "After Decades of Neglect, Jackson's Black Business District Is Coming Back to Life," NPR, November 13, 2022, sec. National.

Index

Page numbers in italics refer to figures.